TITANIC

THE MYTHS AND LEGACY OF A DISASTER

TITANIC

The Myths and Legacy of a Disaster

Roger and June Cartwright

First published 2011

The History Press
The Mill, Brimscombe Port
Stroud, Gloucestershire, GL5 2QG
www.thehistorypress.co.uk

© Roger and June Cartwright, 2011

British Library Cataloguing in Publication Data.
A catalogue record for this book is available from the British Library.

ISBN 978 0 7524 5176 3

Typesetting and origination by The History Press
Printed in EU for The History Press

Contents

Acknowledgements

The authors would like to express their appreciation to all those passengers and crew of the cruise ships they have worked on over the past ten years for their suggestions and the encouragement that has led to the production of this book.

Thanks are also due to those who assisted the authors in Belfast and Halifax, Nova Scotia, and to their editor, Amy Rigg and her team at The History Press.

We are also grateful to Peter Lamont, production designer on the 1997 *Titanic* movie, for his insights and excellent company whilst cruising the Baltic on the MV *Saga Ruby*.

Special thanks are due to David Hoddinott of St John's, Newfoundland, for permission to reproduce his painting *Date with Destiny* and to Gordon Bauwens for the use of *Titanic – A Day to Remember*.

Abbreviations

GRT Gross Registered Tonnage
IMM International Mercantile Marine
RMS Royal Mail Steamer
SS   Steamship

Introduction

Note: the GRT (Gross Registered Tonnage) is not, as many in the media make the mistake of saying, a measurement of weight. It is actually a measurement of enclosed space, i.e. volume – the volume of a merchant ship reflects its capacity and is thus of more importance to the owner. In the case of merchant ships the word tonne comes from the Anglo-Saxon 'tun' meaning barrel. For medieval ship owners the number of barrels the vessel could carry was of prime importance. There are still inns and pubs in the UK named 'The Three Tuns' whose sign is three barrels.

In this book the GRT is rounded up or down to the nearest 500 tonnes. However, since GRT changes as ships are altered, it is indicative rather than substantive. As an example, the *Normandie* of the 1930s had a GRT of 79,280 when she entered service. When the *Queen Mary* came out she exceeded this figure and the French Line refitted *Normandie* with an enclosed café grill at the stern. It didn't weigh much but as it was enclosed it increased the GRT to 82,799 compared to *Queen Mary*'s 80,774, making *Normandie* once again the world's biggest ship at the time and restoring French national pride.

A knot in navigation is the measure of speed at sea, and is equal to 1 nautical mile per hour (approximately 1.15 statute miles per hour).

> What I don't understand is how a big ship like that can sink – it only hit a little iceberg.
>
> Jean Marsh as Rose in *Upstairs, Downstairs*,
> London Weekend Television series of the 1970s.

Titanic is possibly the best known ship in the world. Since her foundering in April 1912, a wealth of myths, conspiracy theories and half-truths about the ship have been repeated. She was too big, she was unsinkable, she was trying to gain the Blue Riband, steerage passengers were denied lifeboat spaces and even that she never actually sank. Since 1912 there have been passenger vessels of four times the tonnage of *Titanic* and disasters (albeit most in wartime) that have led to many, many more casualties at sea and yet the legacy of *Titanic* is still with us.

Ask a random group of people what has been the worst shipping disaster outside wartime and the chances are they will say '*Titanic*'. One thousand five hundred and thirteen lives were lost when *Titanic* foundered. In December 1987, some 4,341 people died when *Doña Paz*, an inter-island passenger ferry owned by Sulpicio Lines, collided with the oil tanker *Victor* off Mindoro in the Philippines.

A second question to ask is 'name the <u>two</u> British-registered transatlantic liners that sank off North America with the loss of over 1,000 lives each in the three years before the First World War'. Most people will name *Titanic* but how many will know of the loss of Canadian Pacific's the *Empress of Ireland* and 1,024 lives in the St Lawrence in 1914?

> Shipbuilding is such a perfect art nowadays that absolute DISASTER, INVOLVING THE PASSENGERS IS INCONCEIVABLE. Whatsoever happens, there will be time before the vessel sinks to save the life of every person on board. I will go a bit further. I will say that I cannot imagine any condition that would cause the vessel to founder. Modern shipbuilding has gone beyond that.

> Captain Smith, later to be the captain of *Titanic*, in an interview to the *Boston Post* 16 April 1907, five years almost to the day before the sinking.

On the bridge of the ship on that fateful voyage was a notice:

> *The safety of all those on board weighs with us beyond all other considerations, and we would once more impress upon you and the entire navigation staff most earnestly that no risk is to be run which can be avoided by the exercise of caution....and by choosing, whenever doubt exists, the course that tends to safety.*

> IMM Instructions to captains, 1912.

Titanic has spawned a succession of articles, novels and motion pictures that stretch from the accurate to the faintly ridiculous. The true story and its legacy is strong enough to stand the test of time without myths.

What is it about this ship and the disaster that befell her that still impacts on our sensibilities 100 years after the event? Even today an organisational reorganisation that occurs against the background of crisis is referred to as 'rearranging the deck chairs on the *Titanic*'. Why is it that we seemed doomed to repeat the technological arrogance of *Titanic*, as will be demonstrated in the book? The author has also worked in the airline industry, the successor to the liner trade, and will show through case studies on the Comet and the DC10 that technological advances in speed and size can easily run ahead of safety just as they did with *Titanic*.

Roger Cartwright, together with his wife June, has presented many talks on the story of *Titanic* both to land-based groups and to cruise ship passengers. Despite dealing with the most famous shipwreck in history, one can guarantee to fill a cruise ship lounge or theatre for a talk on *Titanic*; it is a topic that seems to fascinate people of all ages and cultures.

There are many *Titanic* buffs in the world – people who are extremely knowledgeable about the ship and who can recite the statistics about her. This book is not designed for them. During their travels the authors have often been told that 'everybody knows that *Titanic* was too big, or trying for the Blue Riband etc.' There are many myths about the ship and this book is for the general reader who wants to separate fact from fiction and who wishes to understand why the legacy of *Titanic* is still with us.

When the *Titanic* set sail on her maiden voyage, even had she survived her reign as the largest ship in the world it would have been brief as the Germans were already building a larger competitor. She was not unique (as some commentators later claimed) as she was one of a planned trio of ships, *Olympic*, *Titanic* and *Gigantic* (renamed *Britannic* after the disaster). She was certainly slower than Cunard's *Mauretania* and could never have held the record for the fastest westbound crossing of the Atlantic – the so-called Blue Riband. She was, however, with her sister *Olympic* of 1911, possibly the most luxurious passenger ship up to that time.

Titanic was not even really British. She was built in a UK yard (Harland & Wolff in Belfast), registered in Liverpool and flew the Blue Ensign that indicated that her captain, Captain Smith, was a senior Royal Naval Reserve Officer. Her registered owner was the UK White Star Line but White Star was part of J. Pierpont Morgan's International Mercantile Marine. Britons may have built and crewed *Titanic* but she was paid for with US dollars and owned, ultimately, by a US billionaire.

Titanic carried with her not just the kinetic energy of some 30,000+ tons of steel and fittings (her gross tonnage of 46,000 GRT was, as noted, a measure of volume not weight) moving at 21 knots but also, for reasons that will be explored in the book, emotional energy that seems as strong today as it was in 1912.

This book examines the genesis of the superliners, spawned as it was through the Anglo–German commercial rivalry on the North Atlantic and the influence of US finance. The building of the ship and the fateful voyage will be examined through a series of statements/questions that are often quoted (and form the basis for the co-authors' talks) when referring to *Titanic*; although not all are in fact myths, some are sadly true. *Viz*:

Myth? Steerage class was very poor

Myth? White Star was a British company

Myth? Prior to the *Titanic* disaster White Star Line had a good safety record

Myth? Captain Smith believed that ships were so well built in 1912 that they would not sink

Myth? *Titanic* was ultra large

Myth? Watertight compartments and the notion of unsinkability

Myth? *Titanic* was built using the most modern techniques

Myth? *Titanic* had enough lifeboats according to the Board of Trade

Myth? Captain Smith had an unblemished safety record

Myth? J.P. Morgan was supposed to sail on the ship but cancelled his booking

Myth? *Titanic* nearly had a collision as she left Southampton

Myth? The richest man in the world was on board *Titanic*

Myth? There really was an 'unsinkable Molly Brown'

Myth? Captain Smith and his officers ignored ice warnings

Myth? There was a true love story on board the *Titanic*

Myth? Class distinction played a part in the tragedy

Myth? There had been a written premonition about the disaster

Myth? Bruce Ismay dressed as a woman to obtain a lifeboat place

Myth? The band played 'Nearer my God to Thee'

Myth? An officer shot himself

Myth? The crew wages stopped the moment the ship sank

Myth? There was another ship near to *Titanic* that made no rescue effort

Myth? Over 1,500 men women and children drowned on the *Titanic*

Myth? It was the first SOS ever sent

Myth? *Titanic* wasn't insured

Myth? DNA evidence cannot be wrong

Myth? Britannia still ruled the waves in 1912

Myth? Captain Smith cancelled the lifeboat drill

Myth? The seamen on *Olympic* went on strike and were accused of mutiny

Myth? The surviving *Titanic* crew were treated like pariahs

Myth? The British Inquiry was a whitewash designed to protect the Board of Trade

Myth? A passenger tried to bribe the crew of a lifeboat not to go back and pick up people in the water

Myth? The *Titanic* was in one piece as she went down

Myth? The *Titanic* disaster was the beginning of the end for White Star

Myth? Captain Smith's table and sideboard from *Titanic* are still in existence

Myth? *Titanic* never sank

Myth? The search for *Titanic* was really a secret mission to locate two missing nuclear submarines

Myth? Ice is no longer a problem for shipping

Myth? It remains the worst peacetime shipping disaster ever

Myth? Jack Dawson (from the 1997 movie) did exist

The book also considers both the US and British inquiries into the loss of the ship and the impact that this had on US–UK relations and whether it was the first public manifestation of US supremacy over Britain, as the first inquiry into the loss of a UK-registered ship, sunk in international waters, was in New York and not London! The demise of White Star and its merger with Cunard during the Depression years and the subsequent takeover of Cunard by the Carnival Corporation will form the basis for a further part of the story.

The impact of *Titanic* on safety at sea forms a section on its own, culminating in an examination of the similarities and lessons learned in the *Andrea Doria* sinking in the 1950s. The loss of Comet and DC10 airlines in similar circumstances to *Titanic*, i.e. where safety technology had either been outpaced or ignored, are examined.

The book also looks at the physical legacy of *Titanic*; the wreck itself and its discovery and artefacts (indeed should they have been recovered?) the graveyards, the shipyard and the fates of survivors. Finally, *Titanic* in literature, films and factual books is examined.

The route across the Atlantic from Europe to North America (and vice versa) has always been one of the most important trade routes of the modern world. Linking as it does the old world of Europe with the new opportunities that, from the seventeenth century onwards, were to be found in North America, the means of making the journey became not only commercial but a way of displaying national pride. The largest, fastest and most opulent vessels of their day were placed on the route and if they were British, French, German, Italian or Dutch their entry into New York was a symbol of the national pride of their owners. Similarly, but on a much smaller scale, the arrival of the SS *United States* – the fastest passenger liner ever built – presents a tangible picture of American technology when she steamed into Southampton or Bremerhaven.

Not only were the European, Canadian and US merchant fleet's largest liners placed on the route but it also saw (with only two exceptions) the only four-funnelled liners ever built. One might wonder why the number of funnels is important? At the beginning of the twentieth century most British cruisers had four funnels whilst their German equivalents had three. Russia, however, had a five-funnelled *Askold*. In 1902 she was sent to the Persian Gulf and the local leaders were very impressed: the more funnels, the more powerful. The Royal Navy could not allow itself to be outdone so the captain of the four-funnelled HMS *Amphorite* rigged up two dummy canvas funnels and fed smoke to them. As Wilfrid Pym Trotter has said of the incident, 'thus was British prestige restored' and perhaps more importantly British influence in what was to become a major oil producing region.

Much has been written about the naval armaments race between Britain and Germany before 1914. Less well known is the parallel race between the two countries to produce the largest and fastest transatlantic liner. Douglas R. Burgess has written about this in his excellent study, 'Seize the Trident'. He believes that the *Titanic* disaster was a direct consequence of the race to be either the fastest or the biggest, or both. He comments that it was easier to build bigger and bigger ships but less easy to introduce new navigational methods or to change the culture of captains trained in the age of sail.

The race to produce the biggest and the best reached its zenith between the wars when Britain, France, Italy and Germany vied with each other to impress New York with the *Bremen* and *Europa*, the *Rex*, the beautiful *Normandie* and the stately *Queen Mary* – the Dictatorships against the Democracies! Even after the war, when the speed crown was firmly in American hands with the SS *United States* and the jet airliner had spelt the end of the conventional passenger liner, France and Britain still clung on to the grandeur of the North Atlantic liner, introducing the *France* and the *QE2* in 1962 and 1968 respectively. Both ended their careers as cruise ships. In the 1930–40s a ship of 80,000+ GRT – of which there were only three, *Normandie*, *Queen Mary* and *Queen Elizabeth* – seemed the ultimate. In 2004 the 149,000 GRT *Queen Mary 2* made her debut as the biggest passenger ship ever built (she is a combination of Atlantic liner and cruise ship) and she was supplanted in 2006 by the 154,000 GRT cruise ship *Freedom of the Seas* (Royal Caribbean International) whose *Oasis of the Seas* of 2010 and her sister *Allure of the Seas* at 220,000 GRT are the world's largest passenger ships ever built.

Titanic is part of the North Atlantic story and her legacy is still with us today. Whilst the Olympic Class were the biggest liners of their day, they were far from the most advanced. *Titanic*'s technology at her introduction in 1912 was a generation earlier than that of her main rivals, Cunard's *Mauretania* and *Lusitania*. So why was a technologically regressive ship built and then billed as a superliner? It is that story and the legacy it has left that forms the basis of this book.

About the Authors

Scottish-based maritime historian Dr Roger Cartwright has entertained and informed British, American, Canadian, Australian, New Zealand and European cruise ship passengers on some thirty of the world's best-known cruise liners with his maritime history-themed talks. Roger has worked in both education and management training in the UK, USA, Germany and India. He is an internationally published author on the history of the cruise industry and a variety of management topics. He also worked as a consultant to a major airline in both the United Kingdom and the United States of America. His work with the Royal Navy has provided him with an in-depth knowledge of maritime history, whilst the many case studies and books he has written about the cruise industry have made him an acknowledged authority of cruise companies, cruise liners and the history of cruising. Roger has also been involved in government studies into mergers within the cruise industry. Roger is proud to be a life trustee of the Canadian Naval Memorial, the corvette HMCS *Sackville* berthed in Halifax, Nova Scotia.

His wife June is an illustrator and works with Roger in sourcing materials and putting together his maritime-themed presentations. She is also an accomplished poet.

Chapter 1

The Context of *Titanic*

Giant ocean liners did not just happen but were part of a natural evolution that involved both technological innovation and social change. The social change was the massive emigration between Europe and North America, particularly to the United States, that occurred from the end of the US Civil War in 1865 until the US Government acted to restrict emigration after the First World War.

The technological innovations in ship design enabled the mass movement of people and that movement in turn encouraged more technological innovation.

Easy movement across the Atlantic did not begin until the liner developed into a safe and efficient form of transportation. The sailing ship was too dependent on the vagaries of the weather to offer a reliable, scheduled service. It was also a very unsafe means of conveyance. Dr Johnson once referred to an ocean voyage as like 'being in prison but with the added possibility of being drowned'. Although the sailing packet ships could advertise the day they would sail, their arrival could not be predicted, making proper schedules difficult. Nevertheless, the seeds of the transatlantic mass passenger trade were sown when Jeremiah Thomson, an English emigrant living in New York, and four associates founded the Black Ball (named after the emblem on the fore topsail) Line in 1817. These ships sailed to a schedule, although arrival times were at the whim of the wind. Their *Pacific* actually sailed from New York to Liverpool in a mere seventeen days that year, taking advantage of the winds and the current which flows from North America to Europe. Until the introduction of steam, eastbound passages were nearly always faster than westbound ones.

As early as 1819 the *Savannah* became the first steam vessel to make an Atlantic crossing, followed by several other vessels, although they all made most of the crossing under sail, using their primitive steam engines coupled to paddle wheels only briefly during the voyage.

The *Royal William* was one of these early passenger steamships to cross the Atlantic using steam and because of the involvement of Samuel Cunard she has left her mark on history. Again, much of her voyage was, however, actually under sail. Financed by and Canadian built from Scottish plans, she set off in August 1833 with just seven passengers. Samuel Cunard from Halifax, Nova Scotia, was heavily involved in the financing of the voyage. The voyage itself took nineteen days: not too bad for an eastbound run. It was not a proper commercial service but more of a trial to see whether steam power could be used profitably on such a large ocean. Indeed the *Royal William* had been built for the St Lawrence service and as the river was icebound in winter the ship's owners were keen to see if she could be employed in European waters. Steam ships were not new by this time but they had been mainly used for inland waterway and coastal applications. For one thing coal capacity was limited and early marine steam engines were very inefficient in their use of fuel.

The Cunard family had emigrated to Britain's American colonies in 1683. They were German Quakers who settled in Pennsylvania. As loyalists during the War of Independence they were forced to move at the war's conclusion and set up home in Nova Scotia. Samuel Cunard was born in 1788; his mother was an alcoholic whilst his father, Abraham, owned a timber yard. Cunard obtained work in the engineering department of the Naval Dockyard in Halifax, the major port of entry in North America for Britain after the revolutionary war.

Isambard Kingdom Brunel (voted the second greatest Briton, after Winston Churchill, in a post-Millennium poll in the UK) planned a commercial service to extend the Great Western Railway that he had engineered from London to Bristol onwards by sea to New York. Bristol was, in the early part of the nineteenth century, Britain's premier port for Atlantic voyages. His *Great Western* was beaten from making the first proper commercial voyage by the Irish Sea packet ship *Sirius*, hastily put into service by the rival British and American Steam Ship Company. With a GRT of just 703 and equipped for 100 passengers, *Sirius* was built by the Menses Yard at Leith on the Firth of Forth. Whilst intimately associated with the *Great Western*, Brunel was not a shipbuilder and as such much of the detailed work was carried out by his colleagues William Patterson and Christopher Claxton.

The British and American Steam Ship Company had ordered a huge (for the time) vessel of 1,800 GRT (they had originally planned for four smaller ships) to be named *British Queen*. As the *British Queen* was by no means ready they chartered the *Sirius*, setting off with ninety passengers before *Great Western* had completed her trials. During these trials *Great Western* suffered a fire in her engine room and Brunel was injured, breaking his leg, during the operation to quench the flames. *Great Western* finally commenced her maiden voyage from Bristol to New York on schedule on 8 April 1838, four days behind *Sirius*. To the chagrin of the company accountants she was carrying only seven of the fifty-seven booked passengers – the remainder having cancelled their bookings after the fire.

Sirius won the race to be first to New York, arriving there on 23 April, having completed the voyage in eighteen days, fourteen hours and twenty-two minutes. Even the best of the sailing ships on the route were taking on average twenty-four days to Europe and, being against the currents, thirty-plus days back.

No sooner were the celebrations in full flow than smoke was seen on the horizon. Was it a ship on fire? No, it was the *Great Western*. She had made up nearly all the time and crossed the Atlantic in fifteen days and twelve hours. *Sirius's* record was short lived. Later the Blue Riband was to be awarded to the passenger vessel that beat the previous westbound (against the prevailing current and winds) time and thus *Great Western* is technically the first holder. The first ship recorded as flying a blue riband, or pennant, from her masthead to show that she had broken the record was the *Rex* in August 1935. *Normandie* flew a blue riband from her masthead as she entered New York harbour on her record-breaking maiden voyage in May 1935. That same year British Member of Parliament Harold K. Hales drew up a set of rules for the trophy that he had commissioned. The last liner to hold the Hales Trophy was the SS *United States* but it is now held by a fast ferry, several of which have been fitted out for record-breaking attempts across the Atlantic. Despite protests, the US Courts ruled that they were eligible despite the fact they were most certainly not liners. The award was not for the quickest crossing but for the average speed, as Bremerhaven to New York is further than Liverpool to New York etc. Hence the Collins liner *Pacific* took the title from Cunard's *Asia* in 1850 by running from Liverpool to New York in ten days, four hours and forty-five minutes at an average speed of 12.46 knots, whereas the *Asia* had covered Liverpool to Halifax (a shorter distance) in only eight days, fourteen hours and fifty minutes, but at an average speed of 12.25 knots. Nevertheless the record-breaker often achieved not just the highest average speed but often the fastest crossing as well.

With a successful crossing under his belt, Brunel's shipping star seemed in its ascendancy. The prize he sought was the lucrative British Admiralty North American mail contract. The Admiralty contract, as issued in 1839, called for a monthly UK to Halifax service operated by ships of at least 300 horsepower. With one ship Brunel could not manage a monthly service, but he offered to provide three ships within two years. The British Government wanted a much earlier start to the contract.

Although the time allowed for bids was short, Cunard took passage to the UK and made a surprise bid to the Admiralty. In association with Robert Napier of Glasgow, a renowned marine engine builder, and ship owners George Burns and the McIvers (David and Charles) from Liverpool, Cunard offered to provide four ships and to operate a weekly service. Brunel had been outflanked and the Admiralty awarded the contract to Cunard. It was the beginning of a company that still exists today, albeit as a Carnival brand.

Cunard's first ships were the *Britannia, Arcadia, Caledonia* and *Columbia*, named after Great Britain, Nova Scotia, Scotland (where the ships were built) and the US.

The four paddle steamers were 207ft long and 34ft wide, with a GRT of 1,150 on a wooden hull. They carried 115 passengers in cramped conditions at a speed of between 9 and 10 knots. They had red and black painted funnels; Cunard had commissioned chemists to produce a heat-resistant paint – henceforth the plain black funnel would be replaced by a visual identification of the owning company.

Cunard did not believe in spending money unnecessarily and the ships were far from luxurious. Charles Dickens sailed on *Britannia* in 1842 and compared his cabin to a coffin! *Columbia* was wrecked in 1843 but with no loss of life. Cunard also introduced red (port) and green (starboard) running lights on the line's vessels. The Cunard Line philosophy was one of conservatism and safety. It is a proud boast of Cunard's transatlantic operation that until the torpedoing of the *Lusitania* in 1915 no passenger lives were lost in accidents. Apparently this is not quite true as a small number of lives may have been lost due to being swept overboard, but that was not seen as being the company's fault.

Brunel soldiered on and tried to compete. Whilst Cunard grew using wooden ships and remaining true to paddle wheel propulsion, Brunel was convinced that iron ships with screw propellers were the answer and he became involved with the experiments carried out by the Admiralty in 1845, in which the paddle sloop HMS *Alecto* and the screw vessel HMS *Rattler* were pitted against each other in a 'tug of war'. The screw vessel won, although recent research using models suggests that the result was not perhaps as clear cut as it seemed at the time.

To prove his belief that screw and iron ships were the way forward, Brunel planned and launched the huge (for the time) 3,270 GRT *Great Britain*. Iron hulled with a propeller, she was so big that part of the lock gates at Bristol had to be removed to get her out. She was originally designed as a large paddle steamer but Brunel decided to fit her with a propeller. Iron vessels were not new but had previously been used for barges on inland waterways; an iron vessel will float but the iron of the time was less easy to shape than wood and could be very brittle and was also less adaptable to the flexing needed to cope with the stresses and strains encountered on the open ocean. It was also harder to make hull repairs whilst at sea. Generations of seamen had grown up with wooden ships and sails – new skills would be needed now. Iron had, however, the advantage of comparative lightness, meaning the engines had less weight to propel through the ocean.

In the summer of 1845 she commenced her maiden voyage to New York but by then the Atlantic was virtually a Cunard lake. Nevertheless she was a very impressive ship but not very successful, being slower than the Cunard vessels.

In September 1846 she left Liverpool (to which port she now operated, spelling the end of Bristol as a passenger terminus) with her largest complement: 180 passengers – the largest number ever carried in a single ship to that date. The iron hull played havoc with her compass and instead of skirting the Isle of Man she ran aground in Dundrum Bay, County Down, Ireland. No lives were lost but the ship was stranded. Re-floating took all winter and a wooden ship would have broken up in the freezing gales.

Unsuccessful against the North Atlantic competition, *Great Britain* was switched to the Liverpool–Australia run in 1856, making thirty-two voyages in twenty-three years. Laid up in 1875, she was sold in 1882 and converted to a sail-only ship. Carrying coal, her cargo caught fire and she put into the Falklands in May 1886 where she was hulked. In the 1930s there was talk of a restoration but no money was available and she was towed to a deserted cove and beached. She remained intact, however, and in 1970 was towed back to her birthplace of Bristol where she was lovingly restored and opened to the public – a fitting monument to her builder and his vision. In appalling weather and with little maintenance she was a survivor from the earliest days of steam ships.

The pioneering *Great Western* was laid up in 1846 after forty-five round trips. Sold as a transport during Crimean War, she was broken up in 1856.

Brunel was not finished with ocean liners, however. In addition to working on the Crystal Palace for the Great Exhibition, he was to build one other ship, and what a ship it was; the mighty *Leviathan* – or as she was later named, *Great Eastern*.

Built for the UK–Australia service, new owners during the building process decided to use her instead on the North Atlantic. She was nearly 20,000 GRT (five times bigger than anything else afloat). Brunel had calculated this would allow her to carry enough coal to reach Australia! She had sails, paddles and a propeller. She was designed to carry 596 cabin and 2,400 steerage passengers from UK to Australia. Nothing as big was seen until White Star introduced their big four: *Celtic, Cedric, Baltic* and *Adriatic* from 1901 onwards.

Built at the J. Scott Russell yard on the Thames, she was laid down as *Leviathan* in 1854 but renamed *Great Eastern* for the Great Steamship Company whilst building. The yard went bankrupt and the project seemed doomed more than once. Brunel and Scott Russell fell out over the way the building was carried out. Everything about her was huge and she had to be launched sideways along rails, but stuck fast at the first attempt on 3 November 1857. This was highly embarrassing as the company had sold tickets for the event.

The ship took a great toll on Brunel's health but finally took to the water on 31 January 1858. Brunel went on board just before her maiden voyage and, despite suffering from nephritus, posed for his photograph. The date was 2 September 1859; he died shortly after, worn out by the stress of the project and his illness. She operated on the North Atlantic from 1860 until 1863 and then found employment as a cable ship for which she was well suited. She laid one of the Atlantic cables (but not the first, which that was laid by HMS *Agamemnon* and USS *Niagara* in 1858).

After her cable duties she languished as a floating exhibition ship and advertising hoardings on the Mersey for Lewis's Bon Marché department store, until she was broken up in 1888–89. As she was being dismantled the remains of two bodies, workmen from the builder's yard, were found in her double hull.

Cunard went on to dominate the North Atlantic but competition was never far away. Initially it came from the United States and the Collins Line, whose driving force was a New Yorker named Edward Knight Collins. Collins entered the North Atlantic trade in 1850 with the most luxurious ships yet seen. His four initial greyhounds, *Arctic, Atlantic, Baltic* and *Pacific*, were of 2,800 GRT, carrying 200 passengers in first class with the later addition of eighty second class and 145 crew. With a speed of 12 knots the Collins Line soon provided a more luxurious alternative to the Cunard vessels, which now looked dated and spartan. However, the loss of *Arctic* in 1854 with 332 dead including Collins's wife and two of his children and then the disappearance of the *Pacific* outbound from Liverpool in 1856 (her wreck was found in 1991 just 60 miles from Liverpool) doomed the company and it ceased operations in 1860.

Who would challenge Cunard next? Cunard was behind the times. *Cambria* and *Hibernia* were slightly larger versions of the Britannia class whilst the four ships of the America class, *America, Canada, Europa* and *Asia*, were slightly bigger and faster again. In 1850 they brought the crossing time down to eight days and fourteen hours between Liverpool and Halifax with a speed of 12.25 knots, only to lose the record to Collins's *Pacific* the same year.

Cunard's response to the Collins challenge was the launching, in 1855 and 1861, of its last two paddle steamers, the *Persia* and the *Scotia* respectively. Cunard still stuck to paddle-wheel propulsion using side-lever steam engines but these ships followed Brunel's lead and were constructed of iron. Of 3,871 GRT, compared to *Britannia's* 1,135, *Scotia* could carry 273 first-class and fifty second-class passengers at 13.5 knots. She took the record but there would be no further improvement on the wooden paddle steamer powered by side-lever steam engines. All the ships covered up to this point also carried a full set of sails, vital as the engines were still not as reliable as they would need to be if they were to be relied on completely. *Persia* also introduced internal bulkheads, the beginnings of the watertight compartment concept. It soon proved itself. In January 1856, five days out of Liverpool on her maiden voyage, *Persia* hit an iceberg head on at 11 knots. Her bow was crumpled and the bulkheads held – she survived although her rivets 'popped' for over 16ft from her bow. Guion Line's *Arizona* had a similar experience in November 1879 and her bulkheads helped her to survive – *Titanic*, as we shall see, was not so lucky.

The propeller, as a means of ship propulsion, had been pioneered by an English farmer, Francis P. Smith, of all people. He was an amateur engineer but in 1836 he had patented a screw device for propelling a vessel. His experimental vessel *Archimedes* interested both the Admiralty and Brunel, and led to the *Great Britain* being screw rather than propeller driven.

Cunard, however, was not interested. It was enough that *Persia* and *Scotia* were built of iron; propulsion would remain traditional but competition was still around and from another British source, a source that would lead directly to *Titanic* – the White Star Line. Nevertheless Cunard was forced to adopt screw propulsion and *Scotia* was the last Cunard paddle-driven vessel on the North Atlantic.

Steerage and emigrants

Steerage was used to refer to the lowest decks of a passenger vessel. This area of the ship came to be used to accommodate passengers travelling on the cheapest class of ticket, and offered only the most basic amenities; initially this typically meant limited toilet use, no privacy and poor food. The name 'steerage' came from the fact that the control lines of the rudder ran on this level of the ship and does not imply accommodation at the stern. Cunard, Brunel and the Collins Line did not carry steerage passengers initially. Such passengers, more often than not those emigrating from Europe to the United States or Canada, were carried on overcrowded sailing ships. These voyages were long, uncomfortable and dangerous.

The potato famine that hit Ireland in 1846 brought about a massive increase in those wishing to leave the old world for the new. Five shipwrecks alone killed over 1,200 emigrants crossing the Atlantic and by 1852 nearly fifty emigrant vessels had been lost. To appreciate the huge number of emigrations to the US, the Ellis Island Centre (where most of the immigrants from the late 1890s onwards were processed) has stated that more than 22 million passengers and members of ships' crews entered the United States through Ellis Island and the Port of New York between 1892 and 1924.

Ellis Island opened in 1892 as a federal immigration station and remained as such until 1954; it is now a museum and educational resource and well worth a visit if you are in New York. Millions of newly arrived immigrants passed through the station during that time – in fact, it has been estimated that close to 40 per cent of all current US citizens can trace at least one of their ancestors to Ellis Island.

America was built by immigrants. From Plymouth Rock in the seventeenth century to Ellis Island in the twentieth, people born elsewhere came to America. Some were fleeing religious persecution and political turmoil. Most, however, came for economic reasons and were part of extensive migratory systems that responded to changing demands in labour markets. Their experience in the United States was as diverse as their backgrounds and aspirations. Some became farmers and others toiled in factories. Some settled permanently and others returned to their homeland. Collectively, however, they contributed to the building of a nation by providing a constant source of inexpensive labour, by settling rural regions and industrial cities, and by bringing their unique forms of political and cultural expression.

Colonial immigration figures were nothing compared to those of the nineteenth century. From 1815 to the start of the Civil War, 5 million people moved to the United States, about half from England and 40 per cent from Ireland. Between the end of the war and 1890 another 10 million came, mostly from north-west Europe – England, Wales, Ireland, Germany and Scandinavia. Finally about 15 million immigrants arrived in the relatively brief period between 1890 and 1914, until the outbreak of war in Europe temporarily arrested the flow. This later group came mostly from eastern and southern Europe and consisted of new immigrant groups – Poles, Russian Jews, Ukrainians, Slovaks, Croatians, Slovenes, Hungarians, Romanians, Italians and Greeks.

These people came largely for the same reasons that colonials had. The American economy had needed both unskilled and skilled workers through much of the nineteenth century. But after the 1880s the demand was almost exclusively for unskilled workers to fill the growing number of factory jobs. Coinciding with this were conditions in some areas of Europe, which were undergoing substantial economic changes in the 1880s as a result of the Industrial Revolution. Southern and eastern Europeans dislocated from their land and, possessing few skills, were attracted to the burgeoning industries in the United States. These 'poor, huddled masses' were to provide the incentive for a huge expansion in the transatlantic passenger trade.

Myth?

Steerage class was very poor

At first emigrants were carried in poor accommodation, initially in sailing vessels and latterly in the most primitive conditions in early steamships. However, pressure on governments brought about improvements and regulations relating to the treatment of steerage passengers. As early as 1848 the British Parliament passed legislation on the ventilation, safety and cleanliness of emigrant accommodation. No longer would they be forced into poor accommodation with women sometimes in fear of their virtue from both the crew and male passengers. Further legislation followed in 1873, following US Congress investigations.

There was an economic imperative that led to improved steerage (later called third class) conditions: those who travelled to the New World in steerage might make their fortunes and visit their old homes, travelling in either first or second class; those who had a reasonable journey might also tell their friends and relatives back home and encourage them to travel on the same line.

The German company Hamburg-Amerika, under Albert Ballin, built a whole town at Hamburg docks to accommodate and process emigrants for its ships, so important was the traffic to Ballin. Ballin and his rivalry with Cunard and White Star plays an important but peripheral role in the *Titanic* story as will be shown later.

One company that was interested in the steerage/emigrant trade was the British Inman Line. Founded in 1850 as the Liverpool and Philadelphia Shipping Company, their first vessel was a speculative venture by the Todd and McGregor yard on the River Clyde – the iron-hulled, screw-propelled *City of Glasgow*. It would be a long time before Cunard would accept such a departure from tradition. Sold to the Richardson Brothers of Liverpool, whose junior partner was William Inman, she had already shown that she was seaworthy and had carried first and second class across the Atlantic at half the fare charged by Collins and Cunard.

She was so successful that the Richardsons ordered a series of ships designed for both first class and the emigrant traffic. The line suffered a major tragedy in 1854 when *the City of Glasgow* disappeared without trace in the Atlantic with the loss of 480 souls – the worst Atlantic tragedy to date. Within six months the *City of Philadelphia* was lost by grounding, fortunately without loss. If it had not been for British Government charters during the Crimean War the company may have failed. Inman eventually became an Anglo–American company in 1887, after the death of William Inman. A consortium fronted by the Pennsylvania Railroad acquired the company to add to the railroad's American Steamship Company and the Belgian-flagged Red Star Line.

Cunard was being challenged but still reigned supreme. Cunard and its competitors began to introduce screw-driven vessels and by the 1870s the iron-hulled, screw-driven steamer with piston engines was the norm for an Atlantic liner. As the numbers wishing to cross the Atlantic grew after the US Civil War, so new companies came into being. The Liverpool and Great Western Steamship Company was founded by the US-born Stephen Guion in 1866 and was usually referred to as the Guion Line. Successful at first with some fine fast ships, increasing competition brought about the demise of the company in 1894 by which time the Inman Line was in American hands.

The growth in the emigrant trade can be seen in the table below which compares the first, second and steerage capacity and the percentage of steerage of ships from the *Great Western* until *Titanic* and her near contemporaries.

Ship	Year	Owner	GRT	Total Passengers	First class	Second class	Steerage	Percentage steerage
Great Western	1838	Great Western	1,340	128	128★	0	0	0
Britannia	1840	Cunard	1,135	115	115	0	0	0
Pacific	1850	Collins	2,707	200	200	0	0	0
Persia	1856	Cunard	3,300	250	200	50	0	0
City of Brussels	1869	Inman	3,081	800	200	0	600	75
Adriatic	1872	White Star	3,868	1,166	166	0	1000	85
Britannic	1874	White Star	5,004	1,730	230	0	1,500	87
Arizona	1879	Guion	5,174	1,350	140	70	1,140★★	84
City of New York	1888	Inman	10,499	1,740	540	200	1,000	57
Campania	1893	Cunard	12,950	2,000	600	400	1,000	50
Kaiser Willhelm der Grosse	1897	NDL	14,349	1,506	206	226	1,074	71
Lusitania	1907	Cunard	31,550	2,165	563	464	1,138	52
Titanic	1912	White Star	46,328	2,435	735	674	1,026	42
Aquitania	1914	Cunard	49,430	3,230	618	614	1,998	61

★ plus accommodation for twenty servants.
★★ includes 140 third-class passengers.

Table 1   Capacity 1838–1914

By 1922 when the US began to restrict emigration, over 30 million people had made the transatlantic journey in the hope of starting a new life. Some returned but many stayed and spread out across the USA.

Faster and bigger

Improvements in metallurgy and engine building led to a rapid increase in the size and speed of ships. Paddles gave way to a propeller (screw) and wood was replaced by iron for the hull. Sails disappeared. One screw gave way to two (much safer as a single screw could break leaving the ship reliant on sails alone) and then finally iron gave way to steel. The move to steel was important as the Bessemer Process increased the quality of steel and decreased the price. Steel is lighter and stronger than iron and thus allowed for increases in size without the penalties of carrying extra fuel and putting in even more powerful engines.

The table below shows how rapid this progress was – the last half of the nineteenth century and the years leading to the First World War saw developments in engineering every bit as impressive as the Information and Communication Technology (ICT) revolution of the late twentieth and early twenty-first centuries.

Date	Ship	Company	Size (GRT)	Hull	Propulsion	Screw/ Paddle	Speed (knots)
1840	Britannia	C	1,135	Wood	1SL	2P	9
1850	Pacific	Col	2,707	Wood	1SL	2P	12
1855	Scotia	C	2,200	Iron	1SL	2P	13
1869	City of Brussels	I	3,081	Iron	1LPS	1S	14
1872	Adriatic	WS	3,868	Iron	1Comp	1S	14
1879	Arizona	G	5,147	Iron	1Comp	1S	15
1884	Umbria	C	7,718	Steel	2Comp	1S	19
1888	City of New York	I	10,499	Steel	2TE	2S	20
1889	Teutonic	WS	9,984	Steel	2TE	2S	20
1892	Campania	C	12,950	Steel	2TE	2S	21
1897	Kaiser Wilhelm der Grosse	NDL	14,349	Steel	2TE	2S	22

C = Cunard, Col = Collins, I= Inman, WS = White Star, G = Guion, NDL = Nord Deutsche Lloyd
SL = Side lever engines, LPS = Low Power Steam engines, Comp = Compound Steam Engines, TE = Triple Expansion Steam Engines
P = Paddles, S = Screws

Table 2   Developments 1840–97

Between 1840 and the end of the century, the size of an Atlantic liner had increased over tenfold and its speed was over double. From one inefficient side-lever engine, driving paddles and wooden hull the liner was now twin screwed and had much more efficient triple-expansion engines driving a steel hull.

White Star

The original White Star Line had been involved in the sailing ship trade from the UK to Australia. Thomas Ismay, a director of the National Line, bought the name. His new company, the Oceanic Steam Navigation Company, entered the transatlantic trade under the White Star houseflag. Ordering his first six ships (an initial order for four ships was increased) from Harland & Wolff in Belfast to be launched from 1871 onwards, he introduced a number of innovations into the transatlantic trade. Edward Harland, a personal friend of Ismay, used a box girder form of construction that was both light and strong. Examples of this type of construction can be seen in Robert Stephenson's (son of the locomotive pioneer George Stephenson) designs for the Conway railway bridge and his larger Britannia Bridge over the Menai Straits in North Wales. Stephenson faced the challenge of building a bridge rigid and strong enough to carry a heavy train of many carriages. This was done by making the bridge out of two long iron tubes, rectangular in shape, through which the trains would travel.

When first conceived, the tubular bridge was to have been suspended from cables strung through the openings at the tops of the towers. However, after engineering calculations and tests of the finished tubes it was decided that they were strong enough by themselves to carry the trains. Harland adapted this system for his ocean liners. The relationship between White Star and Harland & Wolff was to become very close indeed.

The company began in 1853 on Queen's Island in Belfast. In that year Robert Hickson and Company opened a shipbuilding yard. Edward James Harland was taken on at the tender age of only twenty-three as general manager in 1854. He had served as an apprentice with the Stephensons, hence his familiarity with the box girder concept.

Within four years he had bought the yard for £5,000, aided by a Hamburg financier operating out of Liverpool, where he had an interest in the Bibby Line-named G.C. Schwabe. Schwabe's nephew, Gustav Wolff, an engineer like Harland, became a partner in what was renamed Harland & Wolff. Of the initial shares in the Oceanic Steam Navigation Company (White Star) valued at £1,750 million Ismay had fifty but Harland and Schwabe had twelve each, giving them a major investment in the new company. Whilst Harland & Wolff built ships for other clients, of the 1,500 ships they built a large number were for White Star, who only ordered from the yard.

The White Star ships were fast. *Oceanic* was the first to make her maiden voyage, in 1870. In May 1872 the 3,638 GRT *Adriatic* took the Blue Riband with an average speed of 14.53 knots in a time of seven days, twenty-three hours and fourteen minutes. Within a year of its start of operations White Star had reduced the Atlantic crossing time to less than eight days.

It is instructive to see just how fast progress in cutting the passage time from Europe to America had been:

Date	Ship	Company	Time
1838	*Sirius*	British & American	18d 14h 22m*
1838	*Great Western*	Great Western	15d 12h 00m
1850	*Pacific*	Collins	10d 04h 45m
1856	*Persia*	Cunard	9d 16h 16m*
1863	*Scotia*	Cunard	8d 03h 00m*
1871	*Adriatic*	White Star	7d 23h 17m*

* from Queenstown

Table 3   Crossing times to New York 1838–71

The White Star ships brought new standards to the trade. Harland's designs were a step change from traditional liners. Stephen Fox has described *Oceanic* as the first modern ocean liner. Harland developed a design that was a deck higher than contemporary ships, with an extended superstructure rather than disconnected deckhouses. The box girder concept allowed him to make his ships less beamy but still safe. Whilst the ships still carried fore and aft sails, they were fitted with the newly developed compound steam engines that were much more efficient.

Harland & Wolff had a somewhat novel means of charging – the building costs plus a premium (around 4 per cent). This meant that the yard could not lose and it was only when they built P&O's *Canberra* in 1961 on a fixed cost basis that monies were lost and the yard's decline began.

White Star was a line that realised that although record breaking brought headlines, luxury was something the better-off would pay a premium for. Thus, on the figures in table 1 above, the GRT/single-passenger ratio (GRT divided by the number of passengers) on the *Lusitania* of Cunard was 14.5 and for the *Aquitania* 15.3; for *Titanic* it went up to 19. The raw figures, of course, disguise the fact that it was first class and to a lesser degree second class that had the majority of the public spaces on the ship.

Not long after its spectacular beginnings tragedy struck the White Star Line. In 1873 the nearly new liner *Atlantic* sank after striking Marr's Rock off Nova Scotia. She had left Liverpool on 20 March for her nineteenth voyage from Liverpool. There were 952 people on board, of whom 835 were passengers.

Fearing that he was in danger of running out of coal, the captain decided to head for Halifax to refuel. During the approach to Halifax, on the evening of 31 March, the captain and third officer were on the bridge until midnight, while the *Atlantic* made her way, at about 12 knots, through a storm and experiencing limited visibility and heavy seas. She was approximately 12½ miles off course.

At around 2 a.m. local time, on 1 April 1873, *Atlantic* struck an underwater rock. Lifeboats were lowered but were washed away as the ship began to sink, killing 562. The ship's manifest indicates there were 156 women and 189 children on board (including two who had actually been born during the voyage). All perished except for one boy, John Hanly. Nearly every member of the crew survived, with a total survivor count of 390 people of the 952 aboard. This was the worst civilian loss of life in the Northern Atlantic to that date. The Canadian Government's investigation was concluded with the statement, 'the conduct of Captain Williams in the management of his ship during the twelve or fourteen hours preceding the disaster, was so gravely at variance with what ought to have been the conduct of a man placed in his responsible position'.

In 1893 the *Naronic* disappeared without trace and in 1899 *Germanic* capsized whilst loading coal in New York in a blizzard – she was raised and sailed again briefly for the company.

The *Republic* was one of White Star's slower ships, mainly engaged in the emigrant trade full time when sailing from Europe to North America. In the early morning of 23 January 1909, while sailing from New York to the Mediterranean with 742 passengers (including a number of wealthy people heading for southern Europe) and crew, and with Captain Inman Sealby, *Republic* encountered thick fog off the island of Nantucket,

The steamer reduced speed and signalled its presence by whistle. At around 5.45 a.m. another whistle was heard and *Republic*'s engines were ordered hard astern and the helm put over. Out of the fog loomed the Lloyd Italiano liner SS *Florida* and hit *Republic* amidships, at about a right-angle. Two passengers asleep in their cabins on *Republic* were killed when *Florida*'s bow sliced into her. On *Florida* three crewmen were also killed when the bow was crushed back to a collision bulkhead. The engine and boiler rooms on *Republic* began to flood and the ship listed. Captain Sealby led the crew in calmly organising the passengers on deck for evacuation. *Republic* was equipped with the new Marconi wireless telegraph system, and became the first ship in history to issue a CQD (Come Quick Distress) distress signal, sent by Jack R. Binns, later to achieve fame on the *Titanic*. *Florida* came about to rescue *Republic*'s complement, and the USCG *Gresham* also responded to the distress signal. Passengers were distributed between the two ships, with *Florida* taking the bulk of them, but with 900 Italian immigrants already on board, this left the ship dangerously overloaded.

The White Star liner *Baltic* also responded to the CQD call, but due to the persistent fog, it was not until the evening that *Baltic* was able to locate the drifting *Republic*. Once on scene, the rescued passengers were transferred from *Gresham* and *Florida* to *Baltic*. Because of the damage to *Florida*, that ship's immigrant passengers were also transferred to *Baltic*, but a riot nearly broke out when they had to wait until first-class *Republic* passengers were transferred – Edwardian class distinction at play. Once everyone was on board, *Baltic* sailed for New York.

Captain Sealby and a skeleton crew remained on board *Republic* to make an effort to save her, but despite assistance from other vessels she sank. At 15,378 tons, she was the largest ship to have sunk up to that time. All the remaining crew were evacuated before she sank, not far from where the Italian Liner *Andrea Doria* was to go down after her collision with the *Stockholm* in 1956.

Myth?

Up to the Titanic disaster, White Star Line had a good safety record

Compared to the almost perfect safety record of Cunard, White Star's was far less impressive. Not long after her introduction, *Olympic* – *Titanic's* elder sister – collided with HMS *Hawke* off Southampton. The captain on the bridge that day was Captain Smith – later to captain *Titanic* on her fateful voyage.

Ismay and the White Star management were undismayed. The North Atlantic was an unforgiving ocean and the company continued to expand.

In the late 1880s, competition for the Blue Riband was fierce amongst the top steamship lines, and White Star decided to order two ships from Harland & Wolff that would be capable of an average Atlantic crossing speed of 20 knots (37km/h). Construction of the *Teutonic* and the *Majestic* began in 1887. When *Teutonic* was launched on 19 January 1889 she was the first White Star ship not to have square rigged sails. The ship was completed on 25 July 1889 and participated in the Spithead Naval Review on 1 August, commemorating Queen Victoria's Golden Jubilee.

Teutonic was built under the British Auxiliary Armed Cruiser Agreement and was Britain's first armed merchant cruiser, sporting eight 4.7in guns. By this time all vestiges of sail had disappeared. Whether he was referring to the idea of arming such a ship or the idea of a highly modern liner is still in dispute, but *Teutonic* is the ship the German Kaiser boarded during the Review and said, 'We must have some of these'. The guns were removed after the military reviews and, on 7 August, she left on her maiden voyage to New York City.

In 1891 *Majestic* brought the Blue Riband to White Star and in 1891 *Teutonic* took it from her sister with an average crossing speed of 20.25 knots (37.50km/h). She later bested her own record with a speed of 20.5 knots (38.0km/h). The following year the *City of Paris* took the honour away, and no White Star ship would ever regain it. White Star, as Albert Balin in Germany was to do (see below), decided that the price of speed was too high and the company would concentrate on size and luxury.

Enter the Germans

The Atlantic was fast becoming a British lake with a few American interlopers as far as the passenger liner trade was concerned. Cunard and White Star did not have the market completely to themselves. Inman and the Guion Line was started in 1866 as the Liverpool and Great Western Steamship Company by the American born Stephen Barker-Guion. The French company CGT also operated a number of vessels. However, Cunard and White Star were the market leaders – they had the largest and fastest steamers on the Atlantic.

The German Nord Deutsche Lloyd Company had entered the trade in the late 1870s with the *Elbe*, but it was a while before the Germans began to compete to any great extent. The Germans with Albert Ballin (HAPAG (Hamburg-Amerika) and NDL (Nord Deutsche Lloyd)) were also in the business, especially for emigrants, with the first four-funnelled liners. As mentioned earlier, Ballin provided very good shore-side facilities in Hamburg for his emigrant passengers.

The snatching of records from the British began with the introduction of the *Kaiser Wilhelm der Grosse* by NDL in 1897. At that time NDL had the largest fleet of international express steamers, eleven ships in total, although they were smaller and slower than their British rivals. Because Hamburg and Bremen are a day's steaming further from New York than the UK, the German ships needed to carry more fuel and supplies, hence they were always slightly slower than their British competitors.

By the end of the nineteenth century Britain and Germany were locked in a naval arms race that was to see the introduction of HMS *Dreadnought* (launched 1906) and was to have its culmination in the Battle of Jutland in 1916. This naval race has been recounted by Peter Padfield in *The Great Naval Race* and the parallel commercial liner competition between Britain and Germany in Douglas R. Burgess Jnr's *Seize the Trident – the race for superliner supremacy and how it altered the Great War*. As will be shown shortly, it also led to *Titanic* and the disaster.

By the early years of the twentieth century Germany had produced a series of four-funnelled liners that were the equal of anything that Cunard or White Star had in service. HAPAG, under the chairmanship of Albert Balin, had won the Blue Riband with the *Deutschland* of 1900 (she was later to become one of the earliest cruise ships when she was refitted and renamed *Viktoria Luise* in 1911). The *Deutschland* was fast and luxurious but the need for speed made her an unpleasant ride and she had a reputation for shaking her passengers to bits! Just as White Star was to abandon the speed contest and concentrate on size and luxury, so too did Balin. This left his rival, NDL, to challenge the British in the speed stakes.

NDL introduced a series of fast ships, *Kaiser Wilhelm der Grosse* (1897), *Kronprinz Wilhelm* (1890) and *Kaiser Wilhelm II* (1902). The first two, at over 14,000 GRT, were bigger than the latest Cunarders – *Campania* and *Lucania* of 1893 were just over 12,000 GRT – whilst the third came in at over 19,300 GRT. Germany may not have ruled the waves but it seemed as if she was about to rule the Atlantic.

The White Star expansion continued with the introduction of the 17,272 *Oceanic* in 1899, the first ship to exceed 700ft in length, and then the 'Big Four', *Celtic* (1901), *Cedric* (1902), *Baltic* (1904) and *Adriatic* (1907). The first three, on their introduction, were at 20,000 GRT + the largest ships in the world, but they were soon to be dwarfed by the two Cunard giants, *Lusitania* and *Mauretania*. Unlike the NDL and current HAPAG German vessels, the White Star vessels were designed for luxury not speed and whilst not slow they could not have gained the record. The stage was set: Cunard and NDL would go for speed whilst White Star and HAPAG would aim for the greatest luxury possible. However, a new invention was to revolutionise the shipbuilding world and allow Cunard to go for both size and speed.

Parsons and the turbine

The conventional method of powering a steam ship used a traditional steam engine with pistons moving in and out of cylinders. It was wasteful and fuel inefficient but was all that there was – or was it? The idea of using steam to create movement by using it to turn a turbine blade directly had been known to the ancient Greeks but the engineering and metallurgy needed seemed beyond the reach of late Victorian engineers.

Born in London, Charles Parsons was the youngest son of the famous astronomer William Parsons, third Earl of Rosse. He attended Trinity College, Dublin, and St John's College, Cambridge, graduating from the latter in 1877 with a first-class honours degree in mathematics. He then joined the engineering firm of W.G. Armstrong in Newcastle (the north-east of England was at the heart of the Industrial Revolution) as an apprentice, an unusual step for the son of an earl. Later he changed firms and worked on torpedo developments. In 1884 he moved to Clarke, Chapman & Co., ship engine manufacturers near Newcastle, where he was head of their electrical equipment development. He developed a turbine engine there in 1884 and immediately utilised the new engine to drive an electrical generator, which he also designed. Parsons's steam turbine made cheap and plentiful electricity possible.

Parsons was also interested in marine applications and founded the Parsons Marine Steam Turbine Company in Newcastle. In June 1897 his turbine-powered vessel, *Turbinia*, gate-crashed Queen Victoria's Diamond Jubilee Fleet Review off Portsmouth, to demonstrate the great potential of the new technology. The *Turbinia* moved at 34 knots. The fastest Royal Navy ships, using other technologies, reached 27 knots and none of the picket boats could intercept her. Eventually she came alongside White Star's *Teutonic* where the White Star directors inspected her.

Within two years, the destroyers HMS *Viper* and *Cobra* were launched equipped with Parsons's turbines, followed by the first turbine-powered passenger ship, the Clyde steamer TS *King Edward*, in 1901, and the first turbine-powered battleship, HMS *Dreadnought*, in 1906. Today, *Turbinia* is housed in a purpose-built gallery at the Discovery Museum, Newcastle.

White Star did not pursue the turbine concept but Cunard did. In an attempt to make a scientific comparison, Cunard built two sisters in 1905 to test the concept – *Carmania* with turbines and *Caronia* with conventional engines. Although not a record-breaker, *Carmania* proved the faster and more economic of the two; the turbine was here to stay. Cunard was to use the experiment to gain both the size and speed records but not before the company nearly fell into American hands, a fate that White Star was unable to avoid.

J.P. Morgan

J.P. Morgan was a towering personality of the late nineteenth and early twentieth centuries. Born in April 1837, he was a US banker and art collector; he was also somewhat of a ladies' man – it was said that he not only collected old masters but old mistresses too! Morgan dominated corporate finance and industrial consolidation in the US; whilst today monopolies are frowned upon, Morgan saw them as highly efficient. In 1892 Morgan arranged the merger of Edison General Electric and Thomson-Houston Electric Company to form General Electric. After financing the creation of the Federal Steel Company he merged the Carnegie Steel Company and several other steel and iron businesses to form the United States Steel Corporation in 1901. He also controlled a number of US railroads and, of course, made the steel for their rails!

Morgan envisaged a 'through bill of lading' that would allow goods to be transported to and from the US and Europe via a single entity; he owned the railways but he needed a shipping operation. Typically for Morgan he envisaged a Morgan monopoly on the North Atlantic.

By 1901, he was one of the wealthiest men in the world. At the height of Morgan's career, during the early 1900s, he and his partners had financial investments in many large corporations and was accused by critics of controlling the nation's high finance. He directed the banking coalition that stopped the 1907 panic.

J.P. Morgan – White Star was the jewel in his International Mercantile Marine crown. (June Cartwright)

Myth?

White Star was a British company

In 1902 J.P. Morgan & Co. financed the formation of International Mercantile Marine Company (IMM), an Atlantic shipping combine which absorbed several major American and British lines. IMM was a holding company that controlled subsidiary corporations that in turn had their own operating subsidiaries. Morgan hoped to dominate transatlantic shipping through interlocking directorates and contractual arrangements with the railroads, but that proved impossible because of the unscheduled nature of sea transport, American antitrust legislation and an agreement with the British Government. One of IMM's subsidiaries was White Star. Ismay senior had bequeathed the company to his son, J. Bruce Ismay and in 1891 Ismay Jnr had become a partner in his father's firm, Ismay, Imrie and Company. In 1899 Thomas Ismay died and Bruce Ismay became head of the family business. However, in 1901 he was approached by the Americans and Lord Pirrie, by now head of Harland & Wolff, who wished to build an international shipping conglomerate. Ismay agreed after considerable angst and persuasion to merge his firm into the IMM.

Morgan also persuaded Balin and the German Kaiser to give him a 51 per cent stake in the German Atlantic companies – now only Cunard stood in the way of his monopoly. Initially Cunard, now run by Lord Inverclyde, expressed interest as the company was short of capital. This began to worry the British Government and eventually legislation was passed keeping Cunard British and providing a loan of £2.5 million and an annual subsidy of £150,000 for two huge and fast liners that could double as armed merchant cruisers in the event of war. The results of these machinations were to be the Olympic Class, of which *Titanic* was the second sister, and Cunard's *Lusitania* and *Mauretania*.

Titanic's sinking in 1912, the year before Morgan's death, was a financial disaster for IMM, which was forced to apply for bankruptcy protection in 1915. Analysis of financial records shows that IMM was overleveraged and suffered from inadequate cash flow that caused it to default on bond interest payments. Saved by the First World War, IMM eventually re-emerged as the United States Lines, which itself went bankrupt in 1986.

Between 1890 and 1913, forty-two major corporations were organised, or their securities were underwritten, in whole or part, by J.P. Morgan and Company. Morgan died in Rome, Italy, in 1913 at the age of seventy-five; perhaps he was also a *Titanic* victim.

Cunard's giants

Cunard was now safe from American predators and had a subsidy from the British Government. The new liners would be revolutionary, at over 31,000 GRT and 790ft long (conventional wisdom of the time said that 750ft was the maximum hull length possible – exceed that and the hull would break; for comparison the largest passenger ship in the world in 2011 was the *Oasis of the Seas* at 1,181ft long and 225,000 GRT!). Their service speed was to be 25 knots and therein lay the problem. Triple expansion engines had reached their maximum possible output. Just making the engines bigger would not produce the increase in speed. Just as the propeller-driven aircraft could not exceed a certain speed due to the behaviour of the air the propeller cut through, so the triple expansion engine had reached its maximum possible speed – around 23 knots. The answer lay in the as yet untried – in a big ship turbine. The experiment of comparing the turbine-engined *Carmania* with her triple expansion sister *Caronia* (both completed in 1905) had proved the worth of the turbine.

The Admiralty, as the Government department responsible for the subsidy, saw the vessels as an important addition to the fleet in time of war, but was sceptical about turbines in large vessels. This view soon changed as the building of the first turbine and all-big-gun battleship HMS *Dreadnought* in 1906 was to show. Initially Cunard had refused to consider turbines at all but it was the only method of achieving the desired speed advantage over the company's rivals and to meet the requirements of the Admiralty.

Turbines were agreed upon and in 1905 *Lusitania* was laid down at the John Brown yard in Glasgow and the *Mauretania* at Swan Hunter and Wigham on the

Tyne. Both were launched in 1906, *Lusitania* undertaking her maiden voyage in September 1907 and gaining the record at 23.99 knots the month after. *Mauretania* debuted in November and in 1909 gained the record at 26.06 knots. *Lusitania* was torpedoed and sank in 1915 but *Mauretania* held the record until 1929 when she lost it to the *Bremen* – a remarkable achievement.

Prior to *Lusitania* Germany had the fastest ship and White Star the largest: *Lusitania* was a step change.

Ship	Date	Company	Size	Speed
Deutschland	1900	HAPAG	16,502	23.15
Adriatic	1907	White Star	24,541	17
Lusitania	1907	Cunard	31,550	26.06

Table 5   The impact of Lusitania

White Star had deliberately exchanged the quest for speed for the pursuit of size. The Germans had sacrificed size for speed – how would they respond?

The German response was to be a trio of superliners of around 50,000 GRT but before that White Star made its challenge in the form of the three 45,000+ GRT ships of the Olympic Class, *Olympic*, *Titanic* and *Gigantic* (renamed after the *Titanic* disaster as *Britannic*). If Cunard could not be challenged on speed, the challenge from both White Star and the Germans would be on size and it would need to be soon or Cunard would have too large a market share. Thus the Olympics were conceived in haste – the seeds of the disaster had been sown.

RMS *Mauretania* – the Olympic class were built as rivals to her and *Lusitania*. (Authors' collection)

Chapter 2

The Olympic Class

It has often been said that the *Titanic* disaster was a kind of 'loss of British inno-cence following the country's lead in the Industrial Revolution'. In fact it can be argued that the loss of innocence, if there ever was one, occurred much earlier with another transport disaster. On the day she set sail on her maiden voyage, in April 1912, *Titanic* was the world's largest ship (a design improvement gave her a slightly larger Gross Registered Tonnage than her sister, *Olympic*). She was a ship that had received much technical praise; she was a wonder of the age.

In 1878, in addition to the great ocean liners, the transport wonder of the year was the world's longest bridge. The bridge was nearly 2 miles long and consisted of eighty-five spans carrying a single rail track from Fife over the River Tay to Dundee in Scotland. Seventy-two of the spans were supported on spanning girders below the level of the track; the remaining thirteen navigation spans were spanning girders above the level of the track (i.e. the train ran through a tunnel of girders) in order to provide sufficient headroom for ships proceeding to and from Perth, which is upriver from Dundee. The bridge was an important link in the east coast route from London to Aberdeen. Whilst the partners in the east coast route, the Great Northern Railway, the North Eastern Railway and the North British Railway (the Scottish partner) had an advantage over their west coast rivals, the London and North Western Railway and the Caledonian Railway as far as Edinburgh, this was lost north of the Scottish capital. The route up the east coast of England was more lightly graded than that up the west coast, but north of Edinburgh North British Railway passengers had to cross the Firth of Forth and then the Firth of Tay by ferry, whilst those on the Caledonian Railway had an easy run through Perth. Bridges across the Tay and the Forth were the answer.

The contract for the first bridge, that across the Tay, had been awarded to Messrs De Bergh & Co. who were to build the bridge to the design of Thomas Bouch. After three years the contract was taken over by a company from Middlesbrough – Hopkins, Gilkes & Co. Bouch's design is described above. It was a modified version of his original as he found that the riverbed was not of the composition his original soundings in the river had indicated.

When the bridge opened in 1878 the Inspector of Railways for the Board of Trade, Major-General Hutchinson, carried out a number of tests and passed the bridge fit for use although he proposed a speed limit for trains and commented on the possible effects of high winds – prophetic words indeed.

Queen Victoria crossed the bridge on her way to Balmoral and knighted the designer. Sir Thomas Bouch, as he now was, was working on a design for a crossing over the Forth of Firth to complete the east coast line.

At approximately 7.15 p.m. on the stormy night of Sunday 28 December 1879, the central navigation spans of the Tay Bridge collapsed into the Firth of Tay at Dundee, taking with it a train, six carriages and seventy-five souls.

At the time a gale, estimated over Beaufort force 10, was blowing down the Tay estuary from the North Sea at right angles to the bridge. The collapse of the bridge, only opened nineteen months previously and passed safe by the Board of Trade, sent shock waves through the Victorian engineering profession and general public. The disaster is one of the most famous bridge failures and to date it is still one of the worst structural engineering failures in the British Isles.

The collapse occurred within the 'high girders', as they were known, the spans that were 27ft high with an 88ft clearance above the high water mark to allow ships to pass It was these spans which fell. Most of the girders below track level remained standing. After the disaster the design of the railway bridge across the Firth of Forth was transferred to Benjamin Baker and Sir John Fowler.

A Court of Inquiry was set up to try and ascertain the reason for the collapse of the bridge. The inquiry reported that, 'The fall of the bridge was occasioned by the insufficiency of the cross bracing and its fastenings to sustain the force of the gale'. The inquiry also indicated that if the piers, and in particular the wind bracing, had been properly constructed and maintained, the bridge could probably have withstood the storm that night. Bouch was held to blame for the collapse, by not making adequate allowance for wind loading with a train on the bridge – it was the additional forces that the presence of the train brought with it that were the immediate cause of the collapse. The wrought-iron girders that survived were used in the building of the replacement bridge that is still in use today, with the piers of the old bridge visible alongside.

The disaster is still remembered locally but on a national scale its immediate effects were considerable. A triumph of British engineering had failed. Man had not tamed the elements! This chapter concludes with the belief that the Olympic Class were built sufficiently well to withstand the elements despite certain design flaws. The below are some words of Captain Smith, the captain of *Titanic*, on that fateful night that show that just like those who extolled the Tay Bridge, arrogance in the face of nature can lead to disaster. The Tay Bridge showed that engineering was not infallible and yet less than twenty years later the man who was to captain the world's largest ship believed in some form of infallibility.

Myth?

Captain Smith believed that ships were so well built in 1912 that they would not sink

Shipbuilding is such a perfect art nowadays that absolute DISASTER, INVOLVING THE PASSENGERS IS INCONCEIVABLE. Whatsoever happens, there will be time before the vessel sinks to save the life of every person on board. I will go a bit further. I will say that I cannot imagine any condition that would cause the vessel to founder. Modern shipbuilding has gone beyond that.

Proclaimed by Captain Smith, later to be the captain of *Titanic*,
in an interview to the *Boston Post*, 16 April 1907,
five years almost to the day before the sinking.

The Olympic Class

Lusitania and *Mauretania* were the wonders of the age. They were not identical, *Mauretania* could always be recognised by her more prominent profusion of ventilators. The interiors were very different: *Lusitania*'s interior was designed by James Miller, famous for his work on the Glasgow Exhibition of 1901. She was a contemporary, light and airy ship. Harold Peto, a renowned country house designer, produced a seagoing version of a stately home for *Mauretania*. With their exceptional (for the time) speed the two ships revolutionised the transatlantic trade. How would the competition respond? Cunard had the largest and fastest Atlantic liners and a safety record second to none. Whilst they had lost two ships over the years and a small number of passengers had been washed overboard, the proud boast that the company had never lost a passenger to shipwreck was true.

White Star made the first response. J. Bruce Ismay was in charge of the IMM and also chairman of White Star itself – the jewel in the IMM crown.

Britain was still the most important maritime nation in the world but the United States was fast becoming the major world economy. The late Edwardian period coincided with the cusp of British decline and the rise of the German and American economies. Britain still ruled the waves and had a huge overseas empire but in terms of industrial output the country was losing ground to her rivals. Germany was building a fleet of battleships to rival the Royal Navy and her Merchant Marine was also growing very quickly. White Star may have been operating under the auspices of the American IMM but the British public saw it as a British company – its ships were registered in Liverpool, its officers and the vast majority of the crew were British and the ships flew the Red Ensign of the British Merchant Marine (or the Blue Ensign if the captain held a rank in the Royal Naval Reserve).

According to the accepted version of events, Ismay for White Star and Lord Pirrie for Harland & Wolff met at Pirrie's London home with their wives in 1907

to plan their response. Pirrie had previously
expressed a wish to build a ship of over 100ft
long and believed that 100,000 GRT was not
an impossibility (it was to be realised in 1996
with the 101,253 GRT *Carnival Destiny*).
Indeed plans by the Americans in 1909 were
for a 55,000 GRT response to the European
liners and in 1937 the US and then in 1938
the French prepared designs for 100,000
GRT liners, but war put paid to those gran-
diose ideas. Germany's response in 1937
would have been the 80,000 GRT *Vicktoria*
of about the same size as the *Normandie* and
Queen Mary, then in service, and the *Queen
Elizabeth* then building. The lack of US
companies and ships in the previous chapter
may surprise readers. Inman became a US
company and there were a number of US
liners after the Collins Line failed. There was
only really one US yard capable of building

J. Bruce Ismay – chairman of White Star.
(June Cartwright)

an Atlantic liner and that was the Cramp shipyard in Philadelphia. Cramp built a
pair of elegant liners for the American Line (formerly Inman). The *St Louis* and
the *St Paul* of 1995 had only two-thirds of the horsepower of the *Campania* and
Lucania but were briefly the third largest passenger ships afloat. The *St Paul* is germane to the *Titanic* story as it was from her that Marconi made the first ship–shore
radio call in 1899.

Ismay and Pirrie decided on a trio of ships, 46,000 GRT, but slower than the
Mauretania and *Lusitania*.

Myth?

Titanic *was ultra large*

Albert Balin of HAPAG reached the same conclusion as Ismay and Pirrie and his
response was to be a trio of 50,000 GRT. Slower is a relative term; White Star's
ships (or HAPAG's) could not compete for the record but it was important that
if they were not as fast as the Cunard pair then they should not be that much
slower. This is a point that we shall return to when we consider why *Titanic* was
going at nearly her maximum speed in a region of ice.

The basic configuration of the new ships was soon accomplished. In 1948 the
basic configuration of the Boeing B52 bomber was worked out, according to Clive
Irving in his book *Wide Body*, in the Van Cleeve Hotel in Daytona over a weekend.
According to the same author the mighty Boeing 747 'Jumbo Jet' was conceived
in just a few pages in an agreement between the chairman of Boeing and the Juan
Trippe of Pan American Airways (Pan Am). Detailed design came much later.

Ismay and Pirrie produced the idea for a trio of 46,000 GRT liners capable of around 22 knots and carrying around 2,600 passengers in three classes and with a crew of around 940 to cater to the needs of the ship and its passengers.

The press announcement for the new vessels was carefully timed to be a day before *Lusitania* arrived in New York on her maiden voyage.

With the basic configuration decided, the question of propulsion needed to be addressed. Surprisingly in this era of detailed project management this was left until after construction had commenced. Whilst such monster (for the time) ships would require an expansion of the Harland & Wolff facilities, the actual engineering was within tried and tested norms. The Olympic Class would

Lord Pirrie's bust outside Belfast City Hall. (Authors' collection)

be big but they would not be revolutionary in terms of their construction.

Olympic was laid down on 16 December 1908 with *Titanic* following on 31 March 1909. As the lead ship, resources were allocated as a priority to *Olympic*. The men who built the ships were mainly Northern Irish Protestants. Harland & Wolff was a Protestant employer – a discriminatory practice that would not be tolerated today but lingered on in a number of firms in Northern Ireland, with its sectarian history, well into the late twentieth century.

With the exception of the managers, most of the workforce lived around the yard in row after row of terraced houses. At the time the company employed over 40,000 men: it was the major employer in Belfast. In 1912 skilled shipyard workers who built *Titanic* earned £2 per week, unskilled workers earned £1 or less per week.

An oft repeated myth was that the hull number for *Titanic* was 3900 04 which, backwards, was supposed to read 'No Pope' and this was said by Catholics to be a bad omen. Unfortunately for the myth the builder's number of *Titanic* was 401 and her Board of Trade official number was 131428 – how the myth started is unknown but it still surfaces today. In researching this book the authors were taken by taxi from the Harland & Wolff yard to the Ulster Folk Museum. The taxi driver repeated the myth (he knew it had no validity) and then made a joke: 'The Protestants built *Titanic* so the Catholics built an iceberg!'

The *Lusitania* and *Mauretania* owed their speed to the use of the recently developed steam turbine which was to replace the more traditional triple expansion steam engines. This was an expensive option that White Star decided not to compete with. It was better, both White Star and Harland & Wolff argued, to build slightly slower but larger and even more luxurious vessels – this was the only way to compete.

Lusitania and *Mauretania* were luxurious but the trio of vessels that White Star and Harland & Wolff sketched out during a meeting between Ismay and Pirrie in 1907 were bigger and just as well appointed. Together they decided on a trio of ships, 46,000 GRT but slower than the *Mauretania* and *Lusitania*. Let Cunard have the record of the two fastest liners, White Star would have the three biggest. As it transpired the Olympic Class, of which *Titanic* was the second vessel, were designed for 22.5 knots maximum speed (21 knots service speed). Rather than the four main turbines of the Cunarders driving four propellers, the Olympics would have two traditional engines and one turbine driving three propellers.

As designed *Titanic* would be 46,329 GRT and carry 2,603 passengers: 905 first class, 564 second class and 1,134 third class/steerage, looked after by 884 crew. The design of the ships was begun by the chief designer at Harland & Wolff, the Hon. Alexander Carlisle, brother-in-law to Lord Pirrie, the chairman. After he retired in 1910 his position was taken by his assistant, Thomas Andrews, who was Pirrie's nephew.

The ships were designed with the latest in safety measures. Electrically operated watertight doors, controlled from the bridge, were fitted to seal off supposedly watertight compartments. Nobody ever said the ship was unsinkable. An article by Gibbs before the maiden voyage said that the safety measures made her 'practically unsinkable'.

Myth?

Watertight compartments and the unsinkability myth

One of the aspects of *Titanic* that has persisted over the years is that the ship was considered unsinkable. This was never claimed. What was said in a number of articles was that the Olympic Class were 'practically unsinkable' due to their watertight bulkheads, doors and compartments. Sadly there was a fatal flaw built into the class at the planning stage. In a similar manner, as examined in chapter 7, the Douglas (later McDonnell Douglas) DC10 jet airliner had an inbuilt safety flaw. Both were supposed to be the latest things in mass transportation, both were conceived as a response to a rival and both had a fatal flaw built into them: *Titanic* resulted in the worst maritime disaster up to that time and the DC10 the worst air disaster, again up to that time.

Watertight compartments were one of the latest safety devices to be introduced. The concept of steel bulkheads that could hold back water had been proved when Guion's *Arizona* had hit an iceberg head on in November 1879 and survived, as covered in the previous chapter. The bow had crumpled but the bulkhead remained firm and watertight. It is impractical to have totally sealed bulkheads in a liner as there is the need for the crew to move to and fro and thus a system of watertight doors was devised. Initially operated manually, which was a slow process and depended on crew members being stationed by the door, by the time of *Olympic* doors could be closed electrically from the bridge. When the *Empress of Ireland*, built for Canadian Pacific in 1906, collided with a collier in

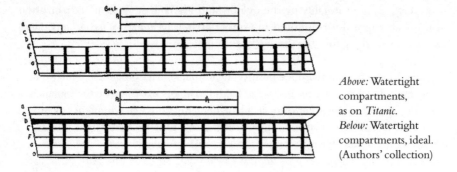

Above: Watertight
compartments,
as on *Titanic.*
Below: Watertight
compartments, ideal.
(Authors' collection)

the St Lawrence in July 1914, the crew were unable to close the watertight doors manually and she sank in fourteen minutes with the loss of over 1,000 lives. The Olympic Class could close the watertight doors very quickly. *Titanic* had fifteen watertight bulkheads and theoretically she could float with two adjacent compartments flooded. After all, the designers pondered, what disaster would flood more than two adjacent compartments?

If the ship had been properly compartmentalised their complacency may have been excusable. However, the Olympic Class's bulkheads were far from ideal. *Titanic* had eight principal decks: boat deck and then decks A–G, plus an orlop deck over the bottom. Deck C was the highest deck within the hull itself. Of the fifteen bulkheads, one only went from the bottom up to F deck, eight to E deck, and only six as far as D deck. The decks themselves were not watertight, with hatchways and staircases penetrating them.

To be completely watertight the bulkheads needed to extend from the top of the ship's double bottom up to a steel main deck, as shown in a simplified form in the bottom diagram. As it was, some of the bulkheads only extended upwards two or three decks and there was no steel lid, as shown in the top diagram.

If too much water entered the forward compartments they would sink lower in the sea and the water would overflow over the top and start filling up the next compartment. This can be modelled using a traditional ice cube maker from a refrigerator in a bowl of water.

However, it is unlikely – and this must be stressed – that, given the fact that the collision with the iceberg opened up six compartments to the sea, *Titanic* or any ship could have survived such damage even if the bulkheads had all been extended up to D deck. If, however, the rivets had been steel at the bow there is the possibility that the ship may have been less badly damaged.

Watertight compartments were one of the latest safety devices to be introduced. Much has been made of the fact that *Titanic* possessed such compartments. Indeed one of the senators in the US Inquiry asked whether any passengers had sought refuge in them.

Within minutes of hitting the iceberg, Thomas Andrews, who lost his life that night, inspected the forepart of the ship and realised the flaw – the ship was going to founder! It was the watertight division that has given rise to the myth that *Titanic* was considered unsinkable. In fact this assertion was never made. What had been written, most notably by the owners and Harland & Wolff in a description of the watertight doors, quoted in Gibbs's article *Deathless Story of the Titanic*, published shortly before the disaster, was:

> Each door is held in the open position by a suitable friction clutch, which can be instantly released by means of a powerful magnet controlled by the captain's bridge, so that in the event of an accident, or at any time when it might be considered advisable, the captain can, by simply moving an electric switch, instantly closing the doors throughout – *practically making the ship unsinkable.*

The italics are in the original. Over the years the word 'practically' has been forgotten about.

Building the ships

Building a ship in the 1900s was a labour-intensive enterprise. Firstly there was the keel, an immense girder running alongside the bottom centreline of the ship. There was then a double bottom of between 5ft 3in and 6ft 3in deep. Divided into forty-four watertight compartments, the double bottom served as both a storage area for water and as a safety feature. If the outer bottom was breached the inner part of the double bottom should prevent water entering the hull proper.

There were 305 frames that formed the skeleton of the vessel spaced between 2 and 3ft apart. These frames extended from the bilges to the bridge deck and were 66ft high. The frames were joined by four longitudinal girders that stretched the length of the ship.

To the skeleton were affixed the plates. Most of the plates were around 30ft long and 6ft wide. Although slightly thinner at the bow and stern, most of the plates were around 1in thick – more than actually necessary. The various joints were made by rivets. The double bottom alone consumed half a million rivets weighing 270 tons.

Myth?

Titanic *was built using the most modern techniques*

The hull was steel, but an earlier type of steel known as steel plate and not the high-tensile steel we know today. Some workers referred to it as 'raw hard iron' according to Michael Davie in *Titanic – the full story of a legend*. Steel is basically an alloy of iron and carbon.

The John Brown yard had switched from iron rivets to stronger ones made of steel. The problem with iron rivets is that impurities may be present, forming a weakened slag. In this state the head of the rivet may under extreme conditions, separate from the body. It is now conjectured that this is what might have happened to *Titanic*. Harland & Wolff used a mixture of iron and steel rivets. Rivets could be hammered either by hand or by hydraulic machinery. According to the specifications for the Olympic Class, iron rivets were to be used at the bow and stern, where hand riveting was to be used, and steel rivets for the remaining three-fifths of the ship, which would use hydraulic riveting. Hand-riveted sections would be double-riveted seams and hydraulic ones triple-riveted seams. Given that the joints were stronger and used steel rivets in the centre three-fifths of the ship it seems that the bow and stern were subsequently weaker than the centre, although it must be stressed they exceeded safety margins by a considerable degree.

A replica of a hull plate from *Titanic* at the Ulster Folk and Transport Museum. (Authors' collection)

Why did Harland & Wolff not use steel rivets throughout? The answer is probably cost. It was harder and more time consuming to hand rivet using steel rivets and that had wage implications. According to Hooper McCarty and Foecke in their excellent forensic analysis of the *Titanic*'s construction, *What Really Sank the Titanic*, the price of iron rivets had increased since 1900 and the price of steel ones had come down as steel making became more efficient and cheaper. However, steel rivets were harder to fit and there was only so much hydraulic riveting capacity at the yard. Three million rivets were used in each vessel and a riveting gang of four men could manage 200 rivets by hand on a fine day.

Olympic was launched on 20 October 1910 and by 29 May 1911 she commenced her sea trials. All the while the hull of her sister, *Titanic*, was a work in progress. *Titanic* was launched on the same day that *Olympic* commenced her trials – a clever piece of public relations by Harland & Wolff and White Star. J.P. Morgan was present at the launching – his money had paid for the ship. The third sister was to have been named *Gigantic* but was re-christened *Britannic* after the loss of *Titanic* and was not completed until 1914. It was not company policy to have lavish launching ceremonies so *Titanic* was never 'christened' with champagne in the traditional way.

Once launched *Titanic* was moved to the Thompson Graving Dock for fitting out. Her engines were installed, coal bunkers and boilers fitted. Her rudder was huge although many have said it was not actually big enough and that a bigger rudder might have enabled her to manoeuvre sufficiently to clear the iceberg, was fitted to the graceful stern. Cabins and public spaces were prepared and her four funnels added to the superstructure. Only three funnels were operational, the fourth being a dummy added for aesthetic reasons; in 1912 four funnels was the fashion for a crack Atlantic liner – *Mauretania* and *Lusitania* had four (functioning) funnels so the Olympics had to have four as well.

The Olympic Class may not have been as fast as the record-breaking Cunarders but in terms of interior décor they were at least their equal. The design of the interiors on the Olympic Class was mainly the work of Aldam Heaton & Co. Heaton established a partnership with Richard Norman Shaw who was a well-known designer of country house interiors. The Edwardian style for an ocean liner was to use land-based ideas in order to convince the passengers that they were not actually at sea. The main staircase was a copy of the one in Belfast City Hall. Bruce Ismay is said to have seen it and remarked that one of those would be good for *Titanic*.

Those rich enough to afford first class also had a small swimming pool and a gymnasium with a Turkish bath. First class had its own lounge, smoking rooms (separate ones for males and females) and a Palm Court. Second-class public rooms were similar, although more modest, but they too had their library and lounges. First and second class had separate promenades along the boat deck. Third class had simple public rooms for eating and dining and a promenade and deck area at the stern. No expense had been spared, especially in first class, and the public areas were very opulent indeed.

As completed, *Titanic* was just over 46,000 GRT, 882ft long, 92ft wide and had a draft of 34ft. Fully booked she could carry 905 first-, 564 second- and 1,134 third-class passengers with 884 crew.

She was built on a financial basis whereby White Star would pay Harland & Wolff the actual construction costs, plus around 4 per cent commission – the builder's profit was guaranteed. Her cost was £1.5 million and she was only insured for £1 million – White Star carried the highest portion of insurance liability of the major shipping companies.

She was laid down on 31 March 1909 and launched on 31 May 1911. Her fitting out and sea trials (one day) lasted until 1 April 1912. The ship had twenty-nine boilers with 159 furnaces and was designed for a service speed of 21 knots.

Once the slipway was clear work began on the third ship – *Gigantic*, later renamed *Britannic*. She was a ship that had a short career as she was sunk in the First World War. She is the forgotten member of the trio.

A group of craftsmen led by Thomas Andrews was to accompany the liner on her maiden voyage. One didn't travel but of those who did none survived.

Belfast was proud of *Olympic* and *Titanic* – these were men who took great pride in their work. The ships were to become known as 'The Loved' (*Olympic*), 'The Dammed' (*Titanic*) and 'The Forgotten' (*Britannic*), and to Belfast the loss of *Titanic* was perhaps more keenly felt than anywhere else.

The designers

The chief designer at Harland & Wolff was the Hon. Alexander Carlisle. Born at Ballymena, County Antrim, on 8 July 1854, the eldest son of Mr John Carlisle, he was sent to the Royal Academical Institution, Belfast, of which his father was headmaster. At the age of sixteen he was apprenticed to Messrs Harland &

Wolff, and during the next forty years held successively the positions of chief draughts-man, under manager, shipyard manager, and, finally, general manager of the whole business and chairman of the board of directors.

In 1879 his sister, Margaret Montgomery Carlisle, married Mr William Pirrie (afterwards Lord Pirrie), who had become a partner in Harland & Wolff in 1874. Mr Carlisle retired from the general managership and chairmanship in 1910, but remained as adviser and consultant. He was a member of the Departmental Committee on Accidents in Factories and Workshops, 1908, and of the Merchant Shipping Advisory Committee on Life-saving Appliances, 1911, an ironic position given the tragedy that was to befall his *Titanic* design the year afterwards.

Thomas Andrews – the ship's designer who died on *Titanic*. (June Cartwright)

The early twentieth century was, as has been shown, a period of great development in the yards, during which many famous liners were built, and in this work Carlisle took his full share. He was the main designer of White Star liners, including the Olympic Class. After his retirement his position was taken by Thomas Andrews, who was Lord Pirrie's nephew.

Thomas Andrews was born at Ardara House, Comber, County Down, Ireland (the whole of Ireland was then part of Great Britain), to Thomas Andrews, a member of the Privy Council of Ireland, and Eliza Pirrie. His older brother, John Miller Andrews, was a future Northern Ireland Prime Minister. From 1884 Andrews began attending the Royal Belfast Academical Institution until 1889 when, at the age of sixteen, he began a premium apprenticeship at Harland & Wolff where his uncle, Viscount (later Lord) Pirrie, was part owner.

At Harland & Wolff, he began with three months in the joiners' shop, followed by a month in the cabinetmakers' and then a further two months working on the ships. The last eighteen months of his five-year apprenticeship saw him working in the drawing office. By 1901, Andrews had worked his way up through the many departments of the company and became the manager of the construction works. That same year he also became a member of the Institution of Naval Architects. In 1907 he was appointed head of the draughting department at Harland & Wolff. During his long years of apprenticeship, study and work, Andrews had become well liked in the company and amongst the shipyard's employees – his death on *Titanic* was a major loss to the company.

On 24 June 1908, he married Helen Reilly Barbour. Their daughter, Elizabeth Law Barber Andrews (known by her initials, 'ELBA'), was born on 27 November 1910. The couple lived at 'Dunallan', 12 Windsor Avenue, Belfast. The houses on Windsor Avenue were later renumbered after additional properties were built.

No.12 is now No.20 and is the headquarters of the Irish Football Association. The fact that Thomas Andrews lived there is recorded on a plaque on the wall. The local story is that the 'new' No.12 was bought by somebody who intended to open a B&B guest house with the unique selling point that Thomas Andrews lived there, but of course that was a new house built long after the disaster.

It is believed locally that Andrews took Helen to view the RMS *Titanic* one night, shortly before Elizabeth was born. After Thomas's death, Helen married Henry Peirson Harland (of the Harland & Wolff family) and died on 22 August 1966.

In 1907, Andrews began to work with Carlisle on the plans for the Olympic Class. As he had done for the other ships he had overseen, Andrews familiarised himself with every detail of the ships in order to ensure that they met the specifications required by White Star.

By July 1908 the specification for No.400, the first vessel, was presented to the White Star directors. The vessel was to be 850ft long with a maximum beam of 92; 3,104 passengers would be carried in three classes. Accommodation, especially for first class, was to be sumptuous, with the swimming pool, gymnasium and Turkish bath. On the last day of July 1908 a letter of agreement was signed for two vessels (a third would later follow). Harland & Wolff, as was customary for the company, would receive the building costs plus around 4 per cent.

The largest vessels that Harland & Wolff had built up to 1908 had been White Star's 'big four' and they were only around 24,000 GRT and 726ft long. New building slips would have to be prepared. Lord Pirrie had foreseen the need for bigger slips when the *Lusitania* and *Mauretania* were announced and two new slips, together with the world's largest gantry, were built for the building of the new vessels. The slips covered 850ft by 270ft.

Gross Registered Tonnage (GRT), as covered in the introduction, is a measurement of volume not weight; of prime concern to merchant ship owners was the volume of cargo the ship could carry but warships are measured by the amount of water they displace – displacement tonnage. At the time of the *Olympic*'s launch her hull weighed around 24,000 tons. That equates to a great deal of steel.

Engines

The decision about the engines was made some time after construction of *Olympic* had commenced. White Star had responded to the introduction of turbines with a hybrid installation of two reciprocating triple-expansion engines and a central low-pressure turbine, driving three propellers in the 15,000 GRT *Laurentic* of 1908. *Laurentic* and her semi-sister *Megantic* were 16.5-knot ships designed for the UK–Canada route. *Megantic* was fitted with just two screws driven by reciprocating triple-expansion engines and proved less economical and slightly slower. It was therefore decided to use a larger version of the two reciprocating triple-expansion engines and a central low-pressure turbine driving three propellers in the Olympic Class. There was no way that this combination could beat the speeds of the *Lusitania* and *Mauretania*. Two triple expansions plus one turbine

An advertisement for *Titanic*. (Authors' collection)

on 46,000 GRT gave the Olympic Class a horsepower of around 50,000, giving a maximum speed of about 22.5 knots and a service speed of 21 knots, against four turbines and four screws developing an HP of 68,000 on the 32,000 GRT of *Mauretania* and *Lusitania*, allowing them to accomplish 25 knots with ease. The advantage of the Olympic Class configuration was that it was far more economical in terms of fuel, albeit at the sacrifice of a 3-knot speed penalty. This allows one great myth about *Titanic* to be debunked. Even today, when the authors give a talk about *Titanic* somebody nearly always claims that the ship was trying to beat the record for a westbound crossing. She couldn't have beaten either *Lusitania* or

Mauretania's best time as she was moving more hull through the water with less power! The Olympic Class were designed to be the biggest ships in the world, not the fastest – size was what we would call today the USP, the 'unique selling point', and that is what was used in the advertisements.

Rudder and manoeuvrability

One notable area of the design of the Olympic Class is the size of the rudder and how this may have impacted upon the collision of the *Olympic* with HMS *Hawke* and the sinking of *Titanic*.

The old-fashioned stern, with its high, graceful counter and long, thin rudder was an exact copy of an eighteenth-century sailing ship, wrought in steel, a perfect example of the lack of technical development. Compared with the rudder design of the Cunarders, *Titanic*'s was a fraction of the size. No account was made for advances in scale and little thought was given to how a ship, 852ft in length, might turn in an emergency or avoid a collision. The lack of manoeuvrability, given her length, was *Titanic*'s Achilles heel. The size and shape of the rudder needed, especially with a three-screw ship, is something that today would be very carefully worked out. The centre screw would dramatically impact on the way water flowed around the rudder and how the ship would respond to helm orders. The centre screw could not be used to help turn

The stern of RMS *Olympic* in dry dock. (Authors' collection)

the ship in an emergency in the way that the port and starboard ones could. Putting one engine ahead and one astern greatly increases the turning motion. The Cunard record-breakers had four screws and their rudder was not in line with any of them, thus they could use a combination of engines ahead or astern (there were separate astern turbines on the ships) to aid manoeuvrability. After the attack on Pearl Harbour in 1941 it is now known that the Japanese Imperial Navy changed the rudder design on their miniature submarines (five of which had been deployed in the attack); they were made bigger. The reason? The original rudders were too small and adversely effected the manoeuvrability of the vessels – shades of the Olympic Class.

Expansion joints

The Olympic Class were the longest ships yet constructed. The length of the hull required the designers to pay special attention to the stresses that the ship would encounter. Certain areas were strengthened and two expansion joints were put in place, one forward and one between the third and fourth funnels. These joints pierced the superstructure at points in the decks where the stress was likely to be greatest, thus providing relief from such stresses. The expansion joints on *Olympic* and *Titanic* were rather primitive and ended in a point – experience has shown that this is the worst configuration as it leads to stresses at the point. At some time after the disaster the design must have been changed as *Britannic's* expansion joints (as uncovered by a dive team for the History Channel on her wreck in the Aegean) were much more sophisticated.

The possible role of the expansion joints in the disaster are covered in chapter 3 but one must agree with the writer Mark Chirnside who has written the definitive work on the *Olympic* and has made the point on a section of his website (http://www.markchirnside.co.uk/Olympic-Titanic_expansionjoints-achille-sheel-_myth.html) that the expansion joints did not cause the tragedy. However, it may be that they had a role in the *Titanic* breaking up and foundering faster than her officers believed might happen. This issue is covered in the next chapter.

Electricity

Today we are used to the provision of electrical equipment on cars, trains, aeroplanes and ships. In the early years of the twentieth century electricity had not reached the masses. The new generation of liners, however, made full use of electricity not just for operating the vessel but also for passenger convenience. *Titanic* (and of course *Olympic*) had electric lights, electric elevators, electricity in the galleys. Survivors remarked on the fact that the lights were burning almost up to the very end. As mentioned earlier, the watertight doors could be shut electrically from the bridge. Telephones were provided for first class and as will be shown below the ships had the most up-to-date radio equipment.

There were four 400kW engines and dynamos plus two 30kW installations in case the main ones failed, and it is a credit to the designers of the electrical equipment that it worked until the very end.

Fuel

Ships of the time were fuelled by coal. By 1914 the Royal Navy had begun to switch to oil for its major vessels but for the Merchant Marine coal still reigned supreme. Britain had a thriving coal-mining industry and the Industrial Revolution had been built on the coal-fired production of steam.

The Olympic Class were designed with eleven coal bunkers. These provided the fuel for the twenty-nine boilers. There were twenty-four double-ended boilers and five single-ended boilers which were housed in six boiler rooms. Each of the double-ended boilers were 20ft long, had a diameter of 15ft 9in and contained six coal-burning furnaces. The single-ended boilers were smaller at 11ft 9in long with the same diameter and three furnaces. Smoke and waste gasses were expelled through the funnels via trunking that passed through the centre of the ship. It was only when the French liner *Normandie* came into service in the 1930s that the trunking was divided to pass up the sides of the superstructure to allow much clearer spaces for the passengers throughout the ship.

The ship's four funnels were constructed away from the site and were then transported to the shipyard for craning on board after the launch of the vessel. Only three of the funnels were used to expel smoke and waste gasses. The fourth was added to make the ship look more powerful, following the trend for four-funnelled ships pioneered by the Germans. With the exception of two vessels for Union Castle's UK–South Africa mail route, the *Arundel Castle* of 1921 and the *Windsor Castle* of 1922, the only four-funnelled liners were to be found on the North Atlantic. According to some authorities it was a means of impressing emigrants – the more funnels, the better the ship. It is reported that when the German superliners that appeared just before the First World War were seen by the emigrants to have only three (albeit huge) funnels, many of them waved brochures showing older but four-funnelled ships and demanding to travel on those rather than the newer ships.

Mauretania, Lusitania and the later Cunard addition, the *Aquitania* of 1914, had four fully functional funnels but the fourth funnel of the Olympic Class was a dummy, there for aesthetic purposes. This has not stopped artists depicting the White Star ships with smoke coming from the fourth funnel and even the James Cameron movie *Titanic* made the same error. Even White Star's suppliers made the same error as shown by the Vinolia Otto soap advertisement shown in the picture section.

When *Titanic* set off on her maiden voyage she did so in the midst of a coal strike in the UK, as will be discussed in the next chapter. It may come as a surprise to learn that she also set off with a fire in one of her coal bunkers. The fire probably did not contribute in any way to the disaster but it is indicative of the White Star attitude, again a subject for discussion in the next chapter.

Radio

Radio was one of the great improvements to communication in the late nineteenth and early twentieth centuries. Its use at sea was very much a part of the White Star story. As recounted in the previous chapter, in 1909 the *Republic* sent the first CQD signal after she had been rammed by the *Florida*.

The invention of radio may be attributed to the work of a number of people, Michael Faraday, James Clerk Maxwell, Heinrich Hertz and Guglielmo Marconi. Marconi, an Italian, began experimenting with the transmission of radio waves in 1894 from his home in Bologna, Italy, to a receiver placed about 2 miles away, on the other side of a hill. In 1896 Marconi moved to London where he filed a patent for his apparatus. He carried out a number of demonstrations on Salisbury Plain and then across the Bristol Channel. In July 1897 the Wireless Telegraph Trading Signal Company was formed with their headquarters in London. In 1898 the first wireless factory was established in Hall Street, in a former silk factory, employing around fifty people.

In 1900 the company's name was altered to Marconi Wireless Telegraph Co. The Marconi International Marine Communication Co. Ltd was also formed as it was clear that Marconi's work would be of great benefit at sea. In the same year Marconi patented the use of tuned circuits enabling simultaneous transmissions from more stations. By then Marconi had his eye on transatlantic communication, despite the claims of many that, over the horizon, communication by radio waves was impossible. Building of the Poldhu Wireless Station in Cornwall at the extreme western tip of England commenced in October 1900 and it was operational by January 1901. On 12 December that year a letter in Morse was transmitted from Poldhu and received by Marconi personnel in St John's. In 1902, at the invitation of the Canadian Government, Marconi travelled to Cape Breton, Nova Scotia, and began the building of a large radio station there.

Before long Marconi had operators on a number of transatlantic liners. The radio operators remained Marconi employees although they were under the command of the captain. The use of Marconi's staff and apparatus to save lives in the *Republic* incident gave a great boost to the company. By 1912 radio had advanced but reception and range was very dependent upon atmospheric conditions. Shipping companies as we shall see did not equip all their vessels with radio and instead relied upon rockets for night-time signals or kept a limited listening watch using only one operator, who had to rest. The concept of automatic radios on channel 16 that could wake an operator if a distress message was received was a long way in the future. The Olympic Class vessels as prestige liners had two operators; however, they were kept very busy, not only with navigational and company messages but as Marconi was operating a commercial service with passenger messages, some very frivolous indeed. An analogy can be found in the way telephones in the handsets on commercial jet aircraft were used by many when they first came into service in the late 1990s and early twenty-first century: 'Hello, guess where I am – over the Rockies…'.

Interiors

The Olympic Class may not have been as fast as the record-breaking Cunarders but in terms of interior décor they were at least their equal.

The design of the interiors on the Olympic Class was mainly the work of Aldam Heaton & Co., a practice founded by John Aldam Heaton (1828–97). Heaton established a partnership with Richard Norman Shaw who was a well-known designer of country house interiors. As mentioned earlier, the Edwardian style for an ocean liner was to use land-based ideas in order to convince the passengers that they were not actually at sea. Thus views of the ocean were restricted. It was not really until the art deco liners of the 1930s, in particular the *Empress of Britain* and the *Normandie*, that large – almost Gothic – windows were used to let the light of the seascape flood in. In first class especially the passengers would feel that they were in a large country house and not on a ship in the North Atlantic, except that country houses do not pitch and roll – even today designers cannot eliminate the motion of a vessel, they can only try to minimise it!

The third-class (steerage) accommodation was plain and wholesome with many four-berth cabins complete with washing facilities. There were also common public areas and a small amount of deck space. Second class was more elaborate whilst first class was palatial. The best cabins (as they are on today's cruise ships) were the suites with separate living and sleeping quarters.

As far as first class was concerned the main dining room was the social hub of the ship. It is possible to experience the first-class dining room of *Olympic* in two places. There is a reconstruction of it as an alternative restaurant on Celebrity Cruise Line's *Celebrity Millennium* and the White Swan Hotel at Alnwick in the north-east of England acquired many of the fittings from the first-class restaurant from the *Olympic* and these are incorporated into the hotel's restaurant.

There was also a Palm Court and a Ritz Carlton Grill for first class and a resident orchestra.

For full details of the internal arrangements of the ships and for the passengers, Mark Chirnside's books and *Building the Titanic* by Tom McCluskie, Michael Sharpe and Leo Marriot are highly recommended.

Crew

In the days of sail and even of the early steamships the majority of the crew were there to work the ship. As steam gained in prominence so too the proportion of engineers, stokers, trimmers etc. – the men who looked after the engines increased over pure sailors. However, as the number of passengers increased so too did those crew members working in, what we would call today, a customer service role. Cooks, bakers, stewards and stewardesses increased as a proportion of the crew whilst the proportion of pure seamen, including the officers of the navigation team, decreased.

When *Titanic* set sail in April 1912 she carried a crew of 844. The management of the ship from the captain through to positions such as clerks numbered seventy-four. Sailors, including the lookouts, comprised a mere forty-five. Stokers (firemen), trimmers and greasers totalled 271 – the coal-fired boilers were very labour intensive. Stewards, stewardesses, waiters, cooks, bakers etc. made up over half the crew at 445. This trend has continued; a modern cruise ship crew is mainly comprised of customer service staff. Today all of these people are highly trained, not only in the service duties but also in safety. In 1912 there were fewer crew drills and many more casual staff.

Lifeboats

Whatever might be said and written about the adequacy of the propulsion system or the rudder, it is not disputed that there were just not enough lifeboats on the *Olympic* and *Titanic* as planned and built. However, legally there were enough.

Myth?

Titanic *had enough lifeboats according to the Board of Trade*

The maximum 'souls on board', i.e. passengers plus crew, was 3,000. There was lifeboat space provided for 1,178 in twenty boats (ten on the port side and ten on the starboard side).

The British Board of Trade required only room for 825 passengers, provided that the ship had watertight bulkheads. If the ship had been US registered the requirement would have been for 2,142. Although the ships were registered in Britain (White Star was a British company) the finance came from America; however, the British registry meant that US regulations did not apply. The Board of Trade considered that a ship with watertight bulkheads was its own lifeboat; lifeboats were there to rescue people from other ships.

There had been discussions about raising the figures to bring them in line with the actual number of souls on board. The regulations were over twenty years old at a time when the largest liner was 10,000 GRT. There were ample cork lifebelts and lifejackets available but these were more or less useless in the freezing North Atlantic. As will be seen later when the aftermath of the disaster is considered, the idea of a lifeboat place for all on board was enacted with alacrity after the disaster.

Carlisle had planned to add additional lifeboats to the ships – 1,700 double banked or even 2,500 triple banked – although White Star rejected these plans. The company believed that the first-class passengers in particular would prefer more deck space. Carlisle did not argue the point, presumably because the ships exceeded the Board of Trade regulations with the twenty boats they carried. The twenty lifeboats comprised fourteen regular lifeboats, two emergency cutters (for rescuing people overboard etc.) and four Englehardt collapsible boats with canvas sides. With his retirement in 1910 there was little chance of the lifeboat allocation being increased.

Olympic enters service

Olympic was launched on 20 October 1910 and by 29 May 1911 she commenced her sea trials. The immense task of fitting out the new liner was complete. All the while the hull of her sister *Titanic* was a work in progress.

After two days of trials *Olympic* sailed for Liverpool and then to Southampton. She sailed from there on her maiden voyage to New York on 14 June with a call at Queenstown (now Cobh) on the 15th. Bruce Ismay was on board and the ship was commanded by Captain Smith – later to captain *Titanic*. Captain Smith was quoted after the voyage stating that the ships were designed for a Wednesday arrival in New York and not a Tuesday one, in other words speed was not the main concern of White Star, luxury was. They would leave Southampton on a Wednesday lunchtime and arrive in New York early the following Wednesday morning.

Ismay made copious notes for improvements to both *Olympic* and *Titanic*. He noticed that first-class passengers could become wet on the A deck promenade and suggested enclosing the forward part of A deck on *Titanic*. This was done using what became known as 'Ismay Screens' and is one easy way to tell the two ships apart.

Olympic was soon to be back in Belfast. At the start of her fifth westbound crossing on 20 September 1911 she met with a serious accident. With Captain Smith and a pilot on board she was proceeding out of Southampton when she was in collision with the cruiser HMS *Hawke*. HMS *Hawke* lost her ram off the bow and *Olympic* suffered serious damage to her stern. To White Star's chagrin *Olympic* was found to be at fault but, as she was under compulsory pilotage at the time, Captain Smith was exonerated. This would not apply today as a captain remains in command and responsible for his or her vessel even if a pilot is on board. There were considerable legal proceedings and the case was not finally settled until November 1914. By then Captain Smith had gone down with *Titanic* and HMS *Hawke* had been torpedoed and sunk in the North Sea by U9 the

Olympic A deck.

Titanic A deck.   (R. Cartwright)

previous month. Could the restrictions in manoeuvrability due to her apparently undersized rudder and three-screw installation have had a bearing on the collision and should Captain Smith have taken this on board?

Olympic returned to Belfast and it is believed parts were taken from *Titanic* to aid the repairs. She missed three round trips. Further problems were to occur. She hit a submerged object that damaged a propeller on 12 February 1912 – another trip to Belfast and her last meeting with *Titanic*.

Returned to service, she left New York on 23 March, carrying sacks of coal from the US in unused cabins due to a coal strike in the UK. This was Captain Smith's last trip in command: notwithstanding the collision with HMS *Hawke*, he was to take command of *Titanic*. White Star would soon have two huge liners at sea – *Titanic* was ready and it is her story, or the disaster that befell her, that we pick up in the next chapter.

Just how well built were the Olympic Class?

Mark Chirnside has written extensively about the Olympic Class and could be said to eulogise the ships. He shows how *Olympic* was profitable and his books have a wealth of detail. He also quotes from Captain Betram Hayes (captain of *Olympic* for six years) who is reported to have said: 'The finest ship in my estimation that has ever been built, or ever will be'. And this of a ship that had been riveted with iron steel rivets for a considerable portion of her hull, was underpowered for her size, utilised old technology, had far too few lifeboats when she entered service and had a rudder that was too small for safety. Thank goodness we don't build them like that today! *Olympic* had a long career and was a superb troopship in the First World War but compared to the *Mauretania* there is, in these authors' opinion, no comparison. People have their favourite ships but objectively Captain Hayes, loyal as he was to White Star, was wrong.

Chapter 3

Anatomy of a Disaster

Captain Edward John (E.J.) Smith was the highest-paid ship's captain in the world in 1912. He was the Commodore (senior captain) of White Star and as such he commanded the newest vessel in the company. He was in command of *Olympic* when she entered service and in command of her when she collided with HMS *Hawke*.

Edward John Smith was born in Hanley, Stoke-on-Trent (almost as far from the sea as is possible in England), in the Potteries region on 27 January 1850. After leaving school at thirteen he went to Liverpool to begin his seafaring career, where he was an apprentice on the *Senator Weber* owned by A. Gibson & Co. of Liverpool.

On 12 July 1887, Smith married Sarah Eleanor Pennington and their daughter, Helen Melville Smith, was born in Waterloo, Lancashire, in 1898. By the time of the disaster the family lived in a large red-brick, twin-gabled house, named 'Woodhead', in Southampton, the home port for White Star.

He joined White Star in March 1880 as the fourth officer of the *Celtic*. Rising swiftly through the ranks he received his first White Star command, the *Republic*. In 1887 he joined the Royal Naval Reserve as a lieutenant (thus entitling him to append his name with RNR); this meant that in a time of war, Smith could be called upon to serve in the Royal Navy. Later, as a Commander in the Royal Naval Reserve, Smith's ship had the distinction of being able to wear the Blue Ensign of the RNR rather than the customary Red Ensign of the British Merchant Marine.

Captain Edward Smith. (June Cartwright)

In 1895 he was given command of the *Majestic*, a post he held for nine years. During the Boer War Smith and the *Majestic* were called upon to transport troops. He made two trips to South Africa, both without incident, and for his service he was awarded the Transport Medal in 1903. Smith had a reputation as a safe captain.

As he rose in seniority, Smith gained a reputation amongst passengers and crew for a degree of flamboyance, especially in regard to his ship handling. He would speed into New York and make dramatic turns in the channel leading up to the harbour. Greatly respected by his first-class passengers, Smith eventually became Commodore of the White Star fleet in 1904. Thereafter it became routine for Smith to command the line's newest ships on their maiden voyages. In 1904 he was given command of one of the largest ships in the world at the time, White Star's new *Baltic*. Her maiden voyage from Liverpool to New York, sailing on 29 June 1904, went without incident. After three years with the *Baltic*, Smith was given his second new 'big ship', the *Adriatic*. During his command of this ship, Smith received the Royal Naval Reserve's long service decoration, along with a promotion to commander. He would now sign his name as 'Commander Edward John Smith, RD (Reserve Decoration) RNR'.

Myth?

Captain Smith had an unblemished safety record

Smith had built a reputation as one of the world's most experienced sea captains and so was called upon to take first command of the *Olympic*, the largest vessel in the world at that time. The maiden voyage from Southampton to New York was successfully concluded on 21 June 1911, but as the ship was docking in New York harbour, at Pier 59, under command of a harbour pilot and the assistance of no fewer than twelve tugs, one became caught in the backwash of the *Olympic*'s starboard propeller. The tug was spun around, collided with the bigger ship and for a moment was trapped under the *Olympic*'s stern, finally managing to work free and limp to the docks.

On 20 September 1911 *Olympic*'s first major mishap occurred during a collision with HMS *Hawke*, as discussed in the previous chapter. The *Hawke* incident was a financial disaster for White Star, and the out-of-service time for the big liner made matters worse. *Olympic* returned to Belfast and, to speed up the repairs, Harland & Wolff was forced to delay *Titanic*'s completion, in order to use one of her propeller shafts for *Olympic*.

Back at sea in February 1912, *Olympic* lost a propeller blade and once again returned to her builder for emergency repairs. To get her back to service immediately, Harland & Wolff yet again had to pull resources from *Titanic*, delaying her maiden voyage from 20 March to 10 April. Ironically the lost blade led to the death of Captain Smith and many of his passengers and crew, as had *Titanic* sailed on schedule she would not have encountered the iceberg that sank her.

Despite the HMS *Hawke* incident, Smith was appointed in command of RMS (Royal Mail Steamship) *Titanic*. Some believe that Smith intended to retire after the maiden voyage but an article in the Halifax *Morning Chronicle* on 9 April 1912 stated that Smith would remain in charge of the *Titanic* 'until the Company [White Star Line] completed a larger and finer steamer' – i.e. *Gigantic* (later renamed *Britannic*).

Titanic was completed by the end of March 1912 and was scheduled to undertake her sea trials in the Irish Sea (one day) on April Fool's Day. The weather was bad that day and the trials were postponed until 2 April with Captain Smith in command for the first time, although technically the ship was still owned by Harland & Wolff, and thus it was the Harland & Wolff houseflag that was at her masthead. She ran a measured mile and under the watchful eye of the Board of Trade inspectors her systems were tested. An hour after her final certificates were signed by the Board of Trade representatives she weighed anchor bound for Southampton. Unlike *Olympic* she did not visit Liverpool as bad weather had set back her sea trials and she arrived in Southampton in the early hours of 4 April. She remained in Southampton over the Easter period. During this time one of her bunkers was on fire but apparently this was an unremarkable event for the era and little effort appears to have been made to put the fire out. Whilst the fire was not germane to the disaster, the lack of concern about it may point to a degree of arrogance amongst those responsible for the safety of the ship.

Coal strike

At the time the UK was in the grip of a coal strike. Although *Olympic* had brought some coal over from the US, White Star was forced to cancel a number of sailings and some passengers who were booked in first class on the company's older vessels were transferred to second class on *Titanic*. Even though *Titanic's* second class was better than first class on older vessels it did not carry the cachet of a first-class baggage label. A number of those unfortunate enough to have been transferred to *Titanic* were to perish in the icy waters of the North Atlantic a few days later.

Myth?

Morgan was supposed to sail on the ship but cancelled his booking
One intended passenger who did not sail with the ship was J. Pierpont Morgan, her actual owner. He was booked into a suite but cancelled and his suite was taken by a US department store owner, Emil Brandis, who did not survive the sinking. Lord Pirrie of Harland & Wolff was also supposed to be on the voyage but his doctor advised him that the journey would be bad for his health – how true that would have been!

Departure

On the bridge of all White Star ships was an instruction to captains from the management of IMM:

> The safety of all those on board weighs with us beyond all other considerations, and we would once more impress upon you and the entire navigation staff most earnestly that no risk is to be run which can be avoided by the exercise of caution … and by choosing, whenever doubt exists, the course that tends to safety.

On 10 April 1912, Smith, wearing a bowler hat and a long overcoat, took a taxi from his home to Southampton docks. He came aboard the *Titanic* at 7 a.m. to prepare for the Board of Trade muster at 8 a.m. He immediately went to his cabin to receive the sailing report from Chief Officer Henry Wilde. Wilde had been Smith's chief officer on *Olympic* and Smith had requested his transfer to *Titanic* for the maiden voyage – Wilde did not survive. Wilde had never been on board *Titanic* before and thus his comment to his sister that 'I still don't like this ship, I have a queer feeling about it' has helped fuel one of the conspiracy theories (a theory that will be examined later) that the ship in dock was not actually *Titanic* but her sister, *Olympic*.

Due to the coal strike the ship was not, fortunately given what was to happen, full. By the time she left Southampton and had picked up her remaining passengers at Cherbourg and Queenstown she was carrying, it is believed (although there are minor discrepancies about the figures):

First class	317
Second class	258
Third class (steerage)	709
Crew	884

Table 6　Titanic's complement on her maiden voyage

Huge amounts of luggage came aboard. First-class passengers in 1912 tended to travel with a large number of cases and steamer trunks, and many of the third class had all their worldly possessions with them.

Myth?

Titanic *nearly had a collision as she left Southampton*

After departure at midday, the huge amount of water displaced by *Titanic* as she passed (possibly at too fast a speed for such a large vessel) caused the SS *New York* moored outboard of *Oceanic* to break from her moorings and swing towards the *Titanic*. Quick action from the tug *Vulcan*, which pushed the stern of the *New York* away from the fast approaching bow of the *Titanic*, helped to avert a premature end to the maiden voyage.

The White Star offices at Cobh (formerly Queenstown). (Authors' collection)

By dusk she had reached Cherbourg and anchored off the port where the specially built tenders *Traffic* (for first class) and *Nomadic* (second and third class) brought the continental contingent on board. She then set off for Queenstown in Southern Ireland where she arrived at 11.30 the following morning. As usual for large liners she anchored a good 2 miles off the tender jetty.

Queenstown, which has been renamed Cobh, is a popular cruise ship port. The White Star offices are still there, now serving as a museum and café/restaurant, although they have been neglected of late. As will be shown later, Cobh contains memorials to two ocean liner disasters, *Titanic* and the loss of the Cunard liner *Lusitania* during the First World War.

One hundred and thirteen third-class and seven second-class passengers joined at Cobh and 1,385 sacks of mail were loaded on board. Irish emigration to North America had been growing and many in Ireland had relatives in the United States, and as the number of emigrants grew so did the mail trade between the UK and Ireland and North America – *Titanic* was a Royal Mail Steamer (RMS) after all. In fact the first emigrant through the Ellis Island Centre in New York harbour was from Queenstown. Annie Moore arrived aboard the *Nevada* on 1 January 1892, which apparently was her fifteenth birthday. As the first person to be processed at the newly opened facility, she was presented with an American $10 gold coin. Moore and all the other emigrants out of Queenstown are also remembered in the town.

A small number of passengers had used *Titanic* as a means to get to France and Ireland – they were the lucky ones. Among those disembarking at Queenstown was a thirty-two-year-old Jesuit student, Francis M. Browne.

Browne attended the Bower Convent in Athlone, Christian Brothers College in Cork, Belvedere College in Dublin and Castlenock College in Co. Dublin. In 1897 he graduated and then toured through Europe: France, Italy and Switzerland. His brother, Dr James Browne, an eye specialist, came with him and Francis brought a special gift from his uncle Robert – a camera. It was his camera that was to make him famous.

He entered the Jesuit noviciate at Tullabey in Ireland in September 1897 and then progressed to the Róyal University in Dublin. In 1902 Browne passed his examinations and travelled to Chieri near Turin, Italy, to study philosophy until 1906 when he returned to Dublin to teach at Belvedere College.

In 1911 he began his theological studies at Milltown Park, Dublin. The year after, his uncle Robert bought him a ticket for a trip on the *Titanic* from Southampton to Queenstown. On 4 April he received his first-class ticket (No.84 at a cost £4), as a cross-Channel passenger, from White Star Agent James Scott & Co., Queenstown. To reach Southampton he travelled via Holyhead to London on 8 April. He probably spent a night on the train and the following one at his brother's in London. On 10 April he left London at 9.45 a.m. (according to other passengers at 8 a.m.) on the 'Titanic Special' to Southampton from Waterloo station. The next day Father Browne disembarked *Titanic* at Queenstown after a stop at Cherbourg the previous evening.

Browne was ordained to the priesthood on 31 July 1915 and went immediately to the front in Flanders as chaplain of the Irish Guards. He was injured five times, once severely (gas attack). He was decorated by the MC and Bar, the Croix de Guerre and by a personal decoration by the Belgian King. In spring 1920 he was demobilised and he returned to Dublin.

Not long afterwards he was appointed Superior of St Xavier's Church in Dublin. His physical constitution, however, was still damaged due to the gassing in the war and under doctor's orders to seek warmer climates, Father Browne went to Australia. On his way 'down under' he stopped at Cape Town and on his way back he visited Ceylon, Aden, Suez, Saloniki, Naples, Toulon, Gibraltar, Algeciras and Lisbon. Everywhere he went he took photographs, including many of transport subjects. By the end of his life he had collected nearly 42,000 of them. We also owe Browne a great debt for the images he took on board *Titanic*, on the voyage from Southampton to Queenstown, even capturing the near accident with the *New York* and providing the last picture ever taken of Captain E.J. Smith.

From 1925 to 1929 he was back in Dublin at his post. Afterwards he became a member of the Retreats and Mission staff of the Irish Jesuits. He preached all over Ireland until his death in 1960. Father Browne was buried in Glasnerin Cemetery, Dublin.

Myth?

The richest man in the world was on board Titanic

By the time *Titanic* departed Queenstown she carried on board a number of personalities and business leaders of the time. The chairman of White Star, J. Brúce

Ismay, was on board, as was John Jacob Astor, reputedly the richest man in the world (worth the staggering sum of over £30 million in 1912 – a huge sum for those days), together with his young wife. Not quite as rich as many believed, Benjamin Guggenheim was travelling in first class with his valet, as were the Strauses, Isidor and Ida. Isidor was the owner of the Macy's department store in New York and was reputed to be worth over £10 million. As will be seen later, the Strauses provided a true love story on the night of the disaster. The heir to the Widener tramway fortune, twenty-seven-year-old Harry Widener, a renowned bibliophile, was travelling back to the USA with his parents after a European trip. The estimated wealth of Astor, Guggenheim, Straus and Widener Snr was over £70 million, a huge amount in 1912. Also on board in first class was Major Archibald Butt, an aide to President Taft. The President sent the cruiser USS *Chester* to search for his body.

Sir Cosmo Duff Gordon, a British aristocrat, was also in first class and became the subject of a scandal in connection with his alleged behaviour in emergency lifeboat No.1 – this scandal will be covered later when considering the British Inquiry into the disaster. One member of the aristocracy showed great pluck. The Countess of Rothes was on her way to join her husband at his Canadian fruit farm and she became one of the heroines of that fateful night by overruling what she believed were incompetent crew members and taking charge of a lifeboat.

Myth?

There really was 'an unsinkable Molly Brown'

Perhaps one of the best-known heroines was another first-class passenger, Molly (the Unsinkable) Brown, although it is interesting to note that she was never referred to as Molly until after her death.

Born as Margaret Tobin on 18 July 1867, she was one of four children born to Irish immigrants John Tobin and Johanna Collins in Hannibal, Missouri. At age eighteen, Margaret moved to Colorado and gained a position in a department store. She met and married an engineer, James Joseph Brown (known as J.J.), whose parents had also emigrated from Ireland. The Browns had two children. Whilst Margaret had always said she would only marry wealth, J.J. was not rich initially. However, J.J.'s efforts proved instrumental in the production of a substantial ore seam at the Little Jonny Mine and he was awarded 12,500 shares of stock and a seat on the board.

In Leadville, Colorado, Margaret became involved in women's rights and setting up soup kitchens for the poor – a sign that she was an independently minded young woman. In 1894, the Browns moved to Denver which gave the family more social opportunities. Margaret became a charter member of the Denver Woman's Club; she had arrived in society! In 1901 she was one of the first students to enrol at the Carnegie Institute in New York City and became well immersed in the arts and fluent in French, German and Russian. In 1909 she ran, unsuccessfully, for the US Senate.

After twenty-three years of marriage, Margaret and J.J. privately signed a separation agreement and went their separate ways in 1909. Although they were never reconciled, they remained connected and cared for each other throughout their lives. The agreement gave Margaret a cash settlement and she maintained possession of the house on Pennsylvania Street in Denver. She also received $700 a month allowance to continue her travels and philanthropic activities.

After her *Titanic* adventure, to be recounted later (she joined the ship as a first-class passenger in Cherbourg after a European trip), she ran for Senate again in 1914 but dropped out of the race for family reasons.

At the time of J.J.'s death on 5 September 1922, Margaret told newspapers, 'I've never met a finer, bigger, more worthwhile man than J.J. Brown'. J.J. died without a will and it took five years of fighting between Margaret and her J.J. two children to finally settle the estate. Due to their lavish spending, J.J. left an estate valued at only $238,000. Margaret was to receive $20,000 in cash and securities, and the interest on a $100,000 trust fund set up in her name. Her children, Lawrence and Helen, received the rest. From that time on, until her death in 1932, Margaret had no contact with her children.

Her fame as a prominent *Titanic* survivor helped her promote the issues she felt deeply about – the rights of workers and women, education and literacy for children, and historic preservation. During the First World War she worked with the American Committee for Devastated France to rebuild areas behind the front line and helped wounded French and American soldiers. She was awarded the French Legion of Honour for her good citizenship including her activism and philanthropy in America. For the last years of her life she pursued a career as an actress.

Margaret Tobin Brown died of a stroke on 26 October 1932, at the age sixty-five. The death certificate gave the cause of death as cerebral haemorrhage, but an autopsy also found a significant brain tumour.

In 1965, the capsule launched in the Gemini 3 space mission that preceded the Apollo moon missions was unofficially named the *Molly Brown*, a humorous reference to a previous incident with the Mercury capsule *Liberty Bell* that sank, nearly drowning Astronaut John Grissom, off the Florida coast. In 2006 she was honoured as a famous Missourian on the Missouri Walk of Fame.

She has been well represented in the theatre and cinema. In 1960, the Broadway musical *The Unsinkable Molly Brown* opened with Tammy Grimes, who won a Tony Award for her performance. Margaret was portrayed by Debbie Reynolds in the 1964 film version of the stage musical, the role bringing Reynolds her only Oscar nomination. She was played by Cloris Leachman in the 1979 television movie *S.O.S. Titanic* and Kathy Bates played her in the 1997 film *Titanic*. These musicals and films are covered in chapter 10.

Although he claimed to be just another first-class passenger, J. Bruce Ismay, the chairman of White Star, held an ambivalent position on board. His behaviour before the disaster and during the fateful night and its aftermath was to raise many questions – questions that are considered in chapter 4. What is known is that before the disaster he had a private meeting with the chief engineer, J. Bell.

According to Ismay they agreed to gradually open up the boilers, with the intention of trying the ship at full speed on the day after the catastrophe. Rumours that Ismay tried to convince both Bell and Captain Smith to try for the Atlantic record are clearly unfounded – with less horsepower and more bulk than either *Mauretania* or *Lusitania*, *Titanic* was not designed as a record-breaking ship, as described earlier in this book. As will be seen in the next chapter, Ismay tried to claim that he was just a passenger, but as the chairman of the company he was clearly more than that. It is believed that he was shown and even carried around at least one radioed ice warning in the hours prior to the disaster, hardly the actions of a mere passenger.

An Atlantic liner such as *Titanic* was a small-scale representation of late Edwardian society: the aristocracy and the scions of industry and commerce were in first class and the middle classes inhabited second class. One of these passengers who was to gain fame through his association with *Titanic* was a British schoolteacher, Lawrence Beesley. Thirty-four-year-old Beesley survived the sinking and was one of the first of the survivors into print with his *The Loss of the SS Titanic: Its Story and Its Lessons, by One of the Survivors*, published in great haste in June 1912. The phenomenon of survivors cashing in on their experiences is not a new one, although to be fair to Beesley he was concerned that lessons should be learnt from the disaster. He returned to teaching and was still holding a position in the 1950s. It is reported that during the filming of *A Night to Remember* in 1958, which will be covered more fully later, he tried to gatecrash the set during the sinking scene, hoping to go down with the ship a second time. The director, however, spotted him and vetoed this unscheduled appearance, due to Equity rules.

The Hart family of Ilford in England was very unlucky. Owing to the coal strike they were transferred to second class on *Titanic* from another, older, White Star ship where it is quite possible they were booked to travel in first class – although it must be stressed that second class on *Titanic* would have been just as opulent and comfortable as first class on an older vessel. Benjamin Hart, his wife Esther and seven-year-old daughter Eva had decided to emigrate to Winnipeg in Canada where he planned to open a tobacconist's shop.

Apparently Esther felt uneasy about the ship and feared that some catastrophe would happen. To call a ship unsinkable was, in her mind, flying in the face of God. With such fear, Esther slept only during the day and stayed awake in her cabin at night fully dressed.

Eva was sleeping when *Titanic* struck the iceberg. Her father rushed into her cabin to alert his daughter and her mother and, after wrapping Eva in a blanket, he carried her to the boat deck. He placed his wife and daughter in Lifeboat No.14 and told Eva to 'hold Mummy's hand and be a good girl'. It was the last thing her father ever said to her, and the last time she ever saw him.

Eva and her mother were picked up by the *Carpathia* and finally arrived in New York on 18 April. Eva's father perished and his body was never identified.

Eva and her mother returned to England where her mother later remarried. Eva was plagued with nightmares and upon the death of her mother, when Eva was twenty-three, she confronted her fears head on by returning to the sea and locking herself in a cabin for four straight days until the nightmares went away. She died in February 1996 aged ninety-one.

Less is known about the steerage passengers, although it is from their ranks that the last survivor of *Titanic* came. Elizabeth Gladys Dean, better known as Millvina, was born on 2 February 1912, the daughter of Bertram Frank Dean and Georgette Eva Light Dean. In April 1912 she was only nine weeks old and was, with her parents and elder brother Bertram, who all boarded at Southampton, about to emigrate to Wichita, Kansas, where her father hoped to open a shop, like the Hart family

Millvina, her mother and brother were all rescued and returned to England aboard the *Adriatic*. It was on the *Adriatic* that Millvina first became quite a spectacle: that such a tiny baby could have come through the ordeal alive. First- and second-class passengers on the *Adriatic* queued to hold her and many took photographs of her, her mother and brother, several of which were published in newspapers.

Millvina and her brother were raised and educated on various pension funds and Millvina attended Greggs School, Southampton. In her younger years Millvina did not know that she was on the *Titanic* as she had, being only a few weeks old at the time, no memory of the disaster. She only found out when she was eight and her mother was planning to remarry.

Millvina herself never married, working for the government during the Second World War by drawing maps and later serving in the purchasing department of a Southampton engineering firm. It wasn't until she was in her seventies that she became a *Titanic* celebrity: in 1997 she was invited to travel aboard the *QE2* to America to complete her family's voyage to Wichita, Kansas.

In April 1996, by which time Millvina was the last *Titanic* survivor, she visited Belfast for the first time, as guest of honour for a *Titanic*

Millvina Dean in later life. (June Cartwright)

Historical Society convention. She lived in retirement in Southampton, England, and was kept very busy attending conventions, appearing in documentaries, television series and radio shows, signing huge amounts of autographs and relating her tale to school groups. She died on 31 May 2009 after a short illness.

Another family in third class was the Goodwins, believed to be from London. The party included nineteen-month-old Sidney who has been found to be the 'unknown child of the *Titanic*', which will be covered later.

The 709 third-class passengers came from all over Ireland, the rest of the UK, Scandinavia, Northern, Southern and Central Europe, and even the Near East. Fares were relatively cheap and it was the promise of a new life that drove them to the Americas. Of the 709 who were on board by the time *Titanic* left Queenstown, only 175 would see the New World.

A few years ago the authors were delivering a talk about *Titanic* on a British cruise ship when, at the end of the talk, a very elderly lady came up and told them that her mother and elder sister had been booked to travel on the maiden voyage in third class – she herself not yet having been conceived. The sister contracted mumps, however, and White Star refused to let them travel. It is quite possible that they would have died that night and that this lady would never have been born. Even today the legacy of *Titanic* casts a spell over individual lives.

Fares

Like a modern cruise ship the fares from Britain to the US on *Titanic* varied considerably according to the class of travel:

First-class parlour suite	£870 – the best accommodation
First-class berth	£30 – cheapest first class
Second class	£12
Third class	£3 to £8 – depending on number of berths in the cabin

The most expensive first-class ticket was a huge 290 times more expensive than the cheapest third class; £3 was not an inconsiderable sum for an emigrant in 1912.

By 10 April 1912 *Titanic* had a full complement of crew. Smith rejoined the ship from his Southampton home; also joining was his previous chief officer from the *Olympic* Henry Wilde. Wilde's arrival meant that the other officers on *Titanic* had to take a step down in rank – William Murdoch, who had been appointed as chief officer, was relegated to first officer. The officers were joined by seamen, stockers, stewards, stewardesses, cooks, carpenters; in fact the full range of those you would expect to find in a town, albeit a floating one.

Pay varied considerably, the monthly amounts being:

Captain Smith	£105
Radio Operator	£48
Seaman	£5
Look-out	£5 and 5 shillings
Steward	£3 and 15 shillings
Stewardess	£3 and 10 shillings

Table 7   Crew pay

Titanic also carried cargo including:

Over 300 bags of mail and over 700 parcels.
One Renault 35hp automobile owned by passenger William Carter.
One Marmalade Machine owned by passenger Edwina Trout.
Oil paintings.
Seven parcels of parchment of the Torah owned by Hersh L. Siebald.
Three crates of ancient models for the Denver Museum.
Fifty cases of toothpaste for Park & Tilford.
Eleven bales of rubber for the National City Bank of New York.
Eight dozen tennis balls.
A cask of china destined for Tiffany's in New York.
Five grand pianos.
Thirty cases of golf clubs and tennis rackets.
A jewelled copy of *The Rubáiyát* by Omar Khayyám, the binding of which took
two years to execute and the decoration embodied no fewer than 1,500 precious
stones, each separately set in gold.
Four cases of opium.

Table 8   Cargo

All this was lost, although a few items have been recovered since the wreck was
found in the 1980s.

Titanic set sail at noon on 12 April – just as the bugler sounded the lunch signal
(referred to as dinner in third class) and as the passengers filed to their meal – the
ship's whistle sounded, *Titanic* left her berth and nearly ran into disaster. As she
approached the liners *Oceanic* and *New York*, which were crowded with sightseers,
the surge of water ahead of *Titanic* and the weight of people caused *New York*'s
stern lines to part and she swung out into *Titanic*'s path. Quick thinking by a tug
captain averted a collision, as detailed previously; however, if the ships had met
Titanic's voyage would have been delayed.

Once clear of Southampton, Captain Smith set sail for Cherbourg where
Titanic anchored at around sunset. The few passengers who were joining the ship
were brought out by two tenders, one for first class and another for second and
third class. Even though there were only a few passengers to join, propriety had to
be observed and first class had to have their own tender.

After a short stay *Titanic* headed for Queenstown, her final stop before
New York. Local tenders were used and six second-class passengers and
Father Browne, who had used the opportunity to sail from Southampton to
Ireland, disembarked and a fireman, John Coffey, is believed to have deserted
the ship. Seven second- and 130 third-class passengers joined. As the ship left
Queenstown, newly joined Eugene Daly in third class played a *Lament to Erin* on
his bagpipes – he survived.

In the bowels of the ship, in temperatures of over 120 degrees Fahrenheit, the
'Black gang', an army of stokers, fed the boilers with coal. One of the bunkers was
actually on fire during the voyage, an occurrence that was not considered unusual

1 The Thompson Graving Dock at Harland & Wolff today. (Authors' collection)

2 The drawing office at Harland & Wolff. (Authors' collection)

3 Commemorative plaque for Thomas Andrews. (Authors' collection)

4 Thomas Andrews' house on Windsor Avenue, Belfast. (Authors' collection)

5 Soap advertisement featuring *Titanic* (note A deck and smoke coming from the fourth funnel – the ship is actually the *Olympic*). (Authors' collection)

6 *Titanic* sets sail. (Authors' collection)

7 *Titanic*, replica first-class corridor. (Authors' collection)

8 *Titanic*, replica first–class suite. (Authors' collection)

9 *Titanic*, replica steerage cabin. (Authors' collection)

10 *Titanic*, replica radio room. (Authors' collection)

11 *Date with Destiny* by Newfoundland artist David Hoddinott. (© David Hoddinott)

12 *Left:* The memorial to the Belfast men who died – partly obscured by the Belfast Eye. (Authors' collection)

13 *Below:* Memorial to the *Titanic's* engineers, Southampton. (Marc Williams)

14 *Titanic* sinking by John Batchelor. (Dover Publications)

15 *Left: Titanic* mural, Belfast. (Authors' collection)

16 *Below: Nomadic*, one of *Titanic*'s Cherbourg tenders, undergoing restoration in Belfast. (Authors' collection)

17 There is a direct link from *Titanic* through Cunard White Star to today's Cunard
flagship the *Queen Mary 2*. (Authors' collection)

18 *Titanic* on her trials off Northern Ireland, 2 April 1912. (© Artist Gordon Bauwens, 1998. Reproduced by kind permission. Available as art prints from www.gbmarineart.com)

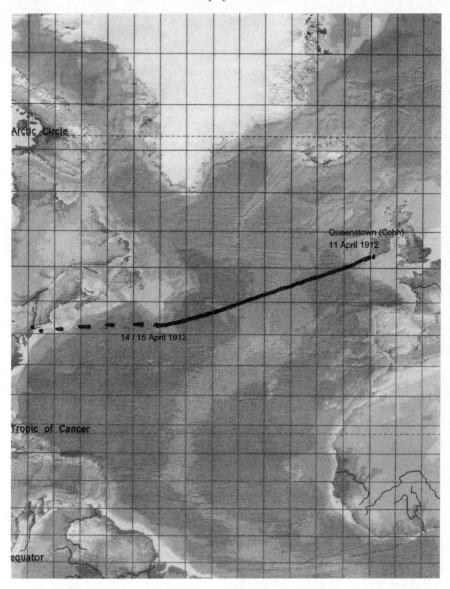

Chart of the voyage from Queenstown. (R. Cartwright)

at the time. Bruce Ismay and the chief engineer, Joseph Bell, discussed how to work the ship up to full speed, although those who spoke to them say they were aware that *Titanic* could not challenge for the record for reasons discussed earlier. Nevertheless Ismay clearly wanted to see what the ship could do.

In the various classes the passengers settled down to their voyage. Most appeared delighted with the standards of accommodation. Many in first class had their servants with them (accommodated in special inside cabins). First class was very formal; ladies might change five or six times a day and every night on a voyage, barring the first and last, one was expected to dress for dinner, which was the high point of the first-class experience.

There was a band for first class, led by Wallace Hartley from Colne in Lancashire, but apart from that and betting on the ship's progress there was little organised entertainment. The only routine was meals. First- and second-class passengers, in their own areas of course, promenaded, gossiped, drank, made business deals and gambled – there was at least one professional gambler on board. Apparently very few first-class passengers used the gym or the Turkish bath – they seem to have been regarded as a gimmick. However, many first-class passengers sent and received 'Marconigrams' – radio at sea was still a novelty and despite the high cost many frivolous messages were sent. At one point sending these messages actually interfered with receiving ice warnings.

Edwardian meals were lavish by today's standards. In first class huge, sumptuous spreads were prepared. Breakfast in first class would include a multitude of dishes and dinner was a very grand affair. The main saloon in first class seated 532 and included the Captain's Table with seating for six. Second-class fare was wholesome and hearty, a typical lunchtime menu offered soup, roast meat dishes, vegetables, a cooked dessert and fruit. Even third class, where language and cultural differences were broken down with singing and dancing in the social halls, was offered four meals a day: breakfast, dinner (lunch), tea and a late supper.

According to records, when *Titanic* set sail she had on board:

Fresh meat	75,000lb
Fresh fish	11,000lb
Salt and dried fish	4,000lb
Bacon and ham	7,500lb
Poultry and game	25,000lb
Fresh eggs	40,000
Sausages	2,500lb
Potatoes	40 tons
Onions	3,500lb
Tomatoes	3,500lb
Fresh asparagus	800 bundles
Fresh green peas	2,500lb
Lettuce	7,000 heads
Sweetbreads	1,000
Ice cream	1,750lb
Coffee	2,200lb
Tea	800lb
Rice, dried beans etc.	10,000lb
Sugar	10,000lb
Flour	250 barrels
Cereals	10,000lb
Apples	36,000
Oranges	36,000

Lemons	16,000
Grapes	1,000lb
Grapefruits	13,000
Jams and marmalade	1,120lb
Fresh milk	1,500 gals
Fresh cream	1,200 qts
Condensed milk	600 gals
Fresh butter	6,000lb
Ales and stouts	15,000 bottles
Wines	1,000 bottles
Spirits	850 bottles
Minerals	1,200 bottles
Cigars	8,000

Table 9   Provisions on board

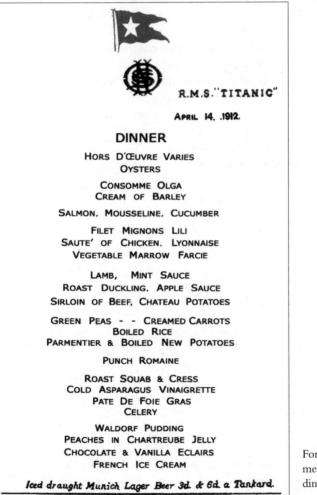

R.M.S. "TITANIC"

APRIL 14. 1912.

DINNER

HORS D'ŒUVRE VARIES
OYSTERS

CONSOMME OLGA
CREAM OF BARLEY

SALMON, MOUSSELINE, CUCUMBER

FILET MIGNONS LILI
SAUTE' OF CHICKEN. LYONNAISE
VEGETABLE MARROW FARCIE

LAMB, MINT SAUCE
ROAST DUCKLING. APPLE SAUCE
SIRLOIN OF BEEF, CHATEAU POTATOES

GREEN PEAS - - CREAMED CARROTS
BOILED RICE
PARMENTIER & BOILED NEW POTATOES

PUNCH ROMAINE

ROAST SQUAB & CRESS
COLD ASPARAGUS VINAIGRETTE
PATE DE FOIE GRAS
CELERY

WALDORF PUDDING
PEACHES IN CHARTREUBE JELLY
CHOCOLATE & VANILLA ECLAIRS
FRENCH ICE CREAM

Iced draught Munich Lager Beer 3d. & 6d. a Tankard.

For many it was the last meal – *Titanic's* first-class dinner menu, 14 April 1912. (Authors' collection)

To prepare this food there were sixteen cooks, fifteen scullions, fourteen bakers and seven butchers, plus extra cooks for the crew. There were no fewer than 324 stewards and eighteen stewardesses (seventeen of whom survived) to serve and look after the passengers in both the restaurants and the cabins. The Ritz Carlton Grill for the first-class passengers employed twenty staff.

The disparity between the numbers of traditional seamen and engineers compared to the number of those catering to the 'hotel function' is even greater on today's cruise ships where the number of hotel staff is many times that of those engaged in navigation, deck and engine room duties. On a large coal-fired ship such as Titanic there were also 167 firemen, seventy-one coal trimmers and thirty-three greasers, making a total of 271 men engaged in keeping the boilers fuelled and working. The deck department consisted of seven quartermasters, six lookouts and thirty-two able seamen.

The senior officers on Titanic for that fateful voyage were:

E.J. Smith	Captain
H.T. Wilde	Chief Mate or Officer
W.M. Murdoch	First Mate or Officer
C.H. Lightoller	Second Mate or Officer (survived)
H.J. Pirman	Third Mate or Officer
J.G. Boxhall	Fourth Mate or Officer (survived)
H.G. Lowe	Fifth Mate or Officer (survived)
J.P. Moody	Sixth Mate or Officer
(All of the mates were qualified to stand a watch on the bridge.)	
W.F.N. O'Loughlin	Surgeon
J. Bell	Chief Engineer
Nineteen assistant engineers	
H.W. McElroy	Purser
R.L. Barker	Purser

Table 10   Senior officers RMS Titanic

Of the above 'senior management team', only Lightoller, Boxhall and Lowe survived.

The crew went about their duties ironing out any problems that occurred and there were very few. One thing that was not done was to hold a lifeboat drill – this was Titanic, what could go wrong?

Disaster in the North Atlantic

Titanic gradually worked up to around 22 knots on that fateful Sunday. Captain Smith, as was part of his duties, inspected the ship with his officers that Sunday and conducted a church service for first and second class. They were allowed to mix at church!

That night Smith dined with a group of first-class American passengers, including Major Butt (an aide to US President Taft), Mr and Mrs Thayer, and Mr and Mrs Widener. Mr and Mrs Widener and Mrs Thayer survived. Mrs Thayer testified that Captain Smith did not drink any alcohol that night and left early to visit the bridge.

The voyage was well into its final third and by 11 p.m. most passengers were in bed. Some men remained in the first-class smoking room talking and enjoying a nightcap. *Titanic* moved through the night at about 22.5 knots.

The myth of supposed unsinkability has already been examined but as the actual disaster is considered it is necessary to examine some of the other myths that have become part of the *Titanic* legacy.

Titanic was trying for a speed record

Titanic, for reasons discussed earlier, could never hope to beat the speed of her rivals *Lusitania and Mauretania*. She had less powerful engines and was a third as big again as the Cunarders. It is clear that Ismay discussed opening up to maximum speed that Sunday evening with Chief Engineer Bell but it is probable that he wanted to demonstrate not that the ship was as fast as the Cunarders (which it wasn't) but that it was not a slow ship.

Myth?

Captain Smith and his officers ignored ice warnings
By April the icebergs calved in the far north have been carried south. In 1912 they were especially numerous and had progressed further south than usual.

During the Sunday afternoon it became colder and colder and *Titanic* was approaching the southern edge of expected ice. Ice is very prevalent in April as the bergs around Greenland glaciers drift further and further south. It is known that ice warnings were received from other ships and some first-class survivors recounted how Ismay spoke to them and showed them an ice warning he had received. Although Captain Smith did not slow down he did take the ship slightly further south than usual in an attempt to avoid the ice (ships crossed the Atlantic on a 'Great Circle' track that led to them steering south-west and then turning to a more due westerly course at the 'turning point'). As night fell, a very calm and starry night but with a haze at sea level, he ordered the temperature of the fresh water tanks checked to ensure the water would not freeze. Second Officer Charles Lightoller, when he was relieved as officer of the watch by Murdoch, said that he had ordered that all lights below the bridge be extinguished so that the glare would not impair the men's vision – they knew they were in the vicinity of ice – they could smell it. Practice at the time was not to slow down for ice or even fog. Only the great explorer Ernest Shackleton told the British Inquiry that he would have reduced speed. Other captains said they would do what Smith did – pass through the danger as quickly as possible. Today the defence of speeding up on the M1 in fog so that you could get away from it quickly would not be expected, but Smith was exonerated of negligence. The inquiry did state that in future ships should slow down near ice or fog. It is easy to be wise after the event.

At around 11.30 p.m., high above the ship in the crow's nest, Fred Fleet, the single lookout, was peering into the icy night. He had no binoculars but in the haze he saw the shape only 500 yards away. He rang his bell to alert the bridge (there was no telephone) and yelled out 'Iceberg dead ahead'. Murdoch acted instantly, ordering an emergency turn to port (left) and hit the switch to close the watertight doors.

There was confusion over the helm orders and this led to a delay

Quartermaster Hichens turned the wheel. If *Titanic* had had a bigger rudder she might have turned more quickly and it is now believed that her rudder was too small for the size of ship.

A novelist whose grandfather sailed on the *Titanic* claims her new book reveals the truth behind the sinking of the ship. Lady Louise Patten has stated that Charles Lightoller, the second officer on board, believed the order to steer the ship away from the danger was misunderstood.

In 1912 different steering systems were used for steam ships and sailing ships and her grandfather maintained this caused confusion when an order was given to turn the ship to starboard. The two steering systems were the complete opposite of one another, so a command to turn 'hard a-starboard' meant turn the wheel right under one system and left under the other. In the older system, 'starboard your helm' would produce a turn to port (this is the way a tiller on a yacht works; pull the tiller to the right and the boat turns left). In the more modern system a starboard helm order actually produces a turn to starboard. Patten believes that Quartermaster Hichens panicked and the real reason why *Titanic* hit the iceberg, which has never come to light before, is because he turned the wheel the wrong way. However, she also claims that the iceberg was spotted 2 miles away and most sources say that it was much closer. *Olympic* used the same system so that it is unlikely that confusion occurred. Her book is well worth reading, but as a work of fiction.

Titanic turned slowly but as it was she scraped against an underwater protruding portion of a relatively small iceberg. It was too late, there was no big gash but it is believed that the rivets (many of them iron as discussed earlier) popped and the plates they held opened up along 300ft of her hull – six compartments opened up; she could float with just three flooded.

Some of the crew felt a slight shudder, one thought that the ship had lost a propeller and would have to return to Belfast for repairs after New York. Mrs Thayer, in her suite, felt just a slight jar; Martha Stevenson heard a grinding noise; Lawrence Beesley only felt an extra heave of the engines; to the passengers nothing seemed amiss. The officers were more concerned. Smith rushed to the bridge and was apprised of the collision. Andrews went below to find water rushing in. It was then that he realised the fatal flaw. There was nothing to stop the compartments overflowing into each other – *Titanic* would founder that night. He told Smith and Ismay, who had joined him, the grim news. Grim news it was: there were over 2,200 souls on board and only 1,178 lifeboat spaces.

Smith knew his ship was doomed and was concerned to avoid panic. He ordered a distress message sent out by Jack Phillips and Harold Bride, the two radio operators on board who were employed by the Marconi Company. Initially they sent the usual signal CQD but then decided to use the newly adopted 'SOS'. The messages were answered by a number of ships, including *Titanic's* sister, *Olympic*. All were some distance away and unlikely to arrive within the two hours Andrews believed the ship might stay afloat.

Radio at sea was new in 1912. White Star did not have its own operators and contracted with Marconi for the use of his staff. Radio had proved its worth in 1909 when White Star's *Republic* collided with the *Florida* off Massachusetts. Radio messages were picked up by the *Baltic* which rescued most of the 1,620 passengers from the ships, both of which were lost.

The Marconi operation was a commercial one and priority was given to the first-class passengers. Sending a 'Marconigram' was not cheap. To send a wireless telegram cost 12s 6d for the first ten words and 9d per word thereafter. Nevertheless, over 250 passenger telegrams were sent and received during the voyage.

Phillips and Bride kept transmitting for as long as they had power. It is reported that a crew member tried to steal Phillips's lifejacket but was restrained. Bride survived but Phillips died.

Once the true scale of the disaster became apparent Smith ordered that the passengers be led to the boat stations. There seems to have been little systematic planning. Stewards went from cabin to cabin (there was no PA system) and roused the passengers. Many were reluctant to leave their beds. In the concern to prevent panic little was done to hurry the passengers up. The crew seemed unsure of the procedures they should follow, short of 'women and children first'. *Titanic's* lifeboats could be lowered fully loaded but the officers did not appear to be aware of this. Boats were partially filled, lowered and then passengers were expected to climb down rope ladders to them, otherwise the boats would go to one of the gangway ports lower in the hull to fill up completely – this plan came to nothing. Lifeboat 7 was the first to be launched at 12.45 a.m., sixty-five minutes after hitting the iceberg. It carried only twenty-seven people yet was rated to hold sixty-five.

Myth?

There was a true love story on board the Titanic

The events of the night produced a love story to rival those of many works of fiction. Isidor and Ida Straus, who were returning from a European trip, were in their eighties and had been married for many years. Isidor was the owner of

Macy's department store in New York and was reputed to be worth over £10 million. They were a devoted couple. When Mrs Straus was placed in a lifeboat she asked if her husband could join her as a man of his age would stand no chance in the icy waters. It was agreed that he could but he refused: if the other men were staying he would too. Mrs Straus climbed out of the lifeboat telling the occupants that she and her husband had been together for over fifty years and that they would stay together now. They were last seen sitting on the promenade deck holding hands – a true love story from *Titanic*.

John Jacob Astor, too, placed his young bride (he was newly married) in a boat and then waited calmly. Benjamin Guggenheim and his valet were in their night clothes on the boat deck. Guggenheim is reported to have suggested that they should go and change so that 'they could go down like gentlemen'.

Slowly the true magnitude of the disaster was beginning to dawn on the passengers, especially when signal rockets began to be fired.

Myth?

Class distinction played a part in the tragedy

Although there was press speculation, at the time and ever since, it seems that there was no class distinction once passengers had reached the boat deck. However, third class was aft and lower down in the ship and it took time for news of the evacuation to reach them. Many of the emigrants spoke little or no English and many wanted to take their possessions with them. The boats themselves were positioned nearer to the first- and second-class area. 'Women and children first' was adhered to, although some officers did let men into the boats if there were no women nearby. Major Arthur Peuchen of the Canadian Militia had felt the collision as no more than a large wave hitting the ship. On the boat deck he saw a boat being lowered and offered his services as a yachtsman. He was told that if he was seaman enough to climb down a rope then he could go – he survived.

When the ship went down a few people were picked up out of the freezing water by lifeboats. However, the statistics especially for third class as will be shown later in this chapter were especially shocking – only a quarter surviving in total.

Of the navigation staff only Second Officer Lightoller, Fourth Officer Boxhall and Fifth Officer Lowe survived to give an account of the disaster. Of the eighteen stewardesses, seventeen survived. Keeping the lights on as long as possible, none of the senior engineers survived. Of the pursers staff only two female clerks survived.

Myth?

There had been a written premonition about the disaster

One curious footnote to the *Titanic* story comes in a premonition of the disaster from as early as 1898 in a short story entitled *Futility* about a disaster to a liner called *Titan*, written by Morgan Robertson. The similarities with *Titanic* are amazing:

Titan
800ft long
British
Disaster in April
3,000 passengers + crew = 2,000 on board
24 lifeboats = 500 capacity in boats
Hit iceberg – starboard side
24–25 knots

Titanic
882ft long
British
Disaster in April
3,000 passengers + crew = 2,227 on board
20 lifeboats = 1,178 capacity in boats
Hit iceberg – starboard side
22.5 knots

As half-filled lifeboats were lowered many third-class passengers were struggling to find the boat deck. Bruce Ismay is said to have gone from boat to boat becoming more and more concerned. He truly believed that the women and children were off the ship and he asked an officer if he could get into a boat.

The last boat to leave was an emergency boat from the bridge roof. Launched by Second Officer Lightoller, it capsized and its occupants ended up balancing on the upturned hull.

Myth?

Bruce Ismay dressed as a woman to obtain a lifeboat place
The rumours that he dressed as a woman are unfounded. However, for the chairman of the company to survive when over 1,500 died caused considerable adverse comment. Nevertheless, Ismay did leave *Titanic* in a lifeboat. It is probable that he put on a head covering as even today the advice given at the lifeboat drill on a cruise ship is for passengers to dress warmly and put on some form of head covering to conserve heat.

The band played on

Wallace Hartley, the leader of *Titanic*'s band, began to play as the evacuation began. He led his colleagues further and further aft as the waters engulfed the ship. They made no attempt to escape but continued to play to the over 1,500 people trapped on the vessel once the last boat had left.

Myth?

The band played 'Nearer My God to Thee'

It is believed that the last piece they played was 'Songe d'Automne' (not 'Nearer My God to Thee' as often quoted). Hartley's funeral (his body was recovered) was a huge affair and the town of Colne in Lancashire has long revered this famous son whose leadership inspired the band to play on to comfort the doomed. Hartley's story is recounted in *A Hymn for Eternity: The Story of Wallace Hartley, Titanic Bandmaster* by Yvonne Carroll (see bibliography).

Breakup

The book by Lady Patten mentioned above claims that *Titanic* kept on steaming at full ahead for ten minutes after Bruce Ismay was informed of the incident and that this led to pressure on the bulkheads. The evidence for this assertion is lacking at this time.

However, recent research does suggest that the *Titanic* did founder at a quicker rate than her officers expected. If the officers believed they had much longer to evacuate the ship this fact could explain the apparent slowness in lowering the boats.

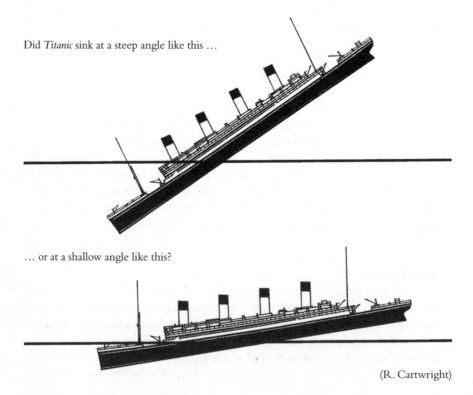

Did *Titanic* sink at a steep angle like this …

… or at a shallow angle like this?

(R. Cartwright)

The Olympic Class had been built with an expansion joint (the second expansion joint) in the upper superstructure. The joint was situated between the third and fourth (dummy) funnels. It is this joint that is believed to have failed due to stress. The more forward expansion joint was subject to less stress, being nearer the bow, and thus less affected by the length of the ship.

Many survivors claimed that the ship had not broken up and had dived beneath the waves complete. However, when the wreck of the *Titanic* was discovered in 1985 the hull was found in two pieces. Many theories were developed as to how the ship broke apart during the sinking process and research was begun to determine how this could have happened. In 1986 a third 17.4m section from the midship region was found.

To help solve this mystery, the Discovery Channel, in developing its award-winning *Titanic: Anatomy of a Disaster* television documentary, approached Gibbs & Cox, Inc. in the US, one of the oldest naval architecture and marine engineering firms in the world, to perform a stress analysis to help determine the possibility of hull fracture at the surface rather than during the dive to the deep.

Engineers analysed the stresses in *Titanic* as the flooding progressed within the bow region, using modern techniques that simply were not available until the 1960s, and certainly were not known to the structural designers of the ship in the first decades of the century. A full-ship model was graphically constructed, employing a modern approach similar to that used for today's US Navy.

Engineers determined that stress levels in the midsection of the ship were at least up to the yield strength of the steel just prior to sinking. When considered alone, stresses at these levels do not necessarily imply catastrophic failure. Additional analyses, focusing on probable locations of initial hull fracture, are required to indicate that the ship sustained possible catastrophic failure at the surface and began to break apart. It was then that the expansion joints began to be considered.

Significant stresses were developed in the vicinity of the two expansion joints, and in the inner bottom of the ship between the forward end of Boiler Room No.1 and the aft end of the Reciprocating Engine Room.

At 2.17 a.m., according to the various investigations after the disaster, the *Titanic* began to go under, her lights blazing in the cold of the sub-Arctic night and with more than 1,500 people still on board. With a rumbling, crashing noise, the bow of the ship sank deeper into the water and the stern rose into the air.

The stern section hung motionless and high out of the water for nearly a minute. The hull fracture was described as the sound of breaking chinaware, but as it continued, it was like a loud roar. A minute later, *Titanic*'s lights flickered and then went out.

Then, at 2.20 a.m., the stern settled back into the water. Following a series of explosions, the submerged forward section began to pull away from the stern. As the forward section began its long descent, it drew the stern almost vertical again. This may account for the belief that the ship was virtually intact when she sank. Once this began, *Titanic* picked up speed as she sank below the surface of the pond-still waters of the North Atlantic. Some of the survivors on the stern stated that it was almost perpendicular as it slid silently and with hardly a ripple beneath the surface. Gibbs & Cox point out that, had the liner been elevated at 90 degrees, the huge boilers would have been ripped from their moorings, which was not the case. Their report suggests that the stern section likely rose from the surface to at least 20 degrees, but not more than 35 degrees, as it filled with water or was dragged down by the bow section.

The failure of the main hull girder of the *Titanic* was the final phase of her sinking process. This began between 2.00 and 2.15 a.m., starting somewhere between funnels 3 and 4. Studies indicate that the plate failures might have started around the second expansion joint, or just behind it.

Stresses in the hull were increasing as the bow flooding continued and the stern rose from the water. Survivor testimony and underwater surveys have confirmed that the forward expansion joint was opened up while the ship was still on the surface, suggesting the significant stresses induced by the flooding of the forward part of the hull. Most probably significant stress developed in the way of the second expansion joint, between its root and the deck structure below it. As the flooding progressed aft, the hull girder was strained beyond its design limitations and the local stresses around this expansion joint soon reached the ultimate strength of the material. It is thought that, in the end, a critical structural failure in the hull or deck plates occurred in the area around the second expansion joint. Once localised, fracture began in the way of this joint; additional plate failures and associated fracturing likely radiated out from this joint.

Assuming that the hull girder failed at the surface then, as Boiler Room No.4 filled with water the stern rose farther out of the water, resulting in some 76m of unsupported hull, which sharply increased the hull girder stresses, in turn accelerating the fracturing of the steel plates. The angle of trim grew to a maximum of 15 to 20 degrees, further increasing the stresses in the hull and deck plating near the aft expansion joint. The stresses continued to build in this area of the ship, where there were large openings for a main access, the machinery casing for the Reciprocating Engine Room, the uptakes and intakes for the boilers, the ash pit door on the port side of Boiler Room No.1 and the turbine engine casing. As the hull girder continued to fail, the bow was first to begin its plunge toward the seabed.

As the bow and stern sections continued to separate, there were some local buckling failures in the inner bottom and bottom structure. This is what caused the stern section to settle back toward the water's surface as the decks began to fail.

An additional stress analysis, based on classical beam theory, indicates that the hull girder stresses exceeded the yield point of the steel. When the bow and stern began to separate, the two main transverse bulkheads bounding Boiler Room No.1 collapsed as they were compressed by the downward movement of the deck structures. The decks, in turn, failed because of the lack of bulkhead support.

When this happened, the unsupported length of the inner bottom suddenly grew to 165ft, encompassing Boiler Rooms Nos 1 and 2, as well as the Reciprocating Engine Room. This condition allowed deformation of the inner bottom structure to extend up further into the ship's machinery spaces, while the deck structure failures continued. It is believed that this compression of the hull girder brought about the failure of the side shell plates and also freed equipment inside the ship, such as the boilers in Boiler Room No. 1, from its foundations.

It is probable from the evidence on the seabed that the fractured stern section concertinaed against the remaining sections of the superstructure forward of the fracture. This explains the buckled metal found at the top of the wreck suggesting that the two parts crashed and ground against each other.

The analysis supports some witnesses' testimonies that the ship likely began to fracture at the surface, and that the fracture was completed at some unknown depth below the water's surface. The resulting stress levels in the strength deck below the root of the second expansion joint (aft), and in the inner bottom structure directly below, were very high because of the unusual flooding occurring in the forward half of the ship. These patterns of stress support the argument that initial hull failure likely occurred at the surface.

Titanic did not sink either quietly or in one piece. She went down in at least two pieces and noisily. Her officers would have been unaware of the impending hull failure and this may have led them to believe that they had longer to evacuate the ship than they really had.

Analysis of the wreck of *Britannic* shows that her expansion joints were much more sophisticated than *Titanic*'s, suggesting that Harland & Wolff were somehow aware of what had actually happened and may have changed the design to one less likely to fail.

Myth?

An officer shot himself

Within days of the disaster, several crew members and passengers began to speak of a suicide by an officer just before *Titanic* sank. It is unclear who may have committed suicide, some claiming it was Smith, Wilde or Murdoch. It is unlikely to have been Murdoch as several members of the crew, including Second Officer Lightoller, said they saw him attempting to free Collapsible Lifeboat A just before the bridge submerged in the final stages of the sinking, when a huge wave washed him overboard into the sea. Surviving radio operator Harold Bride later stated that he saw Murdoch near Collapsible Lifeboat B, but that he died in the water.

In his home town of Dalbeattie, Scotland, there is a memorial to his heroism and a charitable prize has been established in his name. The charitable prize was given a donation by the James Cameron film for its false portrayal of Murdoch after the residents of Dalbeattie complained.

The 1997 film has Murdoch commit suicide; it also has him taking – but later reject – a bribe from villain Caledon Hockley; and shoot two steerage-class passengers (Tommy Ryan and another unidentified passenger) dead in a mob on the deck after Murdoch presumes they intend to storm one of the remaining lifeboats. Murdoch then salutes Chief Officer Henry Wilde and fires his pistol into his own brain, his body crumpling backwards into the sea. After filming producers refused to take out Murdoch's suicide scene, but studio executives later flew to Murdoch's hometown to issue an apology to his surviving relatives for this depiction.

Myth?

The crew wages stopped the moment the ship sank

Not a myth at all. Up to the 1940s it was the norm in the UK (and the USA) for wages to be stopped from the moment that a ship foundered. It was this rule that was to lead to Sir Cosmo Duff Gordon being accused of bribery whilst in a lifeboat – see chapter 5.

When *Titanic* sank there were fewer than 800 people in lifeboats and over 1,500 either dead or doomed in the icy North Atlantic – would rescue come?

Chapter 4

Carpathia Speeds to the Rescue

The Cunard liner *Carpathia*, under the command of Captain Rostron, was on her way to Europe when she picked up *Titanic*'s SOS. Rostron turned his ship around and headed for her position. Passengers donated warm clothing, hot drinks were prepared and, because of the danger of ice, extra lookouts were posted. *Carpathia* was an older ship, built in 1902, and in 1912 she was on the Cunard subsidiary service between North America and the Mediterranean. She was only 13,555 GRT compared with *Titanic*'s 46,000 and her top speed was only 17.5 knots. She was built for 1,704 passengers but reconfigured in 1905 to carry 2,550, mostly in steerage (2,250). She had only 100 first-class and 200 second-class berths.

Carpathia was sailing from New York City to Fiume, Austria-Hungary (today Rijeka, Croatia), on the night of Sunday 14 April 1912. Among her passengers were American painter Colin Campbell Cooper and his wife, journalist Lewis P. Skidmore, photographer Dr Francis H. Blackmarr, and Charles H. Marshall, whose three nieces were, by coincidence, travelling aboard the *Titanic*.

Carpathia's wireless operator, Harold Cottam, had missed previous messages from *Titanic* due to other duties. He then received messages from Cape Race, Newfoundland, stating that they had private traffic for *Titanic*. He thought he would be helpful and sent a message to the *Titanic* stating that Cape Race had

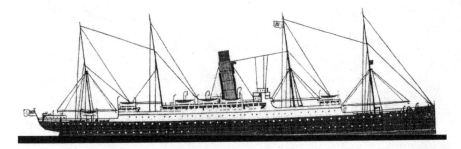

Carpathia – the rescue ship. (R. Cartwright)

traffic for her. In reply he received a distress signal. Cottam awakened Captain Rostron who immediately set a course at maximum speed of 17 knots towards *Titanic's* last known position.

It was a long, cold night for those in the lifeboats. *Titanic* slipped beneath the waves at around 2.45 p.m. A great cry was heard by those in the boats – boats which had been rowed some way from the ship to avoid the suction as she went down. The funnels crashed, there was a rumble as the boilers broke free from their mountings and then silence. Some boats made attempts to save lives. In one boat there were just a few crew and Sir Cosmo Duff Gordon and his party. One of the crew remarked that they had lost everything as their wages had stopped the moment the ship foundered (this was the norm until halfway through the Second World War for both British and US seamen) and Sir Cosmo wrote a cheque out for £5 for each of the men. Later it was claimed that this had been a bribe not to go back and help anyone. The inquiry found that there was no truth in this claim at all but Sir Cosmo was greatly worried by it.

One man who had a lucky escape was Canadian amateur yachtsman Major Arthur Peuchen.

Born in Montreal, Peuchen had been the marshalling officer at the coronation of King George V. He owned a yacht named *Vreda* which had crossed the Atlantic under its own canvas and was, for a time, vice-commodore and rear-commodore of the Royal Canadian Yacht Club.

Peuchen had boarded the *Titanic* at Southampton as a first-class passenger on his fortieth transatlantic voyage. He is believed to have been worried to find out that Captain Smith was in command, because he thought Smith to be a poor commander and that he was too old. On the night *Titanic* sank, Peuchen saw that Lifeboat 6, the boat which contained Quartermaster Hichens and Molly Brown, was poorly manned and came forward to Lightoller, saying he was a yachtsman. Captain Smith was standing nearby and suggested Peuchen go down to the promenade deck so he could break a window and climb into Lifeboat 6. Lightoller replied, however, that Peuchen could slide down the ropes to enter the boat if he was as good a sailor as he claimed. Peuchen then took a rope, swung off the ship, and climbed hand-under-hand down to the boat. He was the only male passenger that Lightoller would allow into a lifeboat that night. He later claimed he did not realise *Titanic* was doomed until he viewed the sinking ship from the lifeboat.

Because Peuchen was a military officer, he came under scrutiny for allowing Hichens to prevent the boat's occupants from going back for survivors and for tolerating the verbal

Margaret (Molly) Brown. (June Cartwright)

abuse Hichens reportedly gave. Peuchen was also criticised for exaggerating his own role, and did not recognise the pivotal role Margaret Brown (the 'unsinkable Molly Brown') played in leading the lifeboat's occupants in rowing and in raising morale. It is possible that Peuchen, as a yachtsman, may have thought that second-guessing an officer in charge would encourage mutiny. Peuchen later publicly blasted Captain Smith and the crew of *Titanic*, claiming their seamanship to be substandard.

Noëlle, Countess of Rothes (Rothes is in Fife, Scotland), embarked at Southampton with her parents, Thomas and Clementina Dyer-Edwardes, cousin Gladys Cherry, and maid Roberta Maioni. Her parents disembarked at Cherbourg for a European tour, whilst the others continued, en route for New York and eventually Vancouver, Canada. The countess, her cousin and maid were rescued in Lifeboat 8. Thomas William Jones, the able seaman in charge of their lifeboat, later said Rothes 'had a lot to say, so I put her to steering the boat', a compliment on her leadership abilities. She took the tiller, asking her cousin to assist her until she went to sit next to and comfort a young Spanish newlywed, Señora María de Satode y Peñasco, whose husband had remained behind on the sinking liner. There she remained for the duration of the night, rowing all the while and helping to boost the morale of other women until their lifeboat was picked up by *Carpathia*. Once aboard *Carpathia*, she devoted herself to the care of the steerage women and children from *Titanic*. As a token of his esteem, Jones later presented her with the brass number plate from their lifeboat. She wrote to him every Christmas and the two maintained correspondence until her death.

One survivor reported that, after the vessel sank, there was a moaning sound from those in the water that gradually subsided, leaving only the sobbing of those in the lifeboats to break the silence of the cold sub-Arctic night.

Carpathia was over 58 miles away when she picked up *Titanic*'s distress calls – she was the nearest ship, or was she?

Myth?

There was another ship near to Titanic *that made no rescue effort*

Californian was a 1901-built steamship owned by the British Leyland Line, like *Titanic* part of J.P. Morgan's International Mercantile Marine. She was primarily designed to transport cotton from North America but also had the capacity of carrying forty-seven passengers and fifty-five crew members, although on 15 April 1912 she was carrying no passengers. Stanley Lord, who had commanded *Californian* since 1911, was the captain of the ship when she left London on 5 April 1912 on her way to Boston.

On Sunday 14 April at around 7 p.m., *Californian*'s only wireless operator, Cyril Evans, reported three large icebergs 15 miles north of the course *Titanic* was heading on. One of *Titanic*'s wireless operators, Harold Bride, intercepted the warning and delivered it to the officer of the watch. Later that evening, while travelling south of the Grand Banks of Newfoundland, *Californian* encountered a large ice field. At 10.21 p.m. local time Captain Lord decided to stop the ship's engines and wait until morning before proceeding further.

At 11 p.m. Lord retired for the night in the chartroom below deck. About fifteen minutes later, he saw through a porthole the arrival of a ship nearby. He went to the wireless room and asked Evans if any ships were in the area. Evans replied: 'Only the *Titanic*.' Lord instructed Evans to wire *Titanic* and inform her that the *Californian* was stopped and surrounded by ice.

On deck, Third Officer C.V. Groves also saw the lights of another ship come into view on the horizon off *Californian*'s starboard side and less than 10 miles away. To Groves, she was clearly a large liner as she had multiple decks brightly lit. Fifteen minutes after spotting the vessel, Groves went below to inform Lord. Lord suggested that the ship be contacted by Morse lamp, which was tried, but no reply was forthcoming.

Titanic's duty wireless operator at that time, Jack Phillips, was busy working off a substantial backlog of personal messages with the wireless station at Cape Race, Newfoundland, 800 miles away. When Evans sent the message that they were stopped and surrounded by ice, the relative closeness made *Californian*'s signal unusually loud in Phillips's headphones. As Evans attempted to transmit his ice message, Phillips was unable to hear a separate, prior message he had been in the process of receiving, and an exasperated Phillips rebuked Evans with: 'Shut up, Shut up, I'm working Cape Race.' Evans listened for a little while longer, but at 11.30 p.m. he turned off the wireless and went to bed. Phillips's impatience may have had disastrous consequences: within ten minutes *Titanic* hit the iceberg.

Ten minutes after that *Titanic*'s lookout, Fred Fleet, claimed to have seen a nearby ship but was it *Californian*?

Twenty-five minutes later *Titanic* sent out her first distress call.

Slightly after midnight Second Officer Herbert Stone took watch from Groves. He, too, tried signalling the ship with the Morse lamp, also without success. Around 12.45 a.m. on 15 April, Stone saw a white flash appear from the direction of the nearby steamer. First he thought it was a shooting star, until he saw another one. He saw five rockets before being joined by an apprentice. He called down the speaking tube to Captain Lord at 1.15 a.m., but it is unclear how many rockets he told the captain about. Lord asked if the rockets had been a company signal. Stone said he didn't know. Lord told Stone to tell him if anything about the ship changed, to keep signalling the ship with the Morse lamp, but did not request that the ship firing rockets be contacted by wireless. Rockets were often used by ships without radio to communicate with each other, each line having its own set of rocket signals.

Later, at the British Inquiry following the *Titanic* disaster, Stone and apprentice Gibson admitted to snippets of the conversation that they had had during their watch that night. 'A ship is not going to fire rockets at sea for nothing,' Stone said, and also, 'Look at her now; she looks very queer out of the water; her lights look queer.' Gibson observed, 'She looks rather to have a big side out of the water' and he agreed that 'everything was not all right with her', that it was 'a case of some kind of distress'.

By 2 a.m. the ship appeared to be leaving the area, or was it *Titanic* sinking? A few minutes later Crewman James Gibson informed Captain Lord as such and that eight white rockets had been seen. Lord, who said that he had been asleep (and later claimed no recollection of the visit), asked whether they were sure of the colour, Gibson said yes and left.

At around 2.20 a.m. local time, *Titanic* sank.

At 3.30 a.m. Stone and Gibson, still sharing the middle watch, spotted rockets to the south. They did not see the ship that was firing them, but at about this same time the rescue ship *Carpathia* was racing up from the south-east, firing rockets to let the *Titanic* know that help was on the way.

At 4.15 a.m., Chief Officer George F. Stewart relieved Stone and almost immediately noticed a brilliantly lit-up steamship with one funnel to the south of *Californian*. This would prove to be the *Carpathia*.

Lord woke up at 4.30 a.m. and went out on deck to decide how to proceed past the ice to the west. An hour later Stewart woke Evans, the wireless operator, and asked him to find out why a ship had fired rockets during the night. Evans turned on the wireless and found out that *Titanic* had sunk overnight. Stewart took the news to Captain Lord who ordered the ship underway. However, instead of proceeding south through clear water to *Titanic*'s last reported position, Lord ordered his ship to head west and into the ice flow. After passing slowly through the flow, the *California* reached clear water, increased speed, and finally turned south. The ship actually passed the *Carpathia* to the east, then turned, and headed north-east back towards the rescue ship, arriving at around 8.30 a.m. Lord later explained that this convoluted route was due to ice conditions, even though there was clear water between his original position and *Titanic*'s reported position. It has been claimed the true explanation for this is that the route was intended to obscure the actual location of the *Californian* – to the north and very close to where *Titanic* had foundered.

At 4 a.m. *Carpathia* had arrived at the scene after working her way through dangerous ice fields. She took on 705 *Titanic* survivors and was just finishing picking up the last of these when *California* arrived. After communication between the two ships, *Carpathia* left the area leaving *Californian* to search for any other survivors, but only found scattered wreckage and empty lifeboats.

As will be shown in the next chapter Lord was castigated by the British Inquiry and spent the rest of his life trying to clear his name.

Myth?

Over 1,500 men women and children drowned on Titanic

Some deaths probably occurred in the breakup of the vessel due to physical reasons – falling, being hit by debris etc. Anybody trapped in the body of the vessel as she went down would have drowned. However, of the 300-plus bodies recovered the vast majority had not in fact drowned but had been kept afloat and upright by their lifejackets. The killer was exposure and hypothermia.

It is not possible to give a full account of what happened to either the lost or those in the lifeboats. There are many books that dedicate the majority of their pages to the actual events of the night and the reader is directed to these (see chapter 10). The following examples hopefully give an indication of what happened.

Amongst those who did not survive was a man believed to be the richest in the world, John Jacob Astor. His second wife, eighteen-year-old Madeleine, became pregnant whilst travelling in Europe and, wanting the child born in the US, the Astors boarded the *Titanic* as first-class passengers in Cherbourg together with Colonel Astor's valet Victor Robbins, Madeleine's maid Rosalie Bidois and nurse Caroline Louise Endres. They also took their pet airedale dog named Kitty. The Astors were deeply fond of Kitty and had come close to losing her on a previous trip when she went missing in Egypt. Kitty did not survive the sinking.

Astor was easily the wealthiest passenger on board the *Titanic*. A short while after the initial crash, Colonel Astor remarked to his wife that the ship had hit an iceberg. He reassured her that the damage did not appear serious. When Second Officer Lightoller came up onto A deck to finish loading Lifeboat 4, Astor helped his wife with her maid and nurse on board and then asked if he might join her because she was in 'a delicate condition', i.e. pregnant. Lightoller told him that men were not allowed to enter until all the women had been loaded, so Astor stood back and just asked Lightoller which boat it was. After Lifeboat 4 was lowered at around 1.55 a.m., Colonel Astor stood alone while others tried to free the remaining collapsible boats. Astor was seen on the starboard wing bridge where doubtless he was seeking information from Captain Smith. He was never seen alive again. His body was later recovered in perfect physical condition by sailors from the cable ship *Mackay-Bennett* on 22 April not far from the sinking. The record of his body reads:

NO. 124 – MALE – ESTIMATED AGE 50 – LIGHT HAIR & MOUSTACHE.
CLOTHING – Blue serge suit; blue handkerchief with 'A.V.'; belt with gold buckle; brown boots with red rubber soles; brown flannel shirt; 'J.J.A.' on back of collar.
EFFECTS – Gold watch; cuff links, gold with diamond; diamond ring with three stones; £225 in English notes; $2440 in notes; £5 in gold; 7 shillings in silver; 5 ten franc pieces; gold pencil; pocketbook.
FIRST CLASS. NAME – J.J. ASTOR

Madeleine, her nurse and her maid survived while Astor's valet died.

Major Archibald W. Butt was another eminent *Titanic* victim. Tall and distinguished looking, Butt was born on 26 September 1865 in Augusta, Georgia. He had served as an aide to Teddy Roosevelt, continuing in his position when William Howard Taft became President in 1908. He developed a strong friendship with both men and by the last year of Taft's presidency his usefulness at official functions at the White House was legendary. At a reception given for the leading members of America's judiciary, he presented an incredible 1,275 people to President Taft in a single hour.

On the night of 14 April Major Butt had dined with Captain Smith at a dinner party given by the Wideners and the Thayers in the à la carte restaurant. After dinner Butt and his friends retired to the Café Parisien, a popular place for *Titanic*'s first class to meet and people watch. When the *Titanic* struck the iceberg at 11.40 p.m., Major Butt was informed by Captain Smith that the ship was doomed and that the lifeboats were being readied. Butt immediately sprang into action and became almost another officer on board the ship. He gave words of encouragement to the weeping women and children, and giving stern commands when needed to the slow and inefficient crew members.

In an interview, Mrs Henry B. Harris said about Major Butt:

I saw Major Butt just before they put me into a collapsible raft with ever so many women from the steerage. Mr. Millet's little smile, which played on his lips all through the voyage, had gone, but when I was put in the boat I saw him wave his hand to a woman in another boat.

But oh, this whole world should rise in praise of Major Butt. The man's conduct will remain in my memory forever; he showed some of the other men how to behave when women and children were suffering that awful mental fear that came when we had to be huddled into those boats. Major Butt was near me, and I know very nearly everything he did.

When the order to take to the boats came he became as one in supreme command. You would have thought he was at a White House Reception, so cool and calm was he. A dozen or so women became hysterical all at once as something connected with a lifeboat went wrong. Major Butt stepped to them and said: 'Really you must not act like that; we are all going to see you through this thing.'

He helped the sailors rearrange the rope or chain that had gone wrong and lifted some of the women in with gallantry. His was the manner we associate with the word aristocrat.

President Taft was so concerned about Butt that he despatched the cruiser USS *Chester* to search for his body. His remains were never identified and thus he could not be buried in the Arlington National Cemetery, but a memorial marker in Section 3 reads:

Military aide to the President (1908–12),
son of Joshua Willingham and Pamela Robertson Butt. Born September 26, 1865 in Augusta, Georgia.
Lost at sea on April 16, 1912, when the steamship Titanic with 1500 souls on board sank in the Atlantic Ocean.
'Greater love hath no man than this, that a man lay down his life for his friends.'

Along with his parents, in April 1912 wealthy Harry Elkins Widener boarded the *Titanic* at Cherbourg. After the collision his father placed his mother and her maid in a lifeboat and the two women were eventually rescued by the *Carpathia*. Harry Elkins Widener and his father both went down with the ship. Their bodies, if recovered, were not identified. A memorial service for them was held at St Paul's Episcopal Church in Elkins Park, Pennsylvania, where stained-glass windows were dedicated in their memory.

One of the friends Harry made on board was seventeen-year-old Jack Thayer. Jack was on board with his father, John Borland Thayer, and his mother, Marian. Jack occupied one cabin while his parents occupied another.

He does not appear to have felt the collision but shortly after 11.30 p.m. Jack noticed that he could no longer feel a breeze streaming through his half-open porthole. He dressed and went to A deck on the port side to see what had happened. Finding nothing, he walked to the bow, where he could faintly make out ice on the forward well deck.

Jack woke his parents, who accompanied him back to the port side of the ship. Noticing that the *Titanic* was developing a list to port, they returned to their rooms and put on warmer clothes and life vests. They returned to the deck, but Jack lost sight of his parents, and after searching for them assumed they had boarded a lifeboat.

Jack and his friend Harry tried to board a lifeboat but were denied because they were men. Jack then proposed to jump off the ship, as he was an accomplished swimmer. But Harry was not much of a swimmer and advised Jack against entering the freezing water.

Eventually, as the ship was sinking quickly, the two men decided to jump and attempt to swim to safety. Harry went first; it was the last time Jack ever saw his friend. Once in the water, Jack reached an improperly launched and overturned collapsible lifeboat, on which he and a number of other men, including Second Officer Lightoller, were able to balance for some hours. They heard the anguished cries of hundreds of men, women and children in the water. After spending the night on the overturned collapsible, Jack was picked up by Lifeboat No. 12. He was so distraught and freezing that he did not notice his mother in nearby Lifeboat 4, nor did she notice him. Lifeboat 12 finally made its way to the *Carpathia*. Jack's father did not board a lifeboat and died in the disaster.

Marian Thayer and a friend had walked on deck that evening before settling into deck chairs outside the aft staircase on A deck to enjoy the sunset. As they sat there they were approached by Bruce Ismay. He sat down and after asking whether the ladies were comfortable and enjoying the trip, he explained to them about the possibility of meeting icebergs in the area. He showed them the ice warning from the *Baltic* that Captain Smith had passed to him.

Earlier that evening the Thayers had dined with Captain Smith and Mrs Thayer was one of those who testified to the fact that Captain Smith did not consume any alcohol during the meal. The family were preparing for bed when the collision occurred. Jack went up immediately to investigate; he returned to their stateroom and they followed him back on deck.

Marian said good-bye to Jack and her husband at the top of the grand staircase on A deck, and she and her friend Miss Fleming then went onto A deck on the port side. The two men thought she was safely off the ship until Chief Second Steward George Dodd told them that she was still aboard and then took them to her.

Jack somehow lost his parents in the confusion on deck but John and Marian eventually made their way back to the port side forward on A deck. By around 12.30 a.m. they and other first-class passengers were waiting by the windows of the enclosed promenade to board Lifeboat 4, which hung in the davits on the other side of the glass. The boat finally left at 1.55 a.m. With only two seamen aboard Mrs Thayer and the other ladies grabbed the oars and helped to row.

During the night when Lifeboat 12, with Lifeboat 4 alongside, picked up the survivors from the upturned Collapsible B, Mrs Thayer was too numbed with cold to see that her son Jack had also been saved. Their reunion had to wait until 8.30 a.m. when Lifeboat 12 arrived at the *Carpathia*. On meeting her son she asked, 'Where's Daddy?' Jack answered, 'I don't know, Mother.'

Unlike the poorer passengers, who were left to make their own arrangements, after they disembarked from the *Carpathia* Marian, Jack and Margaret Fleming made their way to Jersey City, New Jersey, where they boarded a private train back to Haverford. Much later, although still perhaps in shock, on 31 May, Marian dined with Madeleine Astor and Florence Cumings. The guests of honour were Captain Rostron and Dr McGhee of the *Carpathia*.

Marian never claimed from White Star for the loss of her husband's life, but, curiously, she did claim for the loss of their luggage.

Another first class casualty to be lost on *Titanic* was wealthy railroad executive Charles Melville Hays of the Grand Trunk Railway, who was returning home to Canada after hearing news that one of his daughters was having a difficult pregnancy. His wife and her maid survived but he was never to return home.

The story of Violet Jessop – served on all three sister ships; survived two sinkings

In 1910, at the age of twenty-three, Violet Jessop became a stewardess on the *Olympic*. Obviously she did well as she was transferred to the new *Titanic*, which she boarded on 10 April 1912. Violet described in her memoirs that she was ordered up on deck after the collision where she watched as the crew loaded the lifeboats. She was later ordered into Lifeboat 16 and, as the boat was being lowered, one of the *Titanic*'s officers gave her a baby to look after. The next morning Violet and the rest of the survivors were rescued by the *Carpathia*. According to Violet, while on board the *Carpathia*, a woman grabbed the baby she was holding and ran off

Violet Jessop. (June Cartwright)

with it without saying a word, although later in life she received a brief telephone call from a woman who claimed to have been the baby, but rang off before Violet could question her further.

Leaving the sea when war broke out, she became a nurse. In 1916 she was on board the hospital ship *Britannic*, sister to *Olympic* and *Titanic*, when the ship apparently struck a mine and sank in the Aegean. While the *Britannic* was sinking Violet jumped out of a lifeboat to avoid being sucked into the *Britannic's* propellers. She was sucked under the water and struck her head on the ship's keel before being rescued by another lifeboat. She later stated that the cushioning due to her thick auburn hair helped save her life. She had also made sure to grab her toothbrush before leaving her cabin on the *Britannic*, saying later that it was the one thing she missed most immediately following the sinking of the *Titanic*.

After the war Violet continued to work at sea before she married and later retired to Suffolk in the 1950s. She died in 1971. She served on all three ships – *Olympic*, *Titanic* and *Britannic*, was on board for both sinkings and survived to a ripe old age.

Word reaches land

When the first messages reached the radio station at Cape Race the scale of the disaster was not believed. The authors were privileged to travel with a descendant of the lighthouse keeper at Cape Race and were told of his disbelief that anything could have happened to *Titanic*.

Once the scale of the disaster was made known from *Carpathia* whole streets in Britain were plunged into mourning. According to the *Hampshire Chronicle* on 20 April 1912, almost 1,000 local families were directly affected. Almost every street in the Chapel district of Southampton lost more than one resident and over 500 households lost a member.

On board *Carpathia*

Captain Rostron prepared his ship to receive survivors – blankets were collected, hot drinks and food prepared. As the ship proceeded carefully past floating ice the pitiful scene of lifeboats and freezing passengers met the crew and passengers of *Carpathia*.

Harold Bride, *Titanic's* surviving radio operator, was suffering from exposure, but with his feet wrapped up he aided the *Carpathia's* own operator in passing the news to the outside world and sending messages from survivors.

Ismay became a recluse and did not even seem to want to notify his own officials – today we might diagnose his condition as shock or even post-traumatic stress disorder; in 1912 he just appeared callous. All he seemed interested in was to return himself and the surviving crew to the UK as soon as possible. As will be seen in the next chapter he was sufficiently roused to radio his representative in New

York, Philip Franklin, and order him to hold the *Cedric* in New York so that the crew could join her to sail to the UK. He used the anagram of ISMAY, YAMSI, to sign the message. As will be seen, this quick exit from the USA was not to happen.

On 18 April 1912 *Carpathia* docked at Pier 54 on the Hudson River, Little West 12th Street in New York, with the survivors. She arrived at night and was greeted by thousands of people. *Titanic* had been headed for a pier further up the river at 20th Street. *Carpathia* dropped off the empty *Titanic* lifeboats at Pier 59, as property of the White Star Line, before unloading the survivors at Pier 54. As news of the disaster spread, many people were shocked that *Titanic* could sink with such great loss of life despite all of her technological advances. Newspapers were filled with stories and descriptions of the disaster and were eager to get the latest information. Many charities were set up to help the victims and their families, many of whom lost their sole breadwinner or, in the case of third-class survivors, lost everything they owned.

Once *Carpathia* docked, the true extent of the tragedy could finally be understood; the statistics shocked the world:

Category	Number aboard	Number survived	% survived	Number lost	% lost
First class	329	199	60.5 %	130	39.5 %
Second class	285	119	41.8 %	166	58.2 %
Third class	710	174	24.5 %	536	75.5 %
Crew	899	214	23.8 %	685	76.2 %
Total	2,223	706	31.8 %	1,517	68.2 %

Table 11   Survivor statistics

Of a total of 2,223 people aboard *Titanic* only 706, less than a third, survived; 1,517 perished. As discussed above the majority of deaths were caused by hypothermia in the -2°C (28°F) ocean where death could be expected in less than fifteen minutes.

For the rescue work, the members of the crew of the *Carpathia* were awarded medals by the survivors. Crew members were awarded bronze medals, officers silver and Captain Rostron a silver cup and gold medal, presented by Margaret (the Unsinkable Molly) Brown. Rostron was later a guest of President Taft at the White House and was presented with a Congressional Gold Medal, the highest honour the United States Congress could confer upon him.

Carpathia was later used to transfer American troops to Europe during the First World War. She was part of a convoy when she was torpedoed on 17 July 1918, off the east coast of Ireland, by the German U-Boat U55, the explosions killing five of the engine room crew. All of the 218 other people on board, including thirty-six saloon-class and twenty-one steerage passengers, were rescued.

The wreck was discovered on 9 September 1999 about 185 miles west of Lands End, the southernmost point of the English mainland. She was in reasonably good condition.

Marconi & Isaacs

One of the beneficiaries of the disaster (if such a term can be applied to such a tragedy) was the Marconi Company. Whilst radio had not prevented the disaster, it had brought *Carpathia* to the scene. Marconi was just one of the companies that placed its employees on ships. Harold Bride and Jack Phillips, *Titanic's* radio operators, although under Captain Smith's command were actually employed by the Marconi Company. Radio and the Marconi Company had played a major role in the rescue of all but two of the passengers and crew from White Star's *Republic* in 1902. We have already seen how much of the radio traffic was from passengers keeping in touch with friends. Despite the expense, many first-class passengers were keen to take advantage of the new technology just as many airline passengers today use the in-flight telephone service in order to contact friends.

Marconi was, by chance, in New York at the time of the disaster. Together with a reporter, Jim Speers, Marconi boarded *Carpathia* to meet with his surviving employee – Harold Bride. Bride had his feet swathed in bandages as he told his story – a story that was soon published. When it became clear that without radio it was probable that all on board might have been lost Marconi's reputation was further enhanced as was the value of his company. The stock price rose.

The rise in the price of Marconi stock had the makings of a scandal contained within it. The Attorney General of Great Britain was Rufus Isaacs and as such was to play a prominent role in the British Inquiry (see chapter 5). His brother, Godfrey, as managing director of the Marconi Company had acquired a large number of shares in it. On 9 April 1912 he had offered to dispose of some of them to Rufus and his other brother, Harry. There is nothing wrong with that of course. Harry accepted but Rufus, conscious of his position within the government and not wishing for any conflict of interest, declined. As the scale of the disaster and the positive role of the Marconi Company in saving lives became apparent, Rufus Isaacs bought 10,000 shares at £2 each from his brother. He then transferred 10,000 each to two political colleagues, one of whom was David Lloyd George (later to be Prime Minister during the First World War). The shares were in American Marconi rather than British Marconi and so when the matter was raised in the House of Commons, Isaacs denied any wrongdoing on the grounds that these were US shares and thus unconnected with any British Government business. On 8 June 1913 he admitted that buying the shares so soon after the disaster was a mistake. However, his political career was unaffected and he was made Lord Chief Justice in October 1913. Isaacs was heavily criticised by both Rudyard Kipling and the poet Rupert Brooke. Whilst Isaacs did nothing illegal, the affair tarnished the role of the Marconi Company in being instrumental in saving the lives of the survivors.

Myth?

It was the first SOS ever sent

Harold Bride, the surviving radio operator, continued to carry out his duties by helping *Carpathia's* radio operator. Despite have swollen feet, he sent telegram after telegram. When the ship docked in New York he was in much demand for his story and also the story of his colleague and senior, Jack Phillips. He told how they began by sending the distress signal current at the time 'CQD', but then decided to try the new, recently introduced signal of 'SOS'. As said jokingly at the time, 'it might be their last chance to send it'! As for the myth that a crewmember tried to steal Phillips's lifejacket and that Bride held him whilst Phillips knocked him unconscious – that was quoted at the US Inquiry so may well have some truth in it. As it was it was never the subject of any official action.

Myth?

Titanic *wasn't insured*

Titanic was insured but with a higher proportion of the risk than normally carried by the International Mercantile Marine itself. Much of the compensation that would be paid came from IMM and White Star rather than from insurance companies. Apart from the £1.5 million value of the ship there was compensation to survivors and the relatives of those lost.

On 12 January 1913 Irene Harris asked for $1 million for the loss of her husband, just one a number of claims filed that day in New York, following an offer in December 1912 of $664,000 in settlement of all claims arising from the sinking of *Titanic* on 15 April 1912, by White Star.

While surviving first-class passengers or their relatives filed large claims for lost valuables and other possessions (the man who owned the car featured in James Cameron's film – in real-life a new 25 horsepower Renault automobile – claimed $5,000 for its loss), White Star Line employees and their families found themselves having to fight for every penny. Surviving crew members even had their wages stopped the day after the *Titanic* went down, because the company ruled that they no longer had jobs now that the vessel on which they had been employed had sunk (as discussed in the previous chapter). Some relatives even received bills for items of clothing and equipment issued to crewmembers who were lost.

The actual amount paid out is clouded in secrecy. However, in 1961 Roberta Bolling, sixty-eight, who survived the sinking of the *Titanic* nearly fifty years previously, finally received a cheque in compensation for losses and sufferings she encountered that night. The cheque, from trustees administering the compensation fund was for $280!

The US House of Representatives authorised $10,000 appropriations for the families of each of the three postal clerks who lost their lives on the *Titanic*.

Burials

The main recovery ships were the cable ship *Mackay-Bennett*, carrying embalmers on board, which was later joined by the *Minia*. These two ships recovered all but five of the bodies that were found. Amongst those brought ashore was the body of John Jacob Astor. The *Mackay-Bennett* recovered 306 bodies of which 116 were buried at sea due to serious decomposition. The *Minia* recovered seventeen more bodies, including that of Charles M. Hays, the President of the Grand Trunk Railway. Five bodies were later found by other vessels.

Many of the bodies of the more wealthy were returned to their families for burial in their home town. However, there are 150 graves in the Fairview Lawn, the Mount Olivet (Roman Catholic) and the Baron De Hirsch (Jewish) cemeteries. In all the cemeteries those graves where the remains were not identified are marked by the number that represents the order the bodies were recovered. One hundred and twenty-one of the graves are in the Fairview Lawn Cemetery. The *Titanic* section of the cemetery is laid out to represent a plan view of *Titanic* with a gap on the right-hand (starboard) section of the graves to represent the gash caused by the iceberg.

Amongst those buried in the cemetery are the unknown child (see below) and the real J. Dawson – Joseph – a coal trimmer on *Titanic*, whose name was changed to Jack for the 1997 James Cameron movie, *Titanic*, and played by Leonardo DiCaprio.

Above: Titanic graves at Fairview Cemetery, Halifax. (Authors' collection)

Left: Jack Dawson's grave. (Authors' collection)

The grave of Ernest Freeman, J. Bruce Ismay's secretary. (Authors' collection)

Everett Edward Elliot's grave. (Authors' collection)

Also buried in the cemetery is at least one of the ship's musicians (there may be others but many of the bodies remain unidentified), first violinist John Law Hume. Another of the musicians, bass violinist John Frederick Preston Clarke, is buried in the Roman Catholic Mount Olivet Cemetery. Amongst the graves is that of Bruce Ismay's secretary, Ernest Freeman, whose gravestone was erected by J. Bruce Ismay.

The heroism of the ordinary members of the crew is not forgotten. The inscription on the grave of twenty-four-year-old Everett Edward Elliott is most moving and speaks of the heroism of those who remained at their posts to the very end.

One of the spin-offs from the 1997 *Titanic* movie was money to restore and improve the cemetery.

The Mount Olivet Roman Catholic Cemetery contains nineteen graves and the Jewish Baron De Hirsch Cemetery contains ten. One of the most poignant descriptions is that of Grave 328 in the Mount Olivet Cemetery:

Four foot six inches. Age about 14, hair golden brown. Marks: very dark skin, refined features. Lace-trimmed red-black overdress, black underdress, green striped undershirt, black woollen shawl and felt slippers. Probably third class passenger.

Who is she and what was her reason for travelling? We may never know but it would be nice to give her a name.

The unknown child of the *Titanic*

The body of a fair-haired toddler was the fourth pulled from the ocean by the main recovery ship, the cable ship *Mackay-Bennett*, on 17 April 1912. The description read:

NO. 4 – MALE – ESTIMATED AGE, 2 – HAIR, FAIR.
CLOTHING – Grey coat with fur on collar and cuffs; brown serge frock; petticoat; flannel garment; pink woollen singlet; brown shoes and stockings.
No marks whatever.
Probably third class.

The hard-bitten seamen of the *Mackay-Bennett* were moved by their discovery and as the body remained unidentified, probably because his relatives had also perished, they paid for a memorial in the Fairview Lawn Cemetery. The child was buried on 4 May 1912 with a copper pendant placed in his coffin by recovery sailors that read 'Our Babe'.

The body, identified as that of a child around two years old, was initially believed to be that of either a two-year-old Swedish boy, Gösta Pålsson, or a two-year-old Irish boy, Eugene Rice, two other fair-haired toddlers who perished in the disaster.

Myth?

DNA evidence cannot be wrong

In 2002, more than ninety years after the disaster, it was believed that the identity of the unknown child had finally been discovered by means of DNA matching using fragments recovered from the grave.

The 'unknown child' buried with other victims in Halifax, Nova Scotia, was identified as Eino Viljami Panula, a member of a Finnish family all of whom died in the disaster. He was thirteen months old when the *Titanic* sank on 15 April 1912. His mother Maria and four brothers also drowned. Maria Emila Ojala and her five sons were on their way to the US to join her husband, John, who was working in Pennsylvania.

After being informed of this discovery relatives arrived in Halifax to visit the grave, where they decided that the child's body should remain. Magda Schleifer, the granddaughter of Maria's sister, said she had agreed to a DNA blood test when she was approached by a television company planning a film on the *Titanic's* 'ghosts', which was shown in the Channel 4 series *Secrets of the Dead*. Relatives were unaware that any of their family's bodies had been found until approached by television researchers.

Eino Viljami had been in Fairview Lawn Cemetery, along with 120 other *Titanic* victims, ever since, with a gravestone reading 'Unknown Child'.

The grave of the
'unknown child',
now believed to be
Sydney Goodwin.
(Authors' collection)

However, Canadian researchers at Lakehead University in Thunder Bay made further tests, not available in 2002. These tests did not show a match to the Panula family. Further DNA extracted from the exhumed remains and DNA provided by a surviving maternal relative helped positively match the remains to Sydney Goodwin, and the re-identification was announced on 30 July 2007.

Sydney Leslie Goodwin was born on 9 September 1910 in Wiltshire, England. He was the youngest child born to Frederick Joseph Goodwin and his wife Augusta (*née* Tyler). He had older siblings named Lillian Amy, Charles Edward, William Frederick, Jessie Allis and Harold Victor. They were emigrating to the USA to join Frederick's older brother in upstate New York. None of them survived.

Although the bodies of two other children, both older boys, were recovered, it was the unknown child who became a symbol of all the children lost in the disaster. A pair of his shoes was donated to Halifax's Maritime Museum of the Atlantic in 2002 after the misidentification by the descendants of a Halifax police officer who guarded the bodies and clothing of *Titanic* victims. As can be seen in the photograph of the memorial (above) even to this day tributes are still laid at the grave.

Before the bodies were all recovered and buried however the inquiries began, firstly in the USA and then in Great Britain.

Chapter 5

Aftermath

In the famous UK television series *Yes Minister*, Sir Humphrey Appleby (the civil servant) tries to persuade his minister, Jim Hacker MP, that the purpose of an inquiry is to find a mass of non-evidence and that the aim should be protection of individuals rather than discovery of the truth!

Governmental and Public inquiries are a commonplace occurrence today and have indeed engendered certain scepticism. In 1912 the public inquiry was a fairly recent phenomenon. The public and indeed the press were much more deferential to officialdom than they are today. Even in the 1930s the British press made no mention of the relationship between the future King Edward VIII and Wallis Simpson until the abdication crisis had actually developed, such was the deference to the monarchy. US and European newspapers had been reporting the developments for some time but as foreign travel was still rare, the British public remained in blissful ignorance of the developing constitutional crisis.

Initially it was the reporting of the Crimean War and then the US Civil War that brought newspaper discussion of blunders and failings into the homes of ordinary people. The reports by *The Times* of incompetence by senior officers of the British Army during the Crimean War (1853–56) produced not only outrage but far-reaching reforms. The power of the press and public opinion was gaining in strength and was something governments could not ignore.

It was the coming of mass transportation through the railways that brought the need for governments to develop means to inquire into serious incidents. Britain took the lead. In 1840 and 1842 Acts of Parliament empowered the Board of Trade to conduct investigations into railway accidents through the newly formed Railway Inspectorate (many of whose members were Army engineering officers). The first investigation, and most importantly publication of results, took place in August 1840 following an accident on the Hull and Selby Railway. They were able to make recommendations although legislation to compel safety improvements lagged some way behind. Today regulatory authorities such as the US

Federal Aviation Authority (FAA) are able to ground aircraft until safety issues are addressed in extreme cases as will be shown in chapter 8.

In the years since the inquiry into the Tay Bridge disaster (see chapter 2) in 1879, scepticism about official inquiries has grown. Recent inquiries into the assassination of President Kennedy (the 1963 Warren Commission), the 2006 Rogers Commission into the loss of the Space Shuttle Challenger (see chapter 7), the 2003 Hutton Inquiry into the death of Dr David Kelly who was accused of leaking information about Iraq's weapons of mass destruction (or lack of them) to a British journalist, and the 2010–11 Chilcott Inquiry in the UK into the Iraq War of 2003 have all been subject to charges of political interference and cover-up. Were the *Titanic* inquiries useful and fair or could the term 'whitewash' be applied to them?

There were two major inquiries into the *Titanic* disaster. The first, in the US, seemed determined to find somebody to blame, whilst the second, in Great Britain, appears to have had a degree of protection for the authorities as part of its agenda.

Even before *Carpathia* docked the press and the authorities were demanding answers. The world's largest and newest liner had sunk days into her maiden voyage. Even worse, initial reports that all the passengers and crew were safe proved false – over 1,500 lives had been lost in the icy waters of the North Atlantic. How had this happened and who was to blame? Just as today, the need for somebody to blame was apparent from the first news of the disaster. In chapter 8 it will be shown how a baggage handler was initially blamed for the DC10 crash over Paris in the 1970s – in the case of *Titanic* the initial blame fell (and still does to some extent) on a man unconnected with the vessel – Captain Lord of the SS *Californian*. The story of Captain Lord and *Californian* was related in the previous chapter and how he came to be the main culprit in the *Titanic* tragedy, according to the British Inquiry, will be related later in this chapter, as will the attempts – only partially successful – to redeem his reputation; attempts that have never ceased even up to today.

As *Carpathia* steamed into New York the press were waiting. In addition Marconi (who it is believed had intended to sail on *Titanic*) rushed down to the docks. Marconi stood to gain from the tragedy as without his apparatus (then still relatively new) and the heroism of Bride and Phillips, his employees on board *Titanic* (see chapter 4), there might have been no survivors at all. He was anxious to speak with Harold Bride, the surviving radio operator. Whilst the press were kept back by the police, Marconi made it on board.

Whilst the press waited at the dock gates to interview survivors and anybody connected with White Star, Senator Newlands (Democrat, Nevada), the Senate Master at Arms and the private secretary to Senator William Alden Smith (Republican, Michigan), rushed on board *Carpathia* to serve subpoenas on the surviving crew and Ismay: there was going to be an inquiry in the US and it was going to happen before the witnesses could return to the UK.

Senator Smith had no maritime knowledge; however, he was a ranking member of the Senate Commerce Committee and appears to have been moved by the disaster, although it should be noted that he was shortly to be up for re-election and the publicity gained by chairing the inquiry would be personally beneficial to him.

The shift of economic power from Britain to the United States

1912 was at a cusp in the balance of power in the Western world. For much of the nineteenth century the predominant world economic and military power was Great Britain. In 1912 Britain was still the principal imperial and military power, although the threat of German militarism was by then well perceived. Economically Britain's lead in the world was slipping and moving across the Atlantic to the USA. Since the ending of the Civil War in 1865 the US economy had been growing very rapidly.

Myth?

Britannia still ruled the waves in 1912

The man or woman in the street in Great Britain in 1912 was probably unaware of the fact that the country's pre-eminence was passing to the USA. If there were worries in Britain they were about Germany. France was no longer the old enemy (France and Britain was now military allies) but in terms of manufacturing, naval power and even the transatlantic liner trade the main competitor appeared to be Germany.

Whilst there had been disputes between the USA and Great Britain in the nineteenth century, by 1912 relationships between the two great Anglo-Saxon democracies were good. Indeed there was a flourishing trade of aristocratic (but often not very wealthy) British men and women going one way in search of wealthy spouses and wealthy Americans going the other in search of a title! The murder mystery novels of Conrad Allen, including *Murder on the Lusitania* and *Murder on the Celtic*, provide a fascinating insight into the social life on board the Edwardian transatlantic liners. Allen manages to paint an accurate picture of the atmosphere and tensions between British and American passengers (his hero and heroine are an American male and a British female detective working as partners and employed by Cunard, White Star etc. However, he does make mistakes. In *Murder on the Minnesota* he tells the reader that the Cunard vessels *Lusitania* and *Mauretania* had three functioning funnels and one dummy funnel, the latter for aesthetic purposes. However, the Cunarders had four working funnels. It was the White Star trio *Olympic*, *Titanic* and *Britannic* that had the dummy fourth funnel.

From its beginnings in the 1770s the United States had, by 1912, grown to become a huge, integrated, industrialised economy. The country was aided in this growth by a large unified market, a supportive political-legal system, vast areas of highly productive farmlands, huge natural resources such as timber, coal, iron and oil, and an entrepreneurial spirit and commitment to investing in material and human capital. The USA had attracted immigrants numbering from all over the world. The rapid economic development following the Civil War laid the groundwork for its modern industrial economy. By 1890 the USA had overtaken Great Britain for first place in manufacturing output. Railways (called railroads in the USA) greatly expanded the mileage and built stronger tracks and bridges that handled heavier cars and locomotives, carrying far more goods and people at lower rates. It was uneconomic to import rails (of which Great Britain was a major supplier) so a huge steel industry developed. Refrigeration railroad cars came into use. The nation's industrial infrastructure underwent massive development. Coal was found in abundance in the Appalachian Mountains. Oil was discovered firstly in western Pennsylvania. Large iron ore mines opened in the Lake Superior region of the upper Midwest. Steel mills thrived in places where coal and iron ore could be brought together to produce steel. Large copper and silver mines opened, followed by lead mines and cement factories.

The second half of the ninteenth century was the age of tycoons, of which J.P. Morgan was one of the most influential. There was also John D. Rockefeller and Andrew Carnegie amongst many others in the fields of oil, steel, railroads, banking and in Morgan's case shipping. While upper-class European intellectuals generally looked on commerce with disdain, most Americans – living in a society with a more fluid class structure – enthusiastically embraced the idea of money-making. They enjoyed the risk and excitement of business enterprise, as well as the higher living standards and potential rewards of power and acclaim that business success brought.

Whilst Britain may still have a greater military might than the USA, by 1912 it was losing its economic pre-eminence to the US, save in one field – shipbuilding. The US had only a small percentage of the world's tonnage either registered in the US or built in its yards. Belfast, Merseyside, Tyneside and the Clyde were where more than half the world's ships continued to be built, including those for the White Star Line – ostensibly British but owned by the American Morgan.

On the British side of the Atlantic from the 1770s to the 1820s, Britain experienced an accelerated process of economic change that transformed a largely agrarian economy into the world's first industrial economy. This phenomenon is known as the Industrial Revolution, since the changes were all embracing and permanent and eventually global.

By the 1870s, financial houses in London had achieved an unprecedented level of control over industry. This contributed to increasing concerns among policy-makers over the protection of British investments overseas – particularly those in the securities of foreign governments and in foreign-government-backed development activities, such as the railways that were being built throughout the world. As the largest imperial power at the time, Britain was in a position to profit from such developments and to use her ability to build ships and then use the railways to both import raw materials from and export manufactured goods to her colonies. Both were also useful for speeding troops to any trouble spots. At the end of the Victorian era, however, the service sector (banking, insurance and shipping, for example) began to gain prominence at the expense of manufacturing – a problem that still besets Britain today with perhaps a too high reliance on service industries.

Foreign trade tripled in volume between 1870 and 1914, most of the activity occurring between Britain and other industrialised countries. Britain ranked as the world's largest trading nation in 1860, but by 1913 it had lost ground to both the United States and Germany: British and German exports in that year each totalled $2.3 billion and those of the United States exceeded $2.4 billion. More significant was the emigration of their goods and capital. As far as Europe was concerned one major export was people and they went mostly to the USA, carried in mainly British-built (and apparently British-owned) vessels.

By the outbreak of the Franco-Prussian War in 1870 Britain was no longer the sole 'workshop of the world' – its finished goods were no longer produced so efficiently and cheaply that they could often undersell comparable, locally manufactured goods in almost any other market as had been the case previously. German shipbuilding yards, their managers having often been tutored by British consultants, were able to build liners that were in many ways comparable to those produced in Britain.

Britain's share of world trade fell from one-fourth in 1880 to one-sixth in 1913 (it had declined to one-eighth in 1948). Britain was no longer supplying half the needs in manufactured goods of such nations as Germany, France and the United States. Britain was even growing incapable of dominating the markets of India, its 'Jewel in the Crown', China and South America. There was now competition in textiles, chemicals (mainly from the highly efficient German chemical industry) and a host of other products.

In a previous age the British Government would have reacted strongly to the first inquiry into the loss of a British-registered vessel, owned by a company registered in the UK (even if the company itself was ultimately US owned as was White Star) in international waters by a foreign power. It is interesting therefore that the British Government merely instructed its ambassador to the United States, James Bryce, to keep a watching brief over the inquiry. Bryce did discuss the inquiry with President Taft (whose aide, Major Butt, had been lost on the *Titanic*). Taft told Bryce that the matter was entirely for the Senate as it was a Senate committee. The British Board of Trade was concerned about a US inquiry into the loss of a British vessel in international waters and the Foreign Office had asked Bryce to determine what the US agenda was. There is no doubt that Senator Smith and his colleagues were responding to demands for an urgent inquiry by the US press. As many Americans had died on *Titanic* such demands were perhaps not unreasonable. Bryce continued to express his concerns to the British Government throughout the hearings but London declined to intervene.

The US Inquiry

The *Titanic* hearings were conducted by a special subcommittee of the Senate Commerce Committee and chaired by Republican Senator William A. Smith. The hearings began on 19 April 1912, at the Waldorf-Astoria Hotel in New York City. Senators and spectators were to hear dramatic testimony from the surviving passengers and crew. This was the day after the *Carpathia* docked. Despite Ismay's attempts to take the surviving crew back to the UK without delay, Smith

ensured that his witnesses were available to the inquiry. The next week the hearings were moved to the new caucus room of the Russell Senate Office Building
in Washington DC. They were the first hearings to be held in that room. A total
of eighty-two witnesses testified about ice warnings that were ignored, the inadequate number of lifeboats, the ship's speed, the failure of nearby ships to respond
to the *Titanic's* distress calls, and the treatment of passengers of different classes.
Bruce Ismay had tried to leave New York as soon as possible after the *Carpathia*
docked. He had sent messages signed with the code YAMSI (an anagram of
Ismay) from the *Carpathia* asking that White Star's *Cedric* be delayed from sailing
from New York until he and the surviving crew members could board the vessel
and return to the UK. Senator Smith, however, issued a number of subpoenas,
including one for Ismay.

J. Bruce Ismay was the star witness. He had already been dubbed J. 'Brute'
Ismay by sections of the US media and the *Chicago Journal* published a satirical
poem about him, one verse of which read:

> The Captain stood where the Captain should,
> When a Captain's boat goes down;
> But the owner fled when the women fled,
> For an owner must not drown.

Ismay had not helped himself. He had been reclusive and uncommunicative
aboard *Carpathia*, ignoring the pleas of Captain Rostron. He had tried to leave
New York as fast as possible on the *Cedric* together with the surviving crew,
many of whom were material witnesses. In the witness box he was not especially cooperative. Despite his position within IMM and his role as chairman
of White Star he denied he was anything other than an ordinary passenger. As
such he claimed he had no knowledge about bulkheads, lifeboats or navigation.
This was clearly disingenuous. Ismay was at least Morgan's representative. He had
seen ice warnings and after the collision had been on the bridge – hardly the
actions of an ordinary passenger. To his credit he did believe that all the women
and children had been taken off in the lifeboats and the loss of so many women
and children caused him great distress. Ismay did admit to a conversation with
the chief engineer about a full speed trial for *Titanic*; however, evidence from
Captain Rostron of the *Carpathia* suggested that no captain would allow even the
owner to influence his navigational decisions. The myth that Ismay had ordered
Titanic to steam at full speed into an iceberg was dismissed by the inquiry. Despite
rigorous questioning by the committee Ismay was exonerated of any blame for
the disaster. Ismay defended the lack of lifeboats by claiming, correctly, that the
ship was equipped with more spaces than the Board of Trade (and even the US)
regulations required.

Among the surviving officers, Lightoller, Boxhall and Pitman gave evidence
of the collision and the attempts to get the passengers into the boats. Lightoller
gave an account of how he had warned First Officer Murdoch that it was getting
cold and that he had taken action to douse lights at the fore of the vessel before

the collision to improve visibility for the lookouts. Fred Fleet, the lookout on duty that night, gave his account. The vice-president of White Star in the US, Philip Franklin, had gone on board *Carpathia* as soon as she docked in order to speak to Ismay. Questioned by the committee, he claimed no knowledge of the safety equipment on board *Titanic* save that he believed it met all the regulations and exceeded the standards required by Lloyds of London. He was then asked directly as to whether there was any business interest between Harland & Wolff (the builders) and White Star. As was shown in chapter 1 there was a very close relationship but Franklin denied that he had knowledge of any relationship. The fact that Lord Pirrie was both chairman of Harland & Wolff and also a director of the IMM was never revealed.

Franklin claimed that as the crews' wages had ceased the moment the vessel foundered it was imperative that White Star repatriate them as soon as possible. That was why he had initially agreed to use the *Cedric* and had then earmarked another IMM vessel, Red Star Line's *Lapland*.

As regards insurance, Franklin conceded that White Star carried a greater proportion of the value of the vessel itself. Franklin seemed to think this was praiseworthy but in fact it could be said to point to the fact that White Star preferred to take risks and save on insurance premiums.

The first mention of a mystery ship, later claimed to be the *Californian*, was by Ismay. The claim was then repeated by Alfred Crawford, a bedroom steward who had been ordered by First Officer Murdoch to steer for what appeared to be the navigation lights of a nearby ship.

It was known that *Californian* was in the area as she had sent an ice warning to *Titanic*. Captain Lord had signalled *Carpathia* during the recovery operations that she had been stopped in ice and she then followed some days behind the Cunarder into Boston, her intended destination (there is more about *Californian* later in this chapter). It was as a result of stories provided by some of her crew members to the Boston newspapers that specific crew members and her captain, Stanley Lord, were subpoenaed by the committee. What happened then is covered below.

One person whose involvement was virtually ignored by both inquiries was J. Pierpont Morgan. Despite Smith's anti-trust stance there was no attack on Morgan at all despite his being the real owner of *Titanic*. All told the committee examined four officers, thirty-four crew members, twenty-one passengers and twenty-three other witnesses.

The hearings concluded on 28 May 1912, when Senator Smith visited the *Titanic*'s sister ship, *Olympic*, at port in New York, to interview some of its crew. When the *Titanic* sank, the *Olympic* was about 500 miles away.

This finally led to significant reforms in international maritime safety. Whilst Smith achieved notoriety in some quarters for being more colourful than knowledgeable (he was nicknamed 'Watertight Smith' by the British press after asking whether watertight compartments, actually meant to keep the ship afloat, were meant to shelter passengers). In his book on the investigation, *The Other Side of the Night*, Daniel Allen Butler notes that Smith had toured *Titanic*'s sister RMS *Olympic* and knew full well what the watertight bulkheads did, but understood that the general public might not. Other questions were intended to force the officers and crew to answer in simple terms and not attempt to obfuscate with technical jargon that might confuse the public. Smith's questioning, however, seemed to flit from topic to topic without the kind of structure we would expect from a modern inquiry.

Smith not only questioned the crew but also experts and survivors. One of the most interesting was a Mrs J. Stuart White from New York State. She commented that there was resentment amongst some of the first-class survivors that many of the males from the lower orders survived whilst many upstanding first-class males perished. She was also very critical of the four crew members manning the lifeboat she was in. Other survivors also commented that the handling of the lifeboats left much to be desired.

Myth?

Captain Smith cancelled the lifeboat drill

On a modern cruise ship a passenger safety drill is held at the beginning of every cruise (or cruise sector) within twenty-four hours of the passengers joining the vessel. The inquiry was led to believe that there should have been a lifeboat drill on 14 April, but the captain cancelled it to allow people to go to church.

In chapter 8 it will be seen that there was a similar situation on board the *Andrea Doria* in 1956 where there was a very perfunctory drill. Without a proper drill passengers have only a scant understanding of where their muster station is situated. With so many non-English speakers on board and too few lifeboats it is possible that Captain Smith did not want to draw attention to any possibility of disaster and the need to evacuate the ship.

The subcommittee hearing transcripts, which were published on 28 May 1912, are over 1,100 pages long. They were issued as Senate Document 726, 62nd Congress, 2nd session, and are called: '"Titanic" Disaster: Hearings before a Subcommittee of the Committee on Commerce, United States Senate, Sixty-Second Congress, Second Session, Pursuant to S. Res. 283, Directing the Committee on Commerce to Investigate the Causes Leading to the Wreck of the White Star Liner "Titanic"'. Following the success of the 1997 movie, a paperback reprint of the hearings was published in 1998 by Pocket Books, called *The Titanic Disaster Hearings: The Official Transcripts of the 1912 Senate Investigation*.

The final report by the committee contained the panel's conclusions about the causes of the disaster. The report was issued as 'Senate Report 806, 62nd Congress, 2nd session', and is called: '"Titanic" Disaster: Report of the Committee on Commerce, United States Senate, Pursuant to S. Res. 283, Directing the Committee on Commerce to Investigate the Causes Leading to the Wreck of the White Star Liner "Titanic", Together with Speeches Thereon by Senator William Alden Smith of Michigan and Senator Isidor Rayner of Maryland'.

By the time Smith made a report to the Senate many safety improvements had been made:

- Shipping lanes had been moved further south
- Two US Navy cruisers were stationed in a patrol around the Grand Banks thus beginning the International Ice Patrol
- White Star (followed swiftly by other companies) provided lifeboats for all passengers and crew

Smith had succeeded in ascertaining the cause of the disaster and the reason for the huge loss of life:

- *Titanic* was steaming too fast in an area where icebergs were likely (the captain had received radio warnings about the icebergs)
- Captain Smith was overconfident and indifferent to the danger
- There was insufficient communication to the steerage-class passengers thus giving them little chance of escape
- There were too few lifeboats and those that the ship did have were incompetently loaded
- Evacuation procedures were almost non-existent
- Ismay was in no way to blame for the speed of the vessel although his presence on board may have prompted greater risks to be taken as the captain and chief engineer may have wanted to impress him
- Radio procedures were not standardised and needed reform
- Captain Lord of the *Californian* deluded himself about the presence of another ship (see below). He bore a heavy responsibility for the loss of life
- Captain Rostron of the *Carpathia* 'should be honored [sic] throughout the ages'

Poor Captain Lord. He had not caused the collision but he bore the responsibility for the deaths. His ordeal had just begun.

Smith's work convinced the US Government of the need for legislative action to ensure maritime safety. Within a short place of time there were improved US standards regarding bulkheads, crew safety training and lifeboat provision. Rockets were only to be used as a distress signal and regulations concerning radio at sea introduced. All ships carrying over fifty passengers had to be equipped with a radio having a range of at least 100 miles and there had to be direct communications between the bridge and the radio operator(s).

In the months and years following the disaster, numerous preventative safety measures were enacted. Twenty-nine nations ratified the Radio Act of 1912, which required twenty-four-hour radio watch on all ships in case of an emergency. The first International Convention for the Safety of Life at Sea formed a treaty that also required twenty-four-hour radio monitoring and standardised the use of distress rockets.

This was the beginning of the strict inspection regime operated today by the US, UK and many other countries that ensures the maximum safety of ships leaving port. The international regulations known as Safety of Life At Sea (SOLAS) were first developed at a 1913/14 conference in London. Today these regulations are very important and very strict. Ships can and are detained and refused permission to sail if defects are found. For example, *Ocean Glory 1* (built as the *Provence* in 1951) was refused permission to sail from Dover, England, in July 2001 whilst on a segment of a world cruise, as she had failed safety and hygiene tests. She remained at Dover at the end of August 2001, with reports in the newspapers that the crew were still on board, unpaid and running out of food. She never sailed commercially again and was sold for scrap.

In another recent example in August 2008, whilst the *Clipper Pacific* was docked in Seward, Alaska, Coast Guard Inspectors conducted a Port State Control exam on the ship and issued a thirty-two-item deficiency list and detained the vessel temporarily for significant International Ship Management Code violations in respect to oil record books, engineering logs and engineering rough logs. Customs clearance for departure was withheld until a surety bond for $1.1 million was provided by the owner, but was later cleared by US Customs and Border Protection after a Letter of Understanding was received from the owner. Inspectors found issues with the vessel's documentation and non-compliance of the International Ship Management Code for Safety of Life At Sea (SOLAS). There is evidence the vessel's crew operated the oily water separator and potentially inaccurate oil content meter in the US exclusive economic zone in potential violation of United States Code known as the Clean Water Act, 33USC1321 (b) (3). They also failed to report a discharge of oil into a navigable US waterway while draining the bilges of their lifeboats, which is another violation of the regulations. After four days the crew of the vessel had fixed enough of the critical deficiencies that Coast Guard officials were comfortable with the vessel leaving the US port. However, concerns about the oily water discharge system and the fact that it was a foreign-flagged vessel, that might not return to the US, prompted officials in cooperation with Customs and Border Protection to require the vessel's insurance agency, the P&I Club, to issue the $1.1 million surety bond.

The SOLAS 2010 regulations resulted in many old but much loved cruise liners being scrapped as the costs of bringing them into line with the revised regulations would have been prohibitive.

At the time of the *Titanic* disaster the British regulations were, as will be shown below, way out of date.

Myth?

The seamen on Olympic *went on strike and were accused of mutiny*

Like her sister *Titanic*, *Olympic* did not carry enough lifeboats for everyone on board and was hurriedly equipped with additional, second-hand collapsible lifeboats following her return to England. Towards the end of April 1912, as she was about to sail from Southampton to New York, the ship's firemen went on strike because of fears that the ship's new collapsible lifeboats were not seaworthy. The forty collapsible lifeboats were second-hand, having been transferred from troopships, and many were rotten and could not open. The men instead sent a request to the management of the White Star Line that the collapsible boats be replaced by proper wooden lifeboats. Management replied that this was impossible and that the collapsible boats had been passed as seaworthy by a Board of Trade inspector. The men were not satisfied and many ceased work, calling a strike. Some men, however, continued with their duties.

On 25 April a deputation of strikers witnessed a test of four of the collapsible boats. Only one was unseaworthy and they said that they were prepared to recommend the men return to work if it was replaced. These terms were accepted. However, the deputation said that they would not sail aboard the *Olympic* unless the strike-breakers were removed, a condition which the company refused to accept, saying that they would rather abandon the sailing than dismiss men who had remained loyal to the company at a most difficult time.

All fifty-four strikers were arrested on a charge of mutiny (under Merchant Navy Articles) when they went ashore. However, on 4 May 1912, although Portsmouth magistrates found that the charges against the mutineers were proven, they were discharged without imprisonment or fine due to the circumstances of the case and considerable public sympathy in the wake of the *Titanic* disaster. The vast majority of the strikers returned to work, were not disciplined by White Star and the *Olympic* sailed on 15 May.

The *Titanic* crew return home

The surviving crew of the *Titanic* who were not ordered to the US Inquiry returned home on the *Lapland*.

Myth?

The surviving Titanic *crew were treated like pariahs*

When the *Lapland* arrived at her first stop in England, Plymouth on 29 April, the passengers and mail were disembarked. Then the tender *Sir Richard Grenville* came out to collect the 167 surviving crew members. Their union representatives had not been allowed on board the tender and had to come alongside it in a small boat to advise the survivors to say nothing without representation. The survivors were not worried as they believed they would soon be returning to their homes. However, upon landing they were confined in the third-class waiting room in the passenger terminal at Plymouth. Bedding and provisions were allocated and what can only be described as an interrogation by Board of Trade officials began. The survivors were surrounded by a high iron fence and it was clear that they were being treated in a most hostile manner. It had been the intention to hold the survivors overnight but as relatives and the press began to gather it was clear that such an action would be deemed inappropriate. *Lapland* had arrived at 7 a.m. but by 1.30 p.m. the decision was taken to release the surviving seamen and engine room crew after obtaining an oath from them that they would make no press statements. Only then were they allowed to return to the bosom of their friends and families. The next day the remaining survivors – cooks, stewards and steward-esses – were allowed home. Why they were detained longer is not clear – was it perhaps because they had had more contact with the passengers?

The remaining survivors, four officers and thirty-four crew who had been forced to remain behind for the US Inquiry, arrived in Liverpool on board the *Celtic* on 6 May. All of the crew survivors were now home.

Why did the Board of Trade behave in this way? The Board of Trade was responsible for the initial inspection of the *Titanic*. The ship had been cleared to sail even though it was soon to be apparent that one of her coal bunkers was on fire when she left Southampton. The lifeboat provision was in excess of that required by the Board of Trade. Under whose auspices would the British Inquiry be held – the Board of Trade? The Board would be in effect on trial in an inquiry it was itself responsible for!

British Inquiry

The Prime Minister, H.H. Asquith, was aware that two of the UK Shipping Acts required the Board of Trade to hold an inquiry. The fact that there had already been an inquiry in the USA was not of any consequence. British law required a British inquiry. Given the possibility of a conflict of interest he had already been asked a question in the House of Commons as to whether a committee of the Commons should conduct an inquiry. However, precedent and the law required any inquiry to be conducted by the Board of Trade. Actually the law required a Commissioner of Wrecks who would report to the Board of Trade to be appointed; this was sup-posed to insure the independence of the inquiry. However, as Sir Humphrey tells PM Jim Hacker in *Yes Prime Minister*, if you want to ensure that an inquiry makes acceptable findings, just be careful to appoint the right chairperson!

Myth?

The British Inquiry was a whitewash designed to protect the Board of Trade

Even before the arrangements were complete the Bradford and District Trades and Labour Council had complained to the Home Office (responsible for law and order in the UK) that it had no confidence in the inquiry and that it believed it was just 'an attempt to lull public confidence and to whitewash those who are most responsible for the terrible loss of human life.' It is believed that this is the first recorded use of the term whitewash in respect of official inquiries – it certainly was not to be the last. The term was used again by Second Officer Lightoller in 1935 and by Geoffrey Marcos in his 1969 book *The Maiden Voyage*.

Lord Mersey was appointed to head the inquiry. A scion of British society, he was a lawyer who had begun life as John Charles Bigham and started work as a humble shipping clerk in Liverpool. He had also been an MP and in that role had been part of the committee that examined the infamous 'Jameson Raid' (December 1895), designed to ferment revolt against the Boers in the Transvaal and the Orange Free State and what if any role the British Government had played. As the committee cleared the government (much to disgust of many of the public and the Boers) it may well be that it was thought that Lord Mersey as he had become was just the man to protect the government and any other vested interests when the *Titanic* disaster was looked into.

Mersey appointed his son, Captain (Army) the Hon. Clive Bigham, as the secretary to the inquiry. The inquiry, complete with bewigged clerks, barristers, press, public and of course the witnesses, began on 2 May 1912 and lasted until 3 July. Given the inordinate amount of time such inquiries take today, this was a very short period of time in which to ascertain all the facts. Lord Mersey was assisted by five assessors.

The inquiry took testimony from both passengers and crew of *Titanic*, crew members of Leyland Line's *Californian*, Captain Rostron of *Carpathia* and other experts.

The inquiry began in the drill hall of the London Scottish Regiment, whose broad drill floor with two rows of galleries affords accommodation for several hundred persons. The spacious hall was chosen with view to seating an expected crush of spectators. It was not long before there were complaints about the acoustics. In any event the inquiry had to move out later as the hall was needed for a public examination.

Mersey announced that he had twenty-six questions that he wanted answered. Sir Rufus Daniel Issacs, the Attorney-General (the man involved in the Marconi share scandal covered earlier), led the government team whilst White Star, the crew and even the third-class passengers were represented by lawyers. It was clear that the inquiry would cover practically the same ground as the investigation by the committee of the American Senate but would be conducted more in accordance with the procedure of a British court of law and deal definitely with stated cases.

Eight questions would relate to happenings before the casualty; six to warnings given the *Titanic* and the resulting precautions taken; ten to the disaster itself and the consequent events; one to the equipment and construction of the vessel; and the last to rules of the Merchant Ship Act.

A 20ft model of the *Titanic* carrying sixteen miniature lifeboats and a big chart of the North Atlantic Ocean were prominently displayed before the investigators. In front of the platform which they occupied were seated 100 members of the bar representing various interests involved, and 100 representatives of the press.

Sir Rufus announced:

> I desire on behalf of the government to express the deepest sympathy for all those who mourn the loss of relatives and friends among the passengers, the officers and the crew of the ill-fated vessel. The accident exceeded in magnitude and in harrowing incidents any disaster in the history of the mercantile marine. I cannot forbear paying a tribute to those whose devotion to duty and heroic self-sacrifice maintained in the best traditions of the sea.

Sir Robert Finlay, formerly Attorney-General, and now chief counsel for White Star then seconded these remarks.

The only reference to the American investigation was Sir Rufus's announcement that owing to the detention of many witnesses for the Senate inquiry in the United States (as stated above the detained crew members did not arrive back in the UK until 6 May), the testimony would not be presented in a logical manner. The seamen who arrived from New York on the steamer *Lapland* were called first as witnesses to the construction and equipment of the *Titanic*.

Several lawyers representing interested parties requested permission to participate in the proceedings. Lord Mersey recognised Thomas Scanlan, Member of Parliament for the north division of Sligo (Ireland still being part of Great Britain in 1912), who appeared for the Seamen's and Firemen's Union, and an attorney for the Merchant's Service Guild, and took under consideration the application for representation of the Seafarer's Union, the Ship Constructor's Association and the Mercantile Officer's Union.

Little new was revealed as the US Inquiry had covered most of the ground. One issue that was raised, however, was the behaviour of a first-class passenger, Sir Cosmo Duff Gordon. It was an issue that had already been alluded to in the US Inquiry.

Myth?

A passenger tried to bribe the crew of a lifeboat not to go back and pick up people in the water

Sir Cosmo Duff Gordon had been on board *Titanic* with his wife and her secretary, Laura Mabel Francatelli, and rumours that the Duff Gordons had bribed crew in their largely empty lifeboat not to rescue people in the water threatened their reputations. Sir Cosmo explained that the men in the boat had told him that they had lost all their possessions and that (as covered earlier) their pay had stopped at the moment the ship foundered. Sir Cosmo wrote each a personal cheque for £5 on a piece of paper (formal cheque books were not as common in 1912 as they became) to compensate for this. When the men reported his generosity some sections of the press decided that these payments were actually a bribe so that the boat would not be rowed back to pick up others who might swamp it. The British Inquiry into the disaster cleared them completely of any wrongdoing. Duff Gordon was one of many men in first class who were allowed into lifeboats despite the women and children first rule, while many women and children, mostly from third class, never reached the upper deck where the lifeboats were stowed, because it was a first-class deck. First Officer Murdoch was glad to offer Duff Gordon and his wife a place (simply to fill it), after the couple had asked if they could get on.

Gordon died on 20 April 1931 of natural causes. The authors have met one of his descendents and the affair still rankles!

Titanic met all the Board of Trade regulations and thus the inquiry wanted to know why the lifeboat provision was so inadequate. She carried twenty lifeboats, enough for 1,178 people, whilst the existing Board of Trade required a passenger ship to provide lifeboat capacity for only 1,060. *Titanic's* lifeboats were situated on the top deck and although the ship was designed to carry thirty-two lifeboats this number was reduced to twenty because it was felt that the deck would be too cluttered.

Sir Alfred Chalmers of the Board of Trade was asked why regulations governing the number of lifeboats required on passenger ships had not been updated since 1896. Sir Alfred gave a number of reasons for this:

- Due to advancements that had been made in shipbuilding it was not necessary for passenger ships to carry more lifeboats.
- The latest passenger ships were stronger than ever and had watertight compartments making them unlikely to require lifeboats at all.
- Sea routes used were well travelled, meaning that the likelihood of a collision was minimal.
- The latest passenger ships were fitted with wireless technology.
- That it would be impossible for crew members to be able to load more than sixteen boats in the event of a disaster.

He also believed that the provision of lifeboats should be a matter for the ship owners to consider and not the Board of Trade.

Sir Alfred also stated that he felt that if there had been fewer lifeboats on *Titanic* then more people would have been saved as more people would have rushed to the boats in order to fill them to capacity thus saving more people. Even in these days of 'spin' this is an incredible statement.

At the British investigation, Charles Lightoller, as the senior surviving officer, was questioned about the fact that the lifeboats were not filled to capacity. They had been tested in Belfast on 25 March 1912 and each boat had carried seventy men safely. When questioned about the filling of Lifeboat No.6, Lightoller testified that the boat was filled with as many people as he considered to be safe. Lightoller believed that it would be impossible to fill the boats to capacity before lowering them to sea without the mechanism that held them collapsing. He was questioned as to whether he had arranged for more people to be put into the boats once it was afloat. Lightoller admitted that he should have made some arrangement for the boats to be filled once they were afloat. When asked if the crew member in charge of Lifeboat No.6 was told to return to pick up survivors, the inquiry was told that the crew member was told to stay close to the ship. Lifeboat No.6 was designed to hold sixty-five people. It left with forty.

Titanic also carried 3,500 lifebelts and forty-eight life rings; useless in the icy water. The majority of passengers that went into the sea did not drown, but froze to death.

Many people were confused about where they should go after the order to launch the lifeboats had been given. As was shown in the previous chapter there should have been a lifeboat drill on 14 April, but the captain cancelled it to allow people to go to church. Furthermore, many people believed that *Titanic* was not actually sinking but that the call to the lifeboats was actually a drill and stayed inside rather than venture out onto the freezing deck.

The inquiry was concerned that there was a delay of more than an hour between the time of impact and the launching of the first lifeboat – No.7. As a result there was not enough time to successfully launch them all. Collapsible lifeboats A and B were not launched but floated away as the water washed over the ship. Collapsible B floated away upside down. People tried unsuccessfully to right it, although thirty survived the disaster by standing on the upturned boat.

The investigations found that many safety rules were simply out of date, and new laws were recommended. Numerous safety improvements for ocean-going vessels were implemented, including improved hull and bulkhead design, access throughout the ship for egress of passengers, lifeboat requirements, improved life-vest design, the holding of safety drills, better passenger notification, radio communications laws, etc. The investigators also learned that *Titanic* had sufficient lifeboat space for all first-class passengers and most second-class passengers, but not for the steerage passengers. In fact, steerage passengers had no idea where the lifeboats were, much less any way of getting up to the higher decks where the lifeboats were stowed. US immigration regulations required complete isolation of third-class passengers and the route to the boat deck, through the higher classes of accommodation, was somewhat tortuous as a result. A third-class steward, John Hart, had to guide E-deck passengers, in two trips, to the boat deck but many were left behind.

Did either inquiry find Captain Smith negligent? As other captains had said that they would not have reduced speed when encountering ice (only the explorer Sir Ernest Shackleton had given a contrary answer), then Smith was doing what was normal. No, it was decided that any future captain would be negligent in such circumstances but that Smith's reputation should be preserved.

Nor was fault found with *Titanic* herself. It seems that the inadequate bulkheads and lifeboat provision were not involved in the disaster. However, in future there must be adequate bulkheads and enough lifeboats for all the souls on board. The reputation of the Board of Trade and of White Star was upheld. Somebody must be to blame and Senator Smith had first pointed the finger; it must be Captain Lord of the *Californian*.

Myth?

The Titanic *was in one piece as she went down*

The inquiry concluded that the hull of the ship was intact as she sank beneath the waves. It was this conclusion that enabled Clive Cussler to write *Raise the Titanic*, which was followed by the film of the same name. However, as covered in chapter 3 this was not the case, *Titanic* was breaking up as she sank – the inquiry was wrong.

The *Californian* and the agony of Captain Lord

The American inquiry started on 19 April, the day *Californian* arrived in Boston. On 22 April the inquiry discovered that a ship near *Titanic* had failed to respond to the distress signals. The identity of the ship was unknown.

The next day, a small newspaper in New England, the *Daily Item*, printed a story claiming that the *Californian* had refused to come to the aid of *Titanic*. The source for the story was the ship's carpenter, James McGregor, who stated that his ship had been close enough to see *Titanic*'s lights and distress rockets. By sheer coincidence, on the same day, the *Boston American* printed a story sourced by the *Californian*'s assistant engineer, Ernest Gill, which essentially told the same story as the *Daily Item*.

SS *Californian*. (R. Cartwright)

Captain Lord also gave interviews to the Boston area newspapers. In one article, on 19 April (*Boston Traveller*), Lord claimed that his ship was 30 miles from *Titanic*, but in the *Boston Post* (22 April) he claimed 20 miles. He told the *Boston Globe* that his ship had spent three hours steaming around the wreck site trying to render assistance, but Third Officer Grove later stated that the search ended after only two hours. When reporters asked Lord about his exact position the night of the disaster, he refused to answer, supposedly calling such information 'state secrets' – this appears to be an unlikely response and may be what we now call media hype. Lord also claimed that he did not use the wireless because his ship had been stopped and thus the wireless was not working. In fact, only the *Californian*'s engines were stopped; the ship was under steam the whole night (for electricity and heating) and the wireless only needed to be switched on.

As was shown earlier, the American inquiry subpoenaed Gill, as well as Captain Lord and others from the *Californian*, as a result of these stories. During his testimony Gill repeated his claims. Lord's testimony was conflicting and changing. For example, he detailed three totally different ice conditions. He admitted knowing about the rockets (after telling Boston newspapers that his ship had not seen any rockets) but insisted that they were not distress rockets and were not fired from *Titanic* but a small steamship, the so-called mystery ship. Unfortunately for Lord the testimony of Captain J. Knapp, US Navy and a part of the US Navy

Hydrographer's Office, made clear that *Titanic* and the *Californian* were in sight of each other, and that no third vessel had been in the area. How this claim could be made with accuracy is not clear but Knapp was adamant about this.

The so-called scrap log of the *Californian* also came under question. This is a log where all daily pertinent information is entered before being approved by the captain and entered into the official log. Yet the scrap log was missing. In an extraordinary omission, the official log (written after the disaster) never mentioned a nearby ship, or rockets.

On 2 May, the British Inquiry began. Again, Lord gave conflicting, changing and evasive testimony. By way of contrast, the captain of the *Carpathia*, at each inquiry, gave consistent and forthright testimony.

During the inquiry, the crew of the *Californian* also gave conflicting testimonies. Most notably, Captain Lord said he was not told that the nearby ship had disappeared, contradicting testimony from James Gibson who said he reported it and that Lord had acknowledged him.

Also during the inquiries, survivors of *Titanic* recalled seeing the lights of another ship that was spotted after *Titanic* had hit the iceberg. To *Titanic*'s Fourth Officer Boxhall the ship appeared to be off the bow of *Titanic*, 5 miles (8km) away and heading in *Titanic*'s direction. Just like *Californian*'s officers, Boxhall attempted signalling the ship with a Morse lamp, but received no response.

Both the American and British inquires found that *Californian* must have been closer than the 20 or so miles claimed by Lord, and that both ships were visible from each other. Indeed, when the *Carpathia* arrived at the wreck sight, a vessel was clearly seen to the north; this was later identified as the *Californian*. Both inquires concluded that Captain Lord failed to provide proper assistance to *Titanic* and the British Inquiry further concluded that had *Californian* responded to *Titanic*'s rockets and gone to assist, that it '... might have saved many if not all of the lives that were lost'. It is unlikely that all could have been saved from *Titanic* but the death toll would have been substantially reduced.

Captain Lord was not dismissed by the Leyland Line, in spite of the censure of both inquiries. He died in 1962 still attempting to clear his name.

It was the 1950s book by Walter Lord (no relation!) *A Night to Remember* and the subsequent highly successful film that repeated the allegations about the *Californian* that prompted Captain Lord to renew efforts to clear his name. He claimed that it was untrue that the ship had been steaming towards the stricken *Titanic* and then turned away again. His case was taken up by others. Chief amongst his supporters was Leslie Harrison, General Secretary of the Mercantile Marine Service Association. Petitions presented to the UK Government in 1965 and 1968 by the MMSA (Mercantile Marine Service Association), a union to which Captain Lord belonged, failed to reverse the findings of the original inquiries. However, following the discovery of *Titanic* by Robert Ballard (covered in chapter 6), it was realised that *Titanic*'s position as given to the inquiries may not have been accurate and if this was true then the *Californian* might not have been in such close proximity as had been believed. Further investigations were ordered.

In 1992, the British Government's Marine Accident Investigation Branch (MAIB) concluded its 'Reappraisal of Evidence Relating to the SS *Californian*'. The conclusions of the MAIB report were those of Deputy Chief Inspector James de Coverly.

Even with ample evidence to the contrary, the MAIB report stated:

> What is significant, however, is that no ship was seen by *Titanic* until well after the collision. A watch was maintained with officers on the bridge and seamen in the crow's nest and with their ship in grave danger the lookout for another vessel which could come to their help must have been most anxious and keen.
>
> It is in my view inconceivable that *Californian* or any other ship was within the visible horizon of *Titanic* during that period; it equally follows that *Titanic* cannot have been within *Californian's* horizon.

The report went on: 'More probably, in my view, the ship seen by *Californian* was another, unidentified, vessel.' One ship that has often been suggested was a Norwegian sealing ship, the *Samson*, although many authorities dismiss this claim. Some believe that the *Samson* was engaged in illegal sealing off the Canadian coast in or around the time *Titanic* sank.

The original investigator of the 1992 re-appraisal was a certain Captain Barnett. He had concluded that '*Titanic* was seen by *Californian* and indeed kept under observation from 23:00 or soon after on 14 April until she sank,' and that 'he bases this view on the evidence from Captain Lord and the two watch officers'. It was after Barnett's original report was submitted that Captain de Coverly was given the task of further examination.

Nonetheless, both investigators, Barnett and de Coverly, concluded that *Titanic's* rockets had been seen and that Officer Stone and Captain Lord had not responded appropriately to signals of distress. Of that there can be little doubt. To this day there are still defenders of Captain Lord, yet two issues are incontrovertible. Firstly, why didn't Lord simply request that the wireless be turned back on? Secondly, at both inquiries Lord admitted that rockets had been fired. In 1912, it was understood by all seaman that rockets being fired in sequence, no matter their colour, were to be interpreted as a distress signal and that aid should be rendered. It would appear that a call for assistance (even if not from *Titanic*) had been ignored.

The findings of the MAIB remain the official position of the British Government, as reflected in replies to Parliamentary Questions in the years since.

Californian continued normal service until the First World War when the British Government took control of the ship. The ship was torpedoed and sunk by a German submarine on 9 November 1915, 61 miles (98km) south-west of Cape Matapan in the Mediterranean with the loss of one life. Her wreck has never been found.

Those interested in the *Californian* and the mystery ship are recommended to read *Titanic and the Mystery Ship* by Senan Molony and *Titanic and the Californian* by Thomas B. Williams (edited and revised by Rob Kamps).

It seems incredible that Captain Smith, who sailed his ship at nearly full speed into an area of icebergs, icebergs he had been warned about, was not found negligent whilst Captain Lord, who had taken the prudent decision to stop because of the ice, was castigated. Lord should have investigated the rockets but was in no way to blame for the disaster. Yet it was Lord that the inquiries found to be the villain of the story. A clear case of scapegoating and whitewash if ever there was one!

The inquiries were over, recommendations made. Memorials (see chapter 6) were being planned and the survivors could try to rebuild their lives. What now for White Star and Harland & Wolff – would the disaster fade into memory or would it become part of the British psyche?

Chapter 6

The Demise of White Star and Harland & Wolff, a Conspiracy and the Finding of *Titanic*

No sooner had the disaster been announced than mementoes of *Titanic* began to appear. Photographs and postcards abounded and as there were not enough images of *Titanic* available – fakes were sold. Any photograph or postcard of a four-funneled liner could and was altered to be sold as *Titanic*. The photograph below was found in a bric-a-brac store in Newfoundland. The ship is probably the *Olympic* (note the open A deck) but the funnels appear out of proportion. Note how the smoke has been added – the fourth funnel on the Olympic Class being a dummy. Apparently photographs of the *Mauretania* and *Lusitania* were even retouched and passed off as *Titanic*.

Snapped in Sydney, Nova Scotia, but it's not *Titanic*. (Authors' collection)

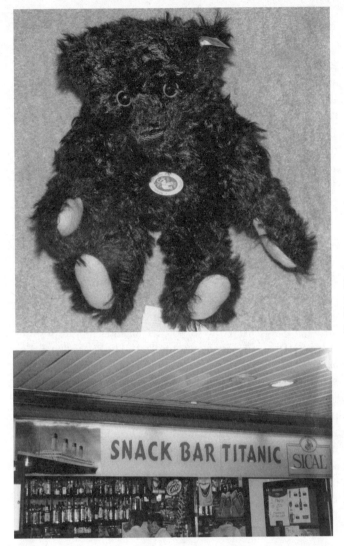

Replica of a Steiff *Titanic* mourning bear. (Authors' collection)

Titanic snack bar in Funchal, Madeira, – but the ship's the *Olympic*. (Authors' collection)

Still today the name *Titanic* sells, even when the ship depicted is actually the *Olympic*.

Perhaps one of the most unusual items to be produced was a black 'mourning' teddy bear made by the German toy maker Steiff: 600 of these bears were shipped to the UK after the tragedy. A recent London auction featured an original of one of these bears. The bear's owner so disliked the bear that it was locked away where it remained for the next ninety years, emerging eventually in pristine condition. The sad-faced 'mourning bear', all original with button in ear and tag intact, was estimated to sell for $22,000–$30,000. Bidding ended at an incredible $136,000! Replicas of the bear cost well over £100 today.

Myth?

The Titanic *disaster was the beginning of the end for White Star*
The year after the disaster White Star made a healthy profit. The disaster played little
part in the eventual demise of White Star and its merger with Cunard in the 1930s.

Just over two years after the *Titanic* disaster the world changed – the First World
War broke out. Just before the outbreak of war there had been another disaster to
a British ocean liner.

On 28 May 1914, the 14,191 GRT (much smaller than *Titanic* but still capable
of carrying over 1,400 passengers) *Empress of Ireland*, one of the crack ships of the
Canadian Pacific Company, at that time a British company, collided with a collier in
the St Lawrence River. *Empress of Ireland*, which was outbound to the UK, sank in
just fourteen minutes with the loss of over 1,000 lives. Lord Mersey presided over the
subsequent inquiry. The losses were not that many fewer than *Titanic* but the *Empress
of Ireland* has largely been forgotten by the public whilst *Titanic* still casts a spell.

Ismay & Morgan

White Star Line chairman J. Bruce Ismay was highly ridiculed by both the press
and the public for surviving the *Titanic* disaster. The press felt Ismay, being president of the White Star Line, should have gone down with the ship as Captain
Smith did. Even before the disaster Ismay had to retire from his position as president of IMM. After the *Titanic* disaster, he asked the IMM board of directors
to allow him to retain his position as chairman of the White Star Line, possibly
because he wanted to regain his reputation. Most likely thinking this was bad
for business, with all of the ridicule and rumours flying around about Ismay, his
request was denied in June 1913.

Morgan himself died in 1913 and IMM was forced to apply for bankruptcy
protection in 1915. Analysis of financial records shows that IMM was overleveraged and suffered from inadequate cash flow that caused it to default on bond
interest payments. IMM eventually re-emerged as the United States Lines, which
itself went bankrupt in 1986.

After the *Titanic* disaster and Ismay's forced retirement, the White Star Line continued, becoming one of the top freight and passengers lines in the world. Despite
surviving the loss of several of its ships either due to war or disaster, and even with
IMM's rocky financial status throughout the years, White Star was still one of the
favourites for the passenger trade. The First World War hurt White Star, as it did
other shipping lines. Very little income could be generated during the war years
with most of White Star's ships either tied up in military service or being sunk.

During the war years (1914–18) both White Star and its bitter rival Cunard lost
vessels. Both lost one of their major vessels: Cunard's *Lusitania* was torpedoed by
U-20 off Old Kinsale Head, Ireland, on 7 May 1915 and sank in eighteen minutes, killing 1,198 of the 1,959 people aboard. The sinking turned public opinion

in many countries against Germany and contributed to the entry of the USA into the war.

Titanic's sister *Britannic* was launched just before the start of the war and was laid up at her builders in Belfast for many months before being put to use as a hospital ship in 1915. In that role she struck a mine off the Greek island of Kea on 21 November 1916, and sank with the loss of thirty lives.

Both companies lost smaller vessels and when the war ended were given German vessels in reparation. Both companies had intended to operate three-ship services from Southampton to New York. Cunard had the *Mauretania* and the 1914, and larger at 46,000 GRT, *Aquitania*. *Aquitania* was destined to become the last of four-funneled liners as she was still in service until 1948. To compensate for the loss of the *Lusitania* Cunard was given the 52,000 GRT Hamburg-Amerika Line *Imperator* which was renamed *Berengaria*. White Star was allocated the 34,351 GRT *Columbus*, renamed *Homeric*, and to replace *Britannic* the company received *Imperator's* sister, the incomplete *Bismarck*. Once the ship was completed in 1922 she was renamed *Majestic*.

After the war the company struggled to keep up maintenance on its ships, which were rapidly becoming obsolete. It was a losing battle. The converted oil-fired *Olympic* was barely able to pass its annual sea-worthiness inspections by the mid-1920s and underwent a series of refits to allow her to pass the inspections. Before she was laid up in 1935 and eventually broken up she managed to collide with the Nantucket Lightship, USS *Nantucket*, on 11 May 1934 causing the death of the seven crew of the lightship. The accident cost White Star $500,000 in damages.

US immigration rules were tightened in 1922 and the steerage trade of immigrants to the US was greatly reduced. Tourism was growing and new ships were catering for the tourist-class trade.

By 1925, the International Mercantile Marine Company (IMM) announced that it was looking at disposing of its non-American holdings including the White Star Line. In 1927, with its sale by IMM, the White Star Line was returned to British interests.

Many people wanted to see what used to be British steamship companies come back into British ownership. One such interested investor was Harland & Wolff's William Pirrie and his new protégé Owen Phillips (soon to become Lord Kylsant). Negotiations for the sale were interrupted when American President Woodrow Wilson intervened and the matter was dropped for the moment.

However, shortly after William Pirrie died, Kylsant quickly took control of Harland & Wolff and named himself chairman. In 1926, Kylsant's conglomeration of interests and holdings, known as the Royal Mail Group, once again entered negotiations for the control of the Oceanic Steam Navigation Company (White Star Line). A few months later it was announced that Lord Kylsant, as chairman of the Royal Mail Steam Packet Company, had purchased the White Star Line for £7 million.

In the early part of 1927, one of Kylsant's first official acts as owner of the newly named White Star Line Limited was to end the earlier 'cost-plus' shipbuilding agreement with his own company, Harland & Wolff, and build ships under a fixed price. This act threatened Harland & Wolff's profit margin and would ultimately affect the quality of the ships it would produce.

There was only one problem; Lord Kylsant didn't exactly have the money to pay for the purchase of the White Star Line. In early 1928, the Royal Mail Steam Packet Company had fallen behind in its payments to the Treasury; in fact it owed substantial amounts of money. Kylsant had already ordered the building of the new 60,000-ton *Oceanic* from Harland & Wolff at a cost of £3.5 million. The keel had been laid, but the ship would never be built. With his operation so deep in debt, Kylsant still continued to make purchases. In 1929 the first payments for the purchase of the White Star Line came due and Kylsant requested an extension on the loan. The common stock had dropped abruptly from 76s to 44s and even Kylsant's brother, Viscount St Davids, publicly accused him of mismanagement.

In 1930, the White Star Line showed an operating loss for the first time. In 1931, the government finally stepped in and conducted its own investigation into the financial situation of the Royal Mail Steam Packet Company. Kyslant eventually ended up in prison and the government had to intervene and form a new company, Royal Mail Group Limited, in order to offer some protection to the company and save jobs. However, many of the individual steam ship lines including White Star were pretty much left to fend for themselves.

Cunard, White Star Line's long-time competitor had also found itself in a serious financial position. Only two years away from the worst stock market crash in US history, Europe had already fallen victim to a depression and Cunard had stopped all plans and construction on their new superliners, the first of which (later to be the *Queen Mary*) was building on the Clyde.

A call of desperation was made by White Star Manager Colonel Frank Bustard to long-time retired J. Bruce Ismay for help. Ismay, now in his seventies, surprisingly agreed to help pull White Star out of trouble but it was too late. A new board of directors had been appointed and it had become obvious that the only answer to survival was for both shipping lines to accept a proposal from the British Government that the companies merge.

The last two ships built for White Star were the 27,778 GRT *Britannic* of 1930 and her sister *Georgic* of 1932. Small by White Star standards, they were motor as opposed to steam ships and lasted until 1961 and 1956 respectively.

In 1934, the government offered to advance the two companies £9.5 million if they would merge into a single organisation. Cunard had already begun construction on the *Queen Mary* but had run out of funds and the building was delayed for two years, causing major unemployment problems on Clydeside. Future plans had been drawn as well for the *Queen Elizabeth*. White Star Line had to stop construction on its new *Oceanic*. The ship was only in an early stage of construction and the steel would eventually be worked into the *Queen Mary*. Both companies knew that the merger was the only answer. The deal was eventually accepted with Cunard holding 62 per cent of the shares. The White Star Line as a stand-alone shipping name was now gone.

Cunard was in a hurry to erase all remnants of White Star and began to phase out share holdings and vessels alike. Double house flags (the Cunard lion over the White Star pennant) were flown on the new Cunard-White Star ships until 1947, at which time Cunard bought the remaining shares held by White Star and liquidated most of its ships and holdings. Cunard went on to produce its magnificent Queens, such as the *Queen Mary* (currently a permanently docked hotel and shopping centre owned and operated by the city of Long Beach, California) and the *Queen Elizabeth*. *The Queen Elizabeth 2* (*QE2*) was recently decommissioned and is now in Dubai, although her future is in doubt. Completing her sea trials in September 2003, the 150,000 GRT *Queen Mary 2* held the title of being the largest cruise ship in the world for about six months and has now been joined by the smaller *Queen Victoria* and *Queen Elizabeth*. These are primarily cruise ships although *QM2* has been designed for transatlantic service.

After more than a century of business Cunard was acquired by the Carnival Group in May 1998. Carnival now owns Princess Cruises, Holland America Line, Windstar Cruises, Seabourn Cruise Line, Costa Cruises, Cunard, P&O Cruises, AIDA, Ibrojet and P&O Cruises Australia, making them the largest cruise group in the world. On 1 January 2005 the business, assets and liabilities of Cunard Line Ltd were transferred to Carnival plc, ending the Cunard name as a business entity – the name still appears on the side of the Cunard-brand ships but purely as a brand.

There is, however, one Harland & Wolff-built White Star vessel still in existence. The tender *Nomadic*, built to bring second- and third-class passengers out to the *Olympic*, had ended up as a restaurant on the River Seine in Paris. Eventually she was purchased by Belfast interests and brought back to Belfast in 2006 where she is undergoing restoration.

Harland & Wolff

The British shipbuilding industry is defunct as far as the passenger liner business is concerned. The *Vistafjord* (now *Saga Ruby*) was the last major liner built in a British yard. She was launched at the Cammell Laird Yard on the River Mersey in 1973. The country which produced so many of the great liners cannot compete with Italy, Germany and France – three of the major cruise ship building countries.

With the rise of the jet-powered airliner in the late 1950s, the demand for Ocean Liners declined. This, coupled with competition from the Far East, led to difficulties for the British shipbuilding industry. The last liner completed by Harland & Wolff was the iconic *Canberra* for P&O in 1961.

In the 1960s the company diversified into large oil tankers and drilling rigs. However, in that decade the British Government started advancing loans and subsidies to British shipyards to preserve jobs. Some of this money was used to finance the modernisation of the yard, allowing it to continue in business. Continuing problems led to the company's nationalisation as part of British Shipbuilders in 1977.

Denationalisation occurred under the Conservative Government in 1989. The company was bought in a management/employee buy-out in partnership with the Norwegian Fred Olsen – well known in the UK for the Fred Olsen Cruise Lines ships operating in the UK cruise market.

For the next few years, Harland & Wolff specialised in building oil tankers and vessels for the offshore oil and gas industry. Faced with competitive pressures (especially as regards shipbuilding), Harland & Wolff sought to shift and broaden their portfolio, focusing less on shipbuilding and more on design and structural engineering, as well as ship repair, offshore construction projects and competing for other projects to do with metal engineering and construction. Harland & Wolff's last shipbuilding project was MV *Anvil Point*, one of six near identical ships built for use by the Ministry of Defence. The ship, built under sub-contract from German shipbuilders Flensburger Schiffbau-Gesellschaft, was launched in 2003.

Belfast's skyline is still dominated today by Harland & Wolff's famous twin Gantry cranes, Samson and Goliath, built in 1974 and 1969 respectively. In recent years the company has indeed seen its ship-related workload increase slightly. Whilst Harland & Wolff has no involvement in any current shipbuilding projects for the foreseeable future, the company is increasingly involved in overhaul, re-fitting and ship repair, as well as the construction and repair of off-shore equipment. In late 2007, the Goliath gantry crane was re-commissioned, having been mothballed in 2003 due to the lack of heavy-lifting work at the yard. In March 2008 the construction of the world's first commercial tidal stream turbine, for Marine Current Turbines, was completed at the Belfast yard.

Many of the buildings from the *Titanic* era remain. The Pump House is now a museum, part of which includes the massive Thompson Graving Dock built to fit out the Olympic Class ships. The drawing office is also intact. Regeneration of the area around the yard was well underway in 2009 and is to be the '*Titanic* Quarter'.

The wasteland that the once thriving Harland & Wolff yard has become. (Authors' collection)

Regeneration – the *Titanic* Quarter, Belfast. (Authors' collection)

White Star has been consigned to the history books and Harland & Wolff is a shadow of its former self. The last *Titanic* passenger survivor, Millvina Dean, died in 2009 whilst the surviving crew members are long gone. Fred Fleet, the lookout, is one of the saddest cases. The man who was the lookout on duty that fateful night, and who spotted the iceberg, served on *Titanic*'s sister ship *Olympic* from 1920 to 1935 in the role of lookout and able seaman. Unemployed during much of the 1930s he served again at sea during the Second World War. When Fleet's wife died shortly after Christmas 1964, he became depressed and committed suicide by hanging in January 1965. His friends said that, in many ways, Fleet could be regarded as the final victim of *Titanic*. People who knew him said that he suffered from terrible guilt throughout his life because he had lived while so many perished, although both inquiries stated he had nothing to reproach himself about. He was buried in an unmarked pauper's grave in Southampton. In 1993 a headstone bearing an engraving of *Titanic* was erected through donations by the Titanic Historical Society.

Second Officer Charles Lightoller served in the Royal Navy during the First World War and was decorated for his service. When he returned to White Star after the war he found that despite his previous loyal service to the company and his defence of his employers at the *Titanic* inquiries opportunities for advancement within the line were no longer available. Lightoller resigned shortly thereafter, taking such odd jobs as an innkeeper and a chicken farmer and later property speculation, at which he and his wife had some success. During the early 1930s he wrote his autobiography, *Titanic and Other Ships*, which he dedicated to his wife. The book was popular and began to sell well. However, it was withdrawn when the Marconi Company threatened a lawsuit, due to a comment by Lightoller regarding the *Titanic* disaster and the role of the Marconi operators. The retired Lightoller did not turn his back on sailing altogether, however, as he eventually purchased his own private motor yacht, which his wife Sylvia named *Sundowner*. He took *Sundowner* to Dunkirk and helped evacuate soldiers and she is now preserved by Ramsgate Maritime Museum. After the war Lightoller managed a small boatyard called Richmond Slipways in London, which built motor launches for the river police.

Lightoller died on 8 December 1952, aged seventy-eight, of chronic heart disease.

Following the *Titanic* disaster Fourth Officer Boxhall briefly served as fourth officer on White Star's *Adriatic* before joining the Royal Naval Reserve as a sub-lieutenant after war broke out. He was promoted to lieutenant in 1915. He later received his own command in the form of a torpedo boat. Boxhall returned to White Star following the war in May 1919, signing on as second officer on board *Olympic* on 30 June 1926. After the White Star-Cunard merger, he served in a senior capacity as first and later chief officer of the *Aquitania*, although he was never made a captain in the Merchant Marine. After forty-one years at sea, he retired in 1940. Boxhall was reluctant to speak about his experiences on the *Titanic*; however, in 1958, he acted as a technical advisor for the film adaptation of Walter Lord's book, *A Night to Remember*.

His health deteriorated sharply in the 1960s, and he was eventually hospital-ised. Joseph Boxhall, the last surviving deck officer of *Titanic*, died of a cerebral thrombosis on 25 April 1967. He was eighty-three. According to his last wishes, his ashes were scattered at sea at 41°46N 50°14W – the position he had calculated as *Titanic*'s final resting place over fifty years earlier.

And what of Bruce Ismay? Ismay kept out of the public eye for most of the remainder of his life. He retired from active affairs in the mid-1920s and settled with his wife in Ireland. He did advise on the problems White Star was experi-encing in the early 1930s (see earlier). His health declined in the 1930s, following a diagnosis of diabetes, which took a turn for the worse in early 1936, when the illness resulted in amputation of part of his right leg. He returned to England a few months later, settling in a small house on the Wirral Peninsular across the River Mersey from Liverpool. Ismay died in London on 17 October 1937 of a cerebral thrombosis at the age of seventy-four, having seen White Star become merged with Cunard. His funeral was held on 21 October 1937 and he is buried in London. He was survived by his wife, Julia Schieffelin. After his death, she renounced her British citizenship in order to restore her American citizenship.

Myth?

Captain Smith's table and sideboard from Titanic *are still in existence*

Apart from the *Nomadic*, a few buildings in Belfast and the graving dock little remains of *Titanic*. There are, however, an interesting sideboard in the Belfast City

Hall and a table in the Board offices in Belfast Harbour. Unremarkable as pieces of furniture it would be difficult to put a value on them. They were both featured in the *Antiques Roadshow* television programme when it was filmed in the Titanic Quarter of Belfast.

The table was designed to be fixed to the floor and, together with the sideboard, was for the use of Captain Smith. The intention was that they would be on board when the vessel left Belfast but they were not quite finished. Ready just before *Titanic* left Southampton they were shipped from Belfast but arrived too late for the maiden voyage. They were put into storage to await the return of the ship – a return that never happened. In the aftermath of the tragedy they were forgotten about until they were retrieved by Harland & Wolff much later.

The sideboard is currently on display by Belfast City Council in the refurbished City Hall whilst the table, complete with replica first-class White Star place settings, is in the Board offices in Belfast Harbour.

Can you have a *Titanic* dining experience?

For those who wish to enjoy a *Titanic*-style dining experience there is a replica of *Olympic*'s first-class dining room on board the cruise ship *Celebrity Millennium* which serves at least one authentic 1914 dish. One does have to pay a surcharge to eat in this venue though.

In the UK, after *Olympic* was scrapped, many items from the first-class dining room were bought by the White Swan Hotel in Alnwick, in the north-east of England. They form part of the hotel's 'Olympic Suite' conference and dining room.

First-class Olympic Class restaurant on board *Celebrity Millennium*. (Authors' collection)

Memorials

There are many memorials dedicated to the disaster, especially in Northern Ireland, England and the USA. A selection is given below:

Thomas Andrews: There is a memorial hall dedicated to the man who completed the design of *Titanic* in Comber, County Down, Northern Ireland. His house at 36 Windsor Avenue, Belfast (it was originally numbered as 12 Windsor Avenue before new houses were built and the whole avenue numbered) is now the headquarters of the Irish Football Association. There is a commemorative plaque on the wall.

Captain Smith: The main memorial to Captain Smith is not in his home town of Stoke-on-Trent. Apparently, after the disasters the authorities in the town decided that it was not appropriate to erect a memorial to him. However, the town of Lichfield just a few miles away did erect a statue of him in Beacon Park, Lichfield. It is believed that following the success of the 1997 *Titanic* movie that Stoke-on-Trent was interested in acquiring the statue, perhaps with an eye to tourism. However, it remains in Lichfield. The original inscription read:

COMMANDER
EDWARD JOHN SMITH
RD RNR
BORN DECEMBER 27 1850
DIED APRIL 15 1912
BEQUEATHING TO HIS
COUNTRYMEN
THE MEMORY AND
EXAMPLE OF A
GREAT HEART
A BRAVE LIFE AND A
HEROIC DEATH

'BE BRITISH'

In 1985 the further inscription was added:

CAPTAIN SMITH WAS CAPTAIN OF THE TITANIC

Crew: The memorial to the stewards is in the ruins of Holyrood church in Southampton. There is also a memorial to the musicians in Southampton. It was in the public library but was destroyed in an air raid during the Second World War. A replica was created and unveiled in 1990 by three survivors – Millvina Dean, Eva Hart and Edith Heisman. There is also a memorial to the musicians in Liverpool located at the home of the Liverpool Philharmonic Orchestra. The town of Colne in Lancashire has honoured bandmaster Wallace Hartley with both a memorial and a blue plaque on the wall of his house. In 2000 the town unveiled a mural about Hartley as part of its Millennium celebrations.

The engineers: They are remembered both in Liverpool near to the famous Liver Building on the waterfront and Southampton. There is a large memorial to them in East Park, Southampton. The inscription is a testament to their courage in keeping lights on and power to the ship as long as they did. It reads:

GREATER LOVE HATH NO MAN
THAN THIS, THAT A MAN LAY
DOWN HIS LIFE FOR HIS FRIENDS

TO THE MEMORY OF THE
ENGINEER OFFICERS OF THE
R.M.S. TITANIC, WHOM SHOWED
THEIR HIGH CONCEPTION OF DUTY
AND THEIR HEROISM BY
REMAINING AT THEIR POSTS 15TH
APRIL 1912

ERECTED BY THEIR
FELLOW ENGINEERS AND
FRIENDS ON 22ND APRIL 1914

Belfast: Outside the City Hall in Belfast is the city's tribute to those from the city who died in the disaster. Sadly in 2009 it was almost completely obscured by the 'Belfast Eye'.

New York: A lighthouse was erected on top of the Seaman's Church Institute in New York in 1913. When the Institute relocated the memorial was moved to the historic South Street Seaport on the East River.

Washington DC: In Washington DC there is a memorial in Rock Creek Park erected by the women of America to honour the men who remained on board so that women and children could be saved.

Macy's: The poignant story of Isidor and Ida Straus (see chapter 3) is remembered by a plaque at one of the entrances of Macy's, the New York department store, owned by the Straus brothers. Erected by the employees its inscription reads:

IDA STRAUS   ISIDOR STRAUS
BORN FEB. 6. 1849.   BORN FEB. 6. 1845.
DIED. APRIL. 15. 1912

'THEIR LIVES WERE BEAUTIFUL AND THEIR DEATHS
GLORIOUS.'
THIS TABLET IS THE VOLUNTARY TOKEN OF SORROWING
EMPLOYEES.

In April 2009 a free exhibit, 'Titanic: Treasures from the Deep' was displayed in
Macy's lower-level parking lot on the west side of the mall.

Cobh: On adjacent street corners
in Cobh (formerly Queenstown),
Eire, which was *Titanic's* last port
of call, there are memorials to both
the victims of *Titanic* and those of
the *Lusitania*, torpedoed in 1915 off
the Irish coast. Cobh also has a small
display dedicated to the emigrants
who sailed from the port when it
was known as Queenstown. There
is also a statue of Annie Moore
who, as a teenager (there is some
dispute as to whether she was fourteen or fifteen at the time), was
an Irish immigrant to the United
States and was the first person to be
admitted through the Ellis Island
facility in New York Harbour on 1
January 1892. She received a gold
$10 piece. There is also a statue to
her at the Ellis Island facility. Those
emigrating on the *Titanic* were following in her footsteps and seeking
a better life – sadly too few of them
were to find it.

The *Titanic* memorial at Cobh (Queenstown).
(Authors' collection)

The Ellis Island facility is a must-visit destination for those who wish to know
more about the emigrant traffic to the United States and indeed those who wish
to understand how immigration helped to build the USA. There are extremely
good displays, and the facility and its online facilities are a useful source of records
including passenger lists. It is possible to search online by passenger name or by
ship. Its free online service can be accessed at: http://www.ellisisland.org.

Finally, in an area of Belfast that was better known for huge slogans of a sectarian
nature at the height of the Troubles not so many years ago there is a whole gable
end of a house adorned with a huge mural commemorating *Titanic*, the crew and
the men who built her.

Myth?

Titanic *never sank*

There is an ingenious conspiracy theory put forward by Robin Gardiner and Dan Van Der Vat that just before *Titanic* left Belfast for her maiden voyage and whilst *Olympic* was being repaired the liners were switched. The repairs to *Olympic* after her collision with HMS *Hawke* were expensive and the contention is that *Titanic* took her name and place and sailed on as *Olympic*. It is known that *Titanic's* maiden voyage was delayed so that some of her parts could be used to repair the *Olympic*. Supposedly, Captain Smith was ordered to engineer an accident on what was now the *Titanic*, but had been the *Olympic*, as an insurance scam. Given the high proportion of risk that White Star carried on its vessels this seems highly improbable. The further contention is that Smith hit an iceberg in the course of the deception. The books on this theory are somewhat technical but contain much information about the Olympic Class and are a good read: *The Riddle of the Titanic* by Robin Gardiner and Dan Van Der Vat, and *Titanic – The Ship That Never Sank* by Robin Gardiner. The latest book on this part of the *Titanic* story is: *Titanic or Olympic: Which Ship Sank?* by Steve Hall and Bruce Beveridge.

Conspiracy theories are good fun but highly unlikely. The number of Harland & Wolff and White Star staff who would have had to have been in on the conspiracy makes it highly unlikely that there is any truth in the idea.

It is probable, however, that *Olympic* survived a torpedo attack in the First World War. When she was broken up a dent was found in the hull that may well have been the result of a dud torpedo hitting the ship. *Olympic* actually sank a U-boat: she was carrying troops across the Atlantic when, on 12 May 1918, she rammed and sank U103.

Finding *Titanic*

Up to the 1980s the technology to search deep in the ocean did not exist. The Cold War and the need to track and if necessary investigate sunken submarines provided a reason for investigating deep ocean exploration. It was a long search but on 1 September 1985 *Titanic* was found by Robert Ballard of the Woods Hole Institute using remote vehicles, 2 miles down, broken into pieces and slowly decaying. The search for *Titanic* had not been easy but the results from the surveys have cast new light on the ship and revived interest in her and the fate of her passengers and crew.

Robert Ballard served in the US Navy achieving the rank of commander. He is renowned as the man who found not only the *Titanic* but also the *Bismarck*, the *Britannic*, J.F. Kennedy's PT109 and many other historic ships.

It was Ballard's work at Woods Hole that spurred his interest in shipwrecks and their exploration. His role in the Navy had involved assisting the development of small, unmanned submersibles which could be tethered to and controlled from a surface ship, and were outfitted with lighting, cameras and manipulator arms. As early as 1973, Ballard saw this as a way of searching for the wreck of *Titanic*. In 1977, he led his unsuccessful first expedition to find the wreck.

In the summer of 1985, Ballard was aboard the French research ship *Le Suroît*, which was using side scan radar to probe for the wreck of *Titanic*. The French ship was recalled and Ballard transferred onto a ship from Woods Hole, the RV (Research Vessel) *Knorr*.

Myth?

The search for Titanic *was really a secret mission to locate two missing nuclear submarines*

Whilst the search for *Titanic* was the reason given out publicly for the operation, it was in fact being funded by the US Navy as part of an operation designed to find the wreckage of two US nuclear submarines, USS *Thresher* and USS *Scorpion*, both of which had disappeared in the 1960s. As far back as 1982 Ballard had approached the Navy about his new deep sea underwater robot craft, the *Argo*, and his 1977 search for *Titanic*.

Whilst the US Navy was not interested in spending that kind of money in searching for the large Edwardian ocean liner, there was interest in finding out what happened to the missing submarines. It was decided that *Argo* presented the best chance of achieving this. The Pentagon agreed to finance Ballard's *Titanic* search provided that he first searched for and investigated the two sunken submarines especially to discover the state of their nuclear reactors after being submerged for such a long period of time, and if their radioactivity was impacting the environment.

Ballard would be placed on temporary active duty in the Navy, in charge of finding and investigating the wrecks. After the two missions were completed, time and funding permitting, Ballard would be free to use the resources to hunt for *Titanic* especially as the three vessels were believed to be not too far apart in the context of the size of the North Atlantic. *Knorr* arrived on site on 22 August 1985 and *Argo* was deployed. Ballard and his team discovered that the submarines had actually imploded from the immense pressure at the depth in which they dropped to. That implosion littered thousands of pieces of debris all over the ocean floor. Following each of the submarines' large trails of debris led Ballard and his team directly to both of them. The trail of debris made it much easier for them to locate the submarines than if they were to search for just a single intact hull.

Ballard concluded *Titanic* may well have partially imploded from pressure in much the same way the two submarines had, and concluded that it too must have also left a scattered debris trail. Basing their search pattern on the search for a debris field rather than a hull, Ballard and his team had *Argo* sweep back and forth across the ocean floor looking for *Titanic*'s debris trail. They conscientiously monitored the video feed from *Argo* as it searched the monotonous ocean floor 2 miles below.

In the early hours of 1 September 1985, observers noted anomalies on the otherwise smooth ocean floor. At first, it was pockmarks, like small craters from impacts. Eventually debris was sighted as the rest of the team was awakened. Finally, a boiler was sighted, and soon after that, the hull itself was found.

Ballard's team made a general search of the vessel's exterior, noting its condition. Most significantly they confirmed that *Titanic* had in fact split in two, and that the stern was in far worse shape than the rest of the ship. This was the first indication of the nature of the break up, as considered in chapter 3. Ballard's team did not have much time to explore as others were waiting to take *Knorr* on other scientific pursuits. Ballard's intention was to keep the exact location a secret to prevent anyone from claiming prizes from the wreck. He considered the site a cemetery and refused to desecrate it by removing artefacts from the wreck – something with which the authors heartily concur.

On 12 July 1986, Ballard and his team returned on board another vessel, *Atlantis II*, to make the first detailed study of the wreck. This time *Alvin*, a deep diving submersible which could hold a small crew, was deployed – humans were going to view *Titanic* directly for the first time since 1912. *Alvin* was accompanied by *Jason Junior*, a small remotely operated vehicle which could fit through small openings to see into the ship's interior. While the first dive saw technical problems, subsequent dives were far more successful and produced a detailed photographic record of the wreck's condition. Each dive took over two hours to reach the wreck.

Now that *Titanic* had been found, the whole world seemed to regain interest. Ballard has not been happy about the way the wreck has been treated since its discovery describing its treatment in the years since as a 'freak show'. Ballard and his crew did not bring up any artefacts from the wreck.

Who owns *Titanic*?

No sooner had *Titanic* been found than the legal battles over ownership of the remnants of the vast liner swallowed by the North Atlantic in 1912 with 1,522 lives began.

Beginning in 1987, a joint US-French expedition, which included the predecessor of RMS *Titanic* Inc (see below), began salvage operations and, during thirty-two dives, recovered approximately 1,800 artefacts which were taken for conservation and restoration.

Establishing present-day ownership has led to lengthy complex court cases because the original owners of the British-registered ship, owned by a US company (IMM), have long since gone. The ship belonged to the White Star Line but when that company was sold to Cunard the *Titanic* was not part of the sale because it was already a wreck and considered unrecoverable.

The American company, RMS *Titanic* Inc (RMST), the successor to the US-French salvage operator, emerged as the owner of the salvage rights and after a series of court battles it was allowed to keep possession and put on touring display the 5,900 artefacts it had lifted from the ship during six dives. However, the courts have since ruled that the company does not own the ship nor the recovered items, which included objects varying from the ship's whistle and children's toys to a section of the hull, but only the salvage rights. RMST claimed that it should have limited ownership as compensation for the huge salvage costs. Another US judge ruled that RMST did not even own the salvaged items outright because a 'free finders-keepers policy is but a short step from active piracy and pillaging'.

Not surprisingly some of the shareholders have pressed for the company to be more aggressive in profiting from the find. Various US government agencies intervened in the case in an effort to prevent the collection being split up and sold to private collectors, and to establish a precedent for how such salvage treasure is handled in the future. The deep diving technologies that proved so useful in finding *Titanic* have since led to other vessels being discovered and thus the ownership precedents set in the *Titanic* case are extremely important.

An international agreement signed by Britain and the US designated the *Titanic* as an international memorial and thus sought to protect it from being plundered or damaged by unauthorised dives.

RMST is owned by Premier Exhibitions, an Atlanta company that has a number of touring exhibitions including a Star Trek-style homage to 'Bodies', an exhibit of preserved human cadavers – an exhibition that has created a great deal of controversy. It says the *Titanic* exhibition has been viewed by 33 million people worldwide including at the National Maritime Museum in Greenwich. RMST has claimed that it wanted to be declared the legal owner of the collection in order to recover some of the costs of salvage which have not been covered by revenues from the touring exhibition. The company values the artefacts at $111 million. If RMST were declared by the US court to be the owner, it would give it the right to sell the collection to a museum. Alternatively, the company has sought a salvage reward of $225 million.

The US State Department and the National Oceanic and Atmospheric Administration in Washington sought to limit ownership rights. The judge in the case, Rebecca Beach Smith, a specialist in maritime law, said she believed the recovered artefacts should remain a single collection and be accessible to the public.

A US court has claimed jurisdiction over the fate of items salvaged from a British-registered ship in international waters on the grounds that part of the wreck is now on American soil and that its rulings under maritime law would be the same in English or any other foreign court.

RMST appealed to the United States Court of Appeals. In its decision of 31 January 2006, the court recognised 'explicitly the appropriateness of applying maritime salvage law to historic wrecks such as that of *Titanic*' and denied the application of the Maritime Law of Finds. The court also ruled that the district court lacked jurisdiction over the '1987 artefacts'. These were the items taken to France. The court therefore vacated that part of the court's 2 July 2004 order. In other words, according to this decision, RMST has ownership title to the artefacts awarded in the French decision (earlier valued at $16.5 million) and continues to be salvor-in-possession of the *Titanic* wreck.

Ballard returned to *Titanic* to find that there is evidence of damage caused by submersibles hitting and landing on the ship. There is a gash to the bow, the mast and crow's nest are badly decayed and the mast bell has been removed. Underwater microbes that form 'rusticles' have been eating away at *Titanic*'s iron since the ship sank and the National Oceanic and Atmospheric Administration estimated that the remaining structure is likely to collapse within the next fifty years, although a recent survey suggests that the ship is in better shape than was previously believed.

Ballard also discovered *Britannic* in the Aegean and that is much better preserved.

Artefacts

The recovered artefacts offer a glimpse into the class-conscious world of mass travel in the Edwardian era. They include coins that were legal tender throughout the Ottoman Empire and dollar notes from some of the many US banks that were permitted to print their own currency. There are crockery items, from elegant first-class plates in cobalt blue and gold to steerage mugs. There are wonderful items of jewellery; there are clothes, spectacles, a top hat, perfume and even the bell Fred Fleet rang to warn the bridge of the iceberg.

Perhaps some of the most poignant items belonged to the 113 children on board, including marbles, one split in half. Almost half of these children were lost, all but one of whom came from third class.

Exhibitions

Since the discovery of the wreck and especially since the 1997 movie *Titanic*, there have been many exhibitions relating to the ship and which give the public an opportunity to view the artefacts.

There have even been exhibitions where those going in are given a ticket bearing the name of somebody on board *Titanic*. On leaving they could check whether they survived the sinking or not. To the authors this appears rather ghoulish. The whole issue as to whether artefacts connected to such a tragedy should be put on public display has generated much debate. At the end of the day *Titanic* is a grave site.

For those who want to know more about the ship, a visit to the *Titanic* section of the Ulster Folk and Transport Museum just outside Belfast is highly recommended. The Pump House Museum at the Harland & Wolff site and the Museum of the North Atlantic in Halifax, Nova Scotia, are also well worth visiting. Both the Ulster Folk and Transport Museum and the Museum of the North Atlantic contain far more than just *Titanic* exhibits. The former also has a wonderful collection of railway locomotives and rolling stock whilst the latter contains much about the Battle of the Atlantic.

There have been exhibitions throughout the world. The authors hope most earnestly that if you do visit such an exhibition that you will remember that

Titanic was not just about glamour, it was part of a tragedy in which over 1,500 lives were lost, families torn apart and hopes and aspirations dashed.

The *Titanic* Museum in Southampton, due to open in 2012, will be a brand new interactive museum situated in the city's former magistrates' court, next to the Civic Centre.

The Maritime Museum in Southampton at the Wool House, Town Quay Road, houses an exhibition devoted to the crew of *Titanic*.

The Merseyside Maritime Museum in Albert Dock, Liverpool, has a *Titanic* display.

The *Titanic* Museum in Indian Orchard, Massachusetts, USA, is a family-run museum and has the Titanic Historical Society's collection of *Titanic* artefacts.

***Titanic* the Experience** in Orlando, Florida, USA, has re-creations of rooms in *Titanic*, and storytellers in period dress. They even host a *Titanic* dinner.

Chapter 7

The Safety Lag

The safety lag refers to the fact that safety mechanisms often lag behind technological improvements. It is often seen in transportation so it is appropriate to look at such issues in respect of not only sea but also land and air transport. It was initially most readily manifested with the development of railways.

Today we are used to the speed and convenience of mass travel. Dozens of jet airliners cross the Atlantic taking a mere eight hours for a journey that would have taken an Edwardian passenger five or more days. Australia is less than a day's flight from London. High-speed rail networks are spreading across the world. London is less than three hours from Paris via the Channel Tunnel and soon there will be a direct London–Frankfurt high-speed rail service.

This chapter uses examples from ships and shipping, railways and the airlines. The airliner superseded the passenger liner as the vehicle for long-distance mass travel from the 1950s onwards. Paradoxically there are now many new passenger liners in service but they are cruise ships designed for holidays rather than a means of transport from point A to point B. There is a synergy between air travel and cruise ships as many cruise passengers reach their ship by air. Once they were rivals, now they are interlinked for mutual benefit.

Before the opening of the first 'modern' railway, the Liverpool and Manchester Railway in 1830, very few people in Britain had travelled more than 5 miles from their homes. The speed of travel for the ordinary person was walking speed – a horse or stagecoach could go faster but not for long periods. In its first year the Liverpool and Manchester carried over 460,000 passengers. The railways allowed towns to grow as it was no longer necessary for workers to live in close proximity to their place of employment. Railways and public transport (initially trams/streetcars) produced a social revolution bringing new opportunities to the working classes. Railways opened up whole continents – it was the railways that fuelled the westward expansion of the United States and Canada for example.

It may seem strange to us but in the very early days of the railways there had to be regulations forbidding passengers from climbing onto the roofs of carriages. It had been the norm to have seats on the roofs of stagecoaches and many passengers on the trains believed that they could sit on the roofs. Railways have bridges and there was the danger of having one's head bashed in! The trouble was that although the technology now existed to travel at 35 or even 40mph people were not psychologically attuned to such an increase in the speed of travel.

The biggest safety issues with the early railways were the newness of steam technology and momentum. Primitive boilers were apt to explode. There were safety valves but these could be faulty or even tampered with. Momentum is a factor of speed and weight: a heavy mass moving at speed is hard to stop. Even if you are running it is harder to stop than if you are walking, and a train weighing many tons travelling at over 30mph is hard to stop. Sadly brakes (a safety component) did not evolve nearly as quickly as the development of ever more powerful and faster locomotives. It was not until 1889 that the British Parliament finally legislated to compel railway companies to fit continuous brakes. This was years after the 9 tons of *Rocket* and her tender had developed into much bigger and faster locomotives – nearly 60 tons of the 1882 Precedent class of express locomotives, capable of over 70mph. As trains were also longer and heavier the momentum was many, many times greater.

Trains, travelling on fixed tracks as they do, cannot manoeuvre out of the way! Ships, of course, can manoeuvre. However, as was discussed in chapter 2, were the Olympic Class as manoeuvrable as they could have been? The *Mauretania* and *Lusitania* had larger rudders for their size than the Olympic Class. They also had four propellers, two on each side, compared to the three (one each side and one centrally) of the Olympic Class. This means that the propellers themselves were able to aid manoeuvrability by varying the speeds on one or other side. As the ships had separate reversing turbines it was harder to run the propellers on one side ahead and those on the other side astern. Doing this greatly aids manoeuvrability. Had *Titanic* had slightly more power and a larger rudder might she have been able to avoid the iceberg?

The other great safety lag on the railways was in the field of signalling. It should be apparent that as trains became heavier and faster so there was an increasing need to regulate their movement to avoid the risk of collision. In the early days the railways used a time interval system. Railway 'policemen' were stationed at intervals along the track and would not let a train proceed until a certain time had elapsed since the last train had past them. It was a system fraught with danger as they would have no way of knowing whether (as happened all too frequently) the previous train had broken down out of their sight. The problem was further compounded by the fact that there was no standard time. Before the railways people set their clocks when the sun was overhead at noon. However, noon in Bristol or Liverpool is some minutes behind noon in London. It was clearly impossible to run a timetable when each station was working to local time. In 1847 what became known as 'railway time', and later Greenwich Mean Time, was based on noon at the Royal Observatory in Greenwich, London. All of Britain was now on the same time.

Eventually Parliament legislated for a better method using firstly semaphore and much later coloured light signals that could lock or unlock points as required and give an indication as to whether the train should proceed or stop. Between the wars systems were developed to automatically apply the breaks if the signal gave a stop indication. These systems were not, however, universal in Britain – even as late as 1997 the system was not universal in the UK. A serious accident at Southall in West London was caused by a train passing a danger signal – 167 years after the opening of the Liverpool and Manchester Railway.

It is perhaps time to provide a reminder of Captain Smith's comments to the *Boston Post* in 1907:

Shipbuilding is such a perfect art nowadays that absolute DISASTER, INVOLVING THE PASSENGERS IS INCONCEIVABLE. Whatsoever happens, there will be time before the vessel sinks to save the life of every person on board. I will go a bit further. I will say that I cannot imagine any condition that would cause the vessel to founder. Modern shipbuilding has gone beyond that.

Today this statement shows not only complacency but an astonishing degree of arrogance. However, he was not alone in showing these traits. Familiarity is said to breed contempt. The railway signalling system in Britain ensured that by 1900 there was possibly no safer place in the world for travellers than a British railway train (or for that matter an Atlantic liner – hence Smith's comments). Safety, however, depended upon human beings doing what they were supposed to do. There was always a danger that a signalman could forget that he had a train standing at a signal and that he (they were all male at the time in Britain) could allow another train to come in behind it at speed leading to a collision. A system was developed to provide protection for trains standing at a signal. Rule 55 ordered the driver or fireman of the train to report to the signal box if the train had been standing for a prescribed length of time (a telephone was provided at signals located some way from the signal box). In addition, signalmen were provided with coloured collars to place over the lever operating the relevant signal to show that there was a train stopped at it and that they should not accept another train into that section. Drivers/fireman were instructed to ensure that where they reported to the signal box that the collars were in place. At important junctions and stations electric track circuits were employed to show the signal man that a section was occupied. What could go wrong?

In 1915 Britain was heavily engaged in the First World War and rail traffic was heavy. There were long coal trains from the English and Welsh coalfields up through Scotland to feed the ships of the Grand Fleet at Scapa Flow.

Gretna in Scotland is perhaps best known for its wedding chapel at the Old Blacksmith's Shop (a popular venue for eloping couples from England as it lies just across the border). It was also the scene, on 22 May 1915, of Britain's worst ever rail disaster. Just outside Gretna was the signal box at Quintinshill which controlled trains on the main West Coast line that ran from London to Scotland. The layout was simple, an up to London (in Britain lines to London are up even if this is the opposite of the direction of travel and down to Glasgow, Edinburgh and beyond) plus a loop line off each of the main lines.

Because of the heavy traffic early in the morning both loops contained a goods train. The signalman had switched a down local passenger rain heading north to the up main line to clear the down main line for an express heading north. The fireman of the local train came to the signal box. The collars had not been placed on the signal lever but he made no comment. By the time the signalman's relief came (he was late) there were three trained railwaymen in the box and all three trains could be clearly seen from it. For reasons that are inexplicable the signalman accepted a troop train from the north and then (correctly) the express from the south. The engine of the troop train, travelling at full speed, ran head first into the local train. Almost immediately the express ploughed into the wreckage. All five trains at Quintinshill were damaged. The troop train was all but obliterated and to make matters worse it was gas lit and had full gas cylinders. Soon it was a charred wreck. Eight lives were lost in the express, two in the local and at least 215 officers and men of the 7th Royal Scots died. It may well have been more as the unit's official roll was destroyed. Despite the most strict rules and safeguards, human frailty had been responsible for a major tragedy. Complacency and arrogance can overcome the strictest safety measures. Captain Smith ran into a known area of ice confident that nothing could happen that would sink his ship. Three years later the signalman at Quintinshill displayed the same complacency and arrogance; *plus ça change, plus c'est la même chose* (the more things change, the more they remain the same).

The steam engine not only revolutionised land transport but also found its applications at sea as was shown in chapter 1. Indeed the railways and the shipping companies and ports were inextricably linked. Liverpool was one of Britain's premier ports and its merchants were keen to deliver their goods to Manchester. The other major port that needed easier access to markets was Bristol. Bristol, on the British west coast, was the nearest west coast port to London.

In 1833 plans were being drawn up to link London and Bristol with a standard gauge (4ft 8½in) railway line following an old, rather convoluted, coach road. A young engineer, Isambard Kingdom Brunel, proposed a radical change. Brunel had worked with his father on a tunnel under the Thames and was a trained engineer, unlike other railway pioneers such as George Stephenson who had had little formal training. Brunel proposed and used a gauge of 7ft which he argued would be more stable and give a smoother and faster ride. He also proposed a flatter route. The railway, which became known as the GWR – Great Western Railway (called by some God's Wonderful Railway and by others the Great Way Round), was the fastest in the world. Later in the 1990s the company was forced to convert its broad gauge lines to standard gauge.

Brunel had great plans for the railway – he wanted to extend it from Bristol to New York as described in chapter 1. Brunel eventually built the three ships mentioned in chapter 1, *Great Western*, *Great Britain* and *Great Eastern*. What is important about *Great Eastern* is that she was in many ways too far ahead of her time. Like the Olympic Class she was underpowered for her size. Brunel had an excuse – the technology he was using was new. White Star and Harland & Wolff could have moved to turbine machinery for all of the power but decided not to. Interestingly, across the road from the *Titanic* mural in Belfast is a pub called the *Great Eastern* which has an illustration of the vessel as its sign – it is somewhat unusual for a public house in Belfast to be celebrating a ship built on the Thames!

HMS *Captain*

The application of steam power to ships required a major change in the way the ships themselves were designed, organised and operated. Initially for larger vessels the Royal Navy (and the French Navy) literally fitted steam engines and a propeller to conventional wooden battleships. Most of the time they operated purely under sail only using steam to enter and leave harbour. To captains used to a spick and span ship the idea of coal dust and smoke was anathema. Engineers were accorded lowly status despite their technical abilities. It was not until 1871 that the Royal Navy introduced its first steam only battleship (HMS *Devastation*) and smaller vessels kept sails until much later. Auxiliary sails were still being fitted to Atlantic liners as late as 1888.

The Royal Navy knew how to operate sailing ships and muzzle-loaded guns. Steam and the new types of breech-loading rifled guns now being introduced were a different matter. Could they be combined – the best of the old and the best of the new perhaps?

Captain Cowper Phipps Coles CB, RN had been placed on half pay after the Crimean War and spent his time creating designs for turret ships. Up to this time the principal armament of warships had been batteries of guns firing from fixed ports in the sides of the ship. On 10 March 1859 he filed a patent for a revolving turret. He was not the only designer working on this idea, although it is not clear how he came by the idea. The USS *Monitor*, constructed by John Ericsson in 1861, incorporated a revolving turret and Ericsson claimed the idea of a revolving protected gun was an old one. The *London Times* suggested that it could well have been Isambard Kingdom Brunel's father, Marc Brunel, who had given Coles the idea. Coles's design aim was to create a ship with the greatest possible all round arc of fire, as low in the water as possible to minimise the target. This proved to be a weakness in designs he created, because he was unwilling to compromise these aims for the practical necessities of the sailing ships operating at that time with their rigging, decks sufficiently high to be clear of heavy seas and other necessary deck items which restricted the guns rotation.

The Admiralty accepted the principle of the turret gun as a useful innovation and incorporated it into other new designs. However, they could not accept his other ideas on ship design. Coles submitted a design for a ship having ten domed turrets each housing two large guns. The design was rejected as impractical, although the Admiralty remained interested in turret ships and instructed its own designers to create better designs. Coles submitted his plans to anyone who might be interested and succeeded in enlisting a number of supporters and a smaller ship was built.

Coles made further proposals which the Admiralty resisted pending completion of the trial ships already under construction. Construction of HMS *Captain* commenced in January 1867.

Captain was designed to have a freeboard of only 8ft but due to mistakes in construction causing increased weight the ship eventually floated 14in lower in the water. She had a full set of sails and the highest masts in the Navy, which were carried on a 'flying deck' over the turrets. She was completed in January 1870 and, initial trials being successful, in May accompanied the Channel fleet and successfully weathered a gale. Vice-Admiral Sir Thomas Symmonds, commanding, commented favourably on her performance. She was hailed as a vindication of Coles' ideas.

In August, the ship sailed again with Coles on board. The weather deteriorated and again she had to face a gale. The squadron commander wisely declined to sail in her. During the night, however, the wind was gusting and unpredictable. It was demonstrated that the ship had a maximum righting moment at an angle of heel around 18 degrees. If she was pushed over more than this, then the force declined and the ship was in mortal danger. Gusts pushed *Captain* past the safe angle and she capsized, even though at the time she was carrying little sail. Coles and the crew perished in the disaster after midnight on the night of 6 September 1870. The idea of combining turrets with sails was now dead and the result was the construction of new battleships that relied purely on their steam engines (engines which were becoming ever more reliable) and turrets beginning, as mentioned above, with HMS *Devastation* in 1871. Coles was so sure of his design that he was prepared to stake his life on it – sadly that was a mistake. It is clear from the records that the British Admiralty had misgivings about the design and yet they seemed prepared to live with these concerns – this cost lives but it was not to be the last time that a defective design was to kill people even though there were those who knew that this might happen.

To examine how attitudes have not changed much the cases of the airship R101, the Douglas DC10 jet airliner and the space shuttle Challenger are examined next. All have tragic issues around them that are echoes of *Titanic*.

Jutland

When the British Grand Fleet and the German High Seas Fleet met at the Battle of Jutland in May 1916 the flamboyant British battlecruiser commander, Admiral David Beatty, saw two of his much vaunted battlecruisers blown up in rapid succession with no losses to the Germans (by the end of the battle three British battlecruisers had blown up whilst only German battlecruiser was lost – and that only sank after taking massive damage). The reasons are too technical to go into here but it was not just the British design that was faulty but also the way the ships were used and operated.

Beatty is reported to have turned to his Flag Captain and said: 'There's something wrong with our bloody ships today'. It is also believed that he further said: '…and something wrong with our system'.

The second quote is often forgotten. There was a design flaw in the battle-cruiser concept if the ships were used as both the British and Germans were doing. They were not designed for fleet actions. A system had been allowed to develop that allowed flash doors between the turrets on the British ships and their magazines holding the high-explosive shells to be kept open despite the obvious risks. This aided the rate of firing but was exceptionally dangerous. The Germans had nearly lost a ship this way earlier in the war and had taken the lesson to heart. *Titanic* had flaws in her propulsion system and watertight division but it was the arrogance and recklessness of Captain Smith and the system that permitted such actions that sank her. At Jutland it was the operating procedures that led to the losses. The battlecruiser concept as defined by the British was proved to be a wrong one both in design and tactics that had cost many lives.

It might be thought that Jutland was a British defeat. Although the Royal Navy lost more ships than the Germans and nearly three times as many men, it was the Germans who slipped away and Admiral Jellicoe who remained on the field of battle still with an overwhelming advantage in ships. The German High Seas Fleet never seriously challenged the Royal Navy again. Despite the losses Jellicoe had not lost the war in an afternoon.

The men were brave but the tactics were out of date and did not make full use of the technological advances. There was something wrong with the ship's design but more than that there was a psychological flaw in the men commanding them – they had not advanced their strategic and tactical thinking to match the new reality.

R101

In 1930 the ocean liner still reigned supreme. Although it was now many years since the Wright brothers had taken to the skies in a heavier than air aeroplane, the range and payloads of such craft were still extremely limited. There was, though, a possible alternative – the airship. Airships, lighter than air machines using hydrogen as the lifting agent, had been pioneered by Count Zeppelin in Germany and had been used in the First World War as bombers. They were cumbersome and the hydrogen was very inflammable but they were much quicker than even the fastest liner: speeds of up to 50 knots were possible. With the technology available in 1930 it was impossible to construct an ocean liner that could match these speeds. The speeds achieved by the fastest ocean liners from 1900 until the outbreak of war in 1939 are shown below:

Year	Ship	Speed (knots)
1900	*Deutschland*	22.36
1910	*Mauretania*	26.06
1929	*Bremen*	27.91
1933	*Rex*	27.92
1935	*Normandie*	30.31
1938	*Queen Mary*	30.99

Table 12   The fastest liners 1900–39

The *Normandie* and the *Queen Mary* both cut down the voyage across the Atlantic to less than four days, although time for departure and docking had to be added on to this. The *Queen Mary* did not gain the record on her maiden voyage as she ran into fog off the coast of the United States; perhaps mindful of the fate of Captain Smith and *Titanic* the master slowed down. There is even an episode of the *Poirot* television series starring David Suchet that is set on this voyage and covers the fact that the liner was forced to slow down. When the *Queen Mary* actually broke the record a few months later Cunard refused to accept the trophy that had recently been commissioned to give to the record breaker. The company declared that they were not in the business of racing and breaking records! This gave them even more free publicity.

For information the fastest ever ocean liner was the SS *United States*. Designed for speed as a possible troopship she entered service in 1952. Her fastest recorded speed in service was 35.59 knots.

Because of the way propellers behave in water it is difficult to gain more speed just by pouring on more power. The same is true of propellers on aircraft (see later). The extra power just goes to breaking up the water around the stern of the ship. The fastest commercial ships today, the superfast ferries, can manage up to 50 knots using gas turbine engines and very sophisticated hull forms, but these were not available in 1930.

Airships in 1930 appeared to offer a faster mode of intercontinental travel, albeit for a select group of people – those who could pay the prices charged as the capacity was limited. It seemed that in still air speeds of over 50 knots might be achieved. Britain, Germany and the USA all entered the airship-building race. Between 1919 and 1930 there had been seven successful flights by airships across the Atlantic with no loss of life. In contrast there had been twenty-seven attempts to fly aircraft across that ocean which had resulted in sixteen failures and twenty-one deaths.

Britain designed two intercontinental airships, *R100* for the Canadian route (built by a private enterprise) and *R101* (built by the government at the Royal Airship Works at Cardington) for the Indian route. These were rigid (hence the R) with the gas bags enclosed within a metal latticework. The basic requirements for the airships were:

Passengers	100
Cargo	30 tons
Range	3,500 miles
Ceiling	2,000ft (approx)

The gas was in the main envelope with all accommodation being in a metal structure fastened beneath it.

The low ceiling height meant that airships needed to fly around hilly terrain rather than over it but this was not an issue on trans-ocean flights. Flying across land, valleys could be followed where the hills and mountains were too high.

When finally completed *R101* was 777ft 2½in long. One million goldbeaters' skins formed from the large intestines of an ox were used to line her gas bags. Her outer skin covered an incredible 5 acres.

Model of the airship *R101* at the model village, Isle of Wight. (Authors' collection)

Hydrogen was to be the lifting agent as helium production was still in its infancy. Whereas hydrogen is highly inflammable, helium is inert. Helium was produced as a by-product from oil wells in the United States and was being used by that country for some of its airships. There was not enough available, however, to provide Great Britain.

As originally designed, these craft had inadequate lifting capacity so extra sections with gas bags were added and the carrying capacity reduced.

After a number of test flights, on 29 July 1930 *R100* began its maiden voyage from the Cardington airship base in England to Montreal in Canada. The airship arrived in Montreal early on 1 August – a very credible journey time. *R100* arrived back at Cardington after a layover in Canada on 16 August.

Rain beating down on the skin during the voyage had caused problems and when the airship was examined it was found that there had been serious deterioration in the outer cover and the gas bags. The refit took three months and included fitting a new bay to give extra lift.

In the meantime *R101* was being completed. Extra gas bag capacity was installed but tests showed that the airship was too heavy and that her diesel engines were not powerful enough. With so much hydrogen around, diesel engines were much safer than petrol ones.

Even though *R101* appeared to have a lifting capacity less than its weight, it was believed that the forward motion would produce enough extra lift to carry the airship on its journey. If Captain Smith can be accused of arrogance and complacency over *Titanic*, this took those failings to a new level!

The *R101* team were under pressure to have the craft ready. The new Viceroy of India, Lord Thomson of Cardington (he had been Secretary of State for Air in a previous role and a prime mover in the *R100/R101* programme, hence taking Cardington as part of his title), wanted to arrive in India during the Imperial Conference to be held in London starting on 1 October 1930.

Thomson placed enormous pressure on the team. It was clear with hindsight that *R101* was in no fit state to make the 5,000-mile voyage to India with stops at Ishmailia, Egypt and Karachi, Pakistan. Because of the prevailing bad, autumnal weather and the need to be ready on time there were no high speed, bad weather or turbulence trials. The captain of *R101*, Flight Lieutenant H. Carmichael Irwin (known as 'Bird') was an experienced airship captain, despite his apparent low rank. He had previously drawn up a comprehensive checklist for airship operations – the powers that be disregarded these and Irwin did not make comment.

It is worth remembering the IMM instructions to captains covered in chapter 3 viz:

> the safety of all those on board weighs with us beyond all other considerations, and we would once more impress upon you and the entire navigation staff most earnestly that no risk is to be run which can be avoided by the exercise of caution … and by choosing, whenever doubt exists, the course that tends to safety.

Lord Thomson issued similar words regarding *R101*:

> … The whole policy of the airship programme is Safety First and Safety Second as well.

Rather like the IMM instructions this missive was not to be followed.

R101 had a mere seven test flights in all before modification and just one afterwards.

On the evening of 4 October 1930 Lord Thomson arrived with his party for the flight to India. The ship was ready and their luggage loaded. Included in the luggage was a 10ft-long carpet weighing 129lb. This was placed in the nose of the airship.

At the very last minute *R101* received a Certificate of Airworthiness, without which the voyage could not go ahead. The airship cast off from the mooring mast, circled Cardington and headed for Egypt. It was fated never to arrive.

Within half an hour one of the five engines developed problems and had to be shut down. Three hours later *R101* had only covered a mere 127 miles. The weather grew worse as the airship headed across the English Channel.

By 2 a.m. *R101* was over France and the weather was worsening. It must be recalled that the airship was overweight. Without forward movement maintaining altitude would be nearly impossible. Her speed over the ground (airspeed less headwind) was a mere 29 knots at an altitude of about 1,200ft. *R101* had to clear the ridge at Beauvais, an area with notorious downdraughts.

It is believed that there was a failure of the outer cover and probably some of the gas bags and as the craft headed into the wind any failure in the outer cover would be made worse. As the gas bags failed the nose dipped sharply (the weight of the carpet could not have helped). Although the crew tried to regain control *R101*, overweight and underpowered, was doomed. She hit the ground near Beauvais and caught fire. Out of fifty-four passengers and crew there were only six survivors.

As with *Titanic* there was an official inquiry. It concluded that the disaster was caused by a substantial loss of gas compounded by a strong downdraught. No mention of the underpowered engines, overweight airship and the lack of testing – another whitewash. Lord Thomson clearly carried a great deal of the responsibility for the flight and subsequent disaster but he was dead and had been a member of the Establishment. There was, however, no Captain Lord to use as a scapegoat so nobody was blamed!

Britain was out of the airship business and the *R100* was broken up. Would there be other airships?

Hindenburg

The answer is yes, and the results just as tragic. If Britain was out of the airship business, old rivals Germany was not. The Nazi Government saw the German airship programme that began again in the 1920s as a means of gaining international prestige. The successor to Count Zeppelin was Dr Eckener and in the 1920s under his leadership the Zeppelin Company began to investigate large commercial airships.

On 18 September 1928, a new German airship named *Graf Zeppelin* in honour of the count flew for the first time. She was the largest airship yet. Eckener's initial concept was to use *Graf Zeppelin* for experimental and demonstration purposes to prepare the way for regular airship travelling, by carrying passengers and mail to cover the costs. In October 1928 the first long-range voyage brought her to Lakehurst, where Eckener and his crew were once more welcomed enthusiastically. *Graf Zeppelin* toured Germany and visited Italy, the Middle East and Spain. A second trip to the United States was aborted in France due to engine failure in May 1929. In August 1929 she left Germany for a circumnavigation around the world. Altogether she made a 30,831-mile journey in safety.

In the following year, *Graf Zeppelin* undertook a number of trips around Europe, and, following a successful tour to Brazil in May 1930, it was decided to open the first regular transatlantic airship line between Germany and Recife in Brazil, the journey taking sixty-eight hours. Eckener intended to supplement the successful craft by another, similar, Zeppelin, projected as *LZ 128*. However, the disastrous accident of the British passenger airship *R101* on 5 October 1930 led the Zeppelin Company to reconsider the safety of hydrogen-filled vessels, and the design was abandoned in favour of a new project. *LZ 129* was designed to be filled with helium.

In 1933 the establishment of the Third Reich in Germany began to overshadow the Zeppelin business. The Nazis were not interested in Eckener's ideals of peacefully connecting people; they also knew very well that airships would be useless in combat and thus chose to focus on aircraft for the Luftwaffe.

However, they were eager to exploit the apparent popularity of the airships for propaganda purposes, something Eckener refused to cooperate with. Goering, the German Air Minister, formed a new airline in 1935, the *Deutsche Zeppelin-Reederei* (DZR), which took over operation of airship flights. Eckener's Zeppelins would now display the Nazi flag on on their fins and occasionally tour Germany to play martial music and propaganda speeches for the people from the air.

On 4 March 1936, LZ 129, named *Hindenburg*, made her first flight. The *Hindenburg* was the largest airship ever built. However, as Eckener had been unable to obtain helium from the United States due to a military embargo, *Hindenburg* was filled with hydrogen.

On 6 May 1937, while landing at the Lakehurst Naval Air Station in New Jersey, following a transatlantic flight, the tail of the ship caught fire and within seconds the *Hindenburg* burst into flames, killing thirty-five of the ninety-seven people on board and one member of the ground crew. The actual cause of the fire has never been definitively determined; lightning has been blamed but this is unlikely. It is possible that a combination of leaking hydrogen from a torn gas bag, and the vibrations caused by a swift rotation performed for a quicker landing, could have started static electricity in the duralumin alloy skeleton. Recent evidence suggests that the doping material used for the outer cover could have been ignited by the static. It took just thirty-four seconds for the *Hindenburg* to be engulfed by flames.

Graf Zeppelin completed more flights, though not for overseas commercial flights to the US, and was retired one month after the *Hindenburg* wreck and turned into a museum.

The career of *Graf Zeppelin* was not quite over. In 1939 she made flights over Britain to spy on the new 'Chain Home' radar sights, although the German engineers spied on the wrong frequencies and concluded that the prominent towers were not part of a British radar system. How wrong they were was to be proved during the Battle of Britain in 1940.

One would have expected the Germans to have learnt from *R101* about the impracticalities of commercial airships. Perhaps, like Captain Smith, they retained too great a faith in their own. The Germans knew all about the risks of hydrogen, the British knew about the state of *R101*. Pride and complacency led to the loss of too many lives in what turned out to be a dead end in air transport.

Recently the successor to the Zeppelin Company has begun to develop large, helium-filled cargo airships. Although slower than conventional ships, their carrying capacity and cost per mile may make them very attractive.

The Second World War brought about many technological advances. Many of the military advances also aided the post-war transportation sectors; none more than the development of the jet airliner. The propeller-driven aircraft has a limit beyond which it can go no faster due to the behaviour of propeller blades in the air. More and more power eventually produces a diminishing increase in speed. Before the war both the British and Germans were experimenting with both rockets and jets that used turbines. Both countries had jet fighters and fighter bombers in service before 1945. It would not be long before somebody decided to put jet technology to commercial use.

The United States introduced the B47 jet bomber and Britain planned its own large military jets, but also a commercial jet airliner – the Comet. The B47 had swept back wings to enable it to fly closer to Mach 1 (the speed of sound), although breaking the sound barrier in a jet aircraft was still some way off, and contained its engines in pods under the wings. Britain's de Havilland Company designing the Comet opted for a much more conservative approach. The Comet's wings were straight and its four engines buried in the wing roots. Boeing, who had built the B47, were also developing a commercial jet – the 707 – a far more radical design with swept back wings and podded engines. It would be faster and carry more passengers over a greater distance than the Comet. Nevertheless the Comet would inaugurate jet air transport although it was to be tinged with tragedy.

Britain's railways have suffered from being first in the field. The loading gauge is smaller and the infrastructure older. In opting for a conservative approach to the Comet de Havilland actually surrendered their commercial advantage. As designed the Comet 1 did not have the range to cross the Atlantic without refuelling nor could it carry enough passengers. During the war larger aircraft had begun to fly at altitudes so high that the pressure of the air was not enough to support life. Pressurisation was developed. The engines pumped air into aircraft so that the pressure remained closer to that on the ground regardless of what the outside pressure was. One of the main problems was building a fuselage that was strong enough to contain the pressurised air. If the fuselage was punctured, air could rush out in an explosive depressurisation that would kill all on board. The Comet was not the first pressurised passenger aircraft but it did fly higher and up to 50 per cent faster than pressurised propeller-driven aircraft. The story of the Comet is integral to that of the DC which follows it in this chapter.

On 2 May 1952 the world's first commercial jet airliner service began from London to Johannesburg with various refuelling stops along the way. There was nothing (yet) as fast as the Comet. De Havilland appeared to have the market to themselves and orders came in even from the United States. Then disaster struck.

The first two crashes of a Comet, both of which occurred on take-off, could be put down to pilot inexperience. Service had been extended to Singapore but exactly a year after the Comet entered revenue service there was a crash of a Comet en route from Singapore to Delhi. The inquiry into the crash concluded that despite some evidence of fatigue in some of the parts it was probable that extremely strong winds and a thunderstorm were responsible.

For a few months there were no further problems. On 10 January 1954 a Comet that had refuelled at Rome for the final leg of its Singapore to London flight disintegrated at around 27,000ft just off the coast of Elba. The authorities did not withdraw the Comet's Certificate of Airworthiness but the operator, BOAC (British Overseas Airways Corporation), grounded the fleet voluntarily.

Very little wreckage had been recovered, although some bodies had been found and autopsied, and the cause of the crash remained a mystery. Ten weeks after the crash flights resumed, on 23 March 1954, but on 8 April 1954 another BOAC

Comet, on charter to South African Airways, was on a leg from Rome to Cairo, as part of a longer flight to Johannesburg, when it crashed in the waters near Naples. The fleet was immediately grounded once again and a large investigation board was formed under the direction of the Royal Aircraft Establishment (RAE). The Royal Navy was tasked with helping locate and retrieve the wreckage so that the cause of the accident could be found. The Comet's Certificate of Airworthiness was revoked and line production suspended while the BOAC fleet was grounded.

Quantities of wreckage and a number of bodies were recovered. Investigators began to reconstruct as much of the aircraft as possible. The question of metal fatigue began to be examined. Before the Elba accident, the aircraft concerned had made 1,290 pressurised flights and at the time of the Naples accident, the aircraft in that crash had made 900 pressurised flights. It was thought that a crack had started at the corner of one of the windows which had widened and caused an explosive depressurisation.

Engineers subjected an identical airframe to repeated re-pressurisation and over-pressurisation and, on 24 June 1954, after 3,057 flight cycles (1,221 actual and 1,836 simulated), the fuselage burst open. Hall, Geoffrey de Havilland and Bishop were immediately called to the scene, where the water tank was drained to reveal the fuselage had ripped open at a corner of the forward port-side escape hatch cut-out. A further test reproduced the same results. By this time two-thirds of the Naples aircraft had been recovered and reconstructed. A fatigue crack growth from a rivet hole at the forward window around the Automatic Direction Finder on the top of the fuselage was found. It was concluded that this had caused a catastrophic breakup of the aircraft in high-altitude flight.

The Comet was redesigned and eventually entered service across the Atlantic but only a few days ahead of the Boeing 707. Less than sixty Comets entered service – the last variant being the large Comet 4 with more range. In contrast Boeing, whose designs for the 707 were much more sophisticated, produced over 900. Being first did not assist either de Havilland or the British aircraft industry.

What did Britain credit was the inquiry into the Comet crashes. This was a prestige project for Britain but, unlike the whitewash of the *Titanic* inquiry, that on the Comets was painstaking and honest. The faults were revealed and acted upon. Other manufacturers took notice of the findings and metal fatigue, whilst always a concern, was looked for much more rigorously.

Given the impeccable inquiry into the Comet – an inquiry determined to find the cause of the crashes and to ensure passenger safety rather than to protect individuals or organisations from blame – the penultimate story in this chapter is at the opposite end of the spectrum. An aircraft with a known design flaw was allowed to enter service despite the fact that the manufacturing company had been informed by one of its suppliers that the defect would eventually cause a major disaster. Furthermore the regulator was dilatory and when disaster occurred an attempt was made to blame a totally innocent individual – just as many believe happened in the *Titanic* case.

Two if not three Comets had been lost to depressurisation – the danger was well known. Any large hole appearing in an aircraft at altitude could cause the air to rush from the aircraft. A small hole is not a problem as the missing air can easily be replenished but a large hole can cause an effect like an explosion. This would be bad enough but if the control cables and the hydraulic tubes are fastened to the underneath of the floor as in many aircraft and the depressurisation causes the floor to fail, control of the aircraft may well be lost.

Aircraft manufactures are aware of this, so are airlines and so are the regulatory authorities. Whilst sabotage can and does cause huge holes to appear in aircraft, normal operations should have safeguards to prevent a hole appearing because of a manufacturing fault. The most likely source for a large hole to appear is if a door becomes detached in flight. The passenger doors are plug doors that open inwards and are larger than the external opening. When closed and locked the positive pressure differential between the inside of the aircraft and the low pressure outside presses the door harder into the frame around the opening – inadvertent opening is almost impossible.

Aircraft carry more than passengers; they have holds for baggage and cargo. If the doors to the holds, which are under the floor, opened inwards this would restrict the space available for payload and make loading and unloading difficult. Therefore these doors need to open outwards. If one of these doors opened at altitude the sudden release of pressure within the fuselage could well cause the floor to fail as the air rushed out. Therefore regulators require strict attention to ensuring that such a door cannot come open in flight.

In the late 1960s two American manufacturers were competing to produce the first medium-range wide-bodied aircraft. A wide-bodied aircraft has two aisles rather than one. The Boeing 747 'Jumbo Jet' was the first of the type but that was designed for long-range flights. What the US airlines believed was needed was a smaller wide body for domestic US flights between major cities.

Both the Douglas and Lockheed companies entered the race. Lockheed was first to begin development with the innovative Tristar, with its Rolls-Royce RB211 engines (Rolls-Royce declared bankruptcy in the middle of the project and had to be rescued by the British Government). Douglas (soon to be taken over by McDonnell to become McDonnell Douglas) came in later with the more conservative DC10. The Tristar could be compared to the *Lusitania/ Mauretania* whilst the DC10 was more akin to the Olympic Class. Douglas had always prided itself that it was not the first into a new field (nor the last) as being first, as de Havilland found with the Comet, is not always a good thing. There were many differences between the two aircraft yet to the passenger they appeared very similar. Both needed new types of engines – turbofans that produced much more power than previous jet engines. These were heavy aircraft and whereas the Boeing 747 had four engines, these aircraft would have only three.

As far as the control cables and hydraulic tubes that allow the pilot to move the heavy control surfaces were concerned these would be underneath the floor. There were three separate systems with crossovers between them (the 747 has four), a concept known as redundancy so that if one or even two systems are damaged the third can take over from them.

In designing the rear cargo door for the DC10 Douglas accepted a suggestion from the launch customer for the aircraft – American Airlines – that the locking system should use electric actuators. Most aircraft (and indeed the DC for its front cargo door) preferred hydraulic actuators. The basic concept is simple although the engineering complicated. An electric motor lowers the door (it is hinged at the top) and then actuators are used to move a locking system into place to latch the door firmly closed. The DC10 used an unusual locking system that resembled a claw that was rotated around a bar by the electric actuators. A handle is then pulled down that puts locking pins behind the mechanism so that it cannot come loose. Fail-safe one might think. It is fail-safe as long as the locking pins are in place. The Douglas system was not. The Douglas system relied on the actuator driving the mechanism 'over-centre' (most light switches are over-centre mechanisms – once the switch has been moved to 'on' it can only go back to 'off' if an equal amount of force is used). A hydraulic system is safer than an electric one as the electric system can stall and the mechanism can appear properly shut even if it has actually failed – a drop in voltage to the actuator can cause this. If this happens, in theory the locking pins will not go into place and it will be impossible to pull the handle controlling them down.

Convair, the contractor responsible for building the fuselages (modern airliners have their sections built in different places, even different continents and then brought together for final assemble), was aware of the problems that the rear cargo door could cause. In an internal memorandum it was noted that the loss of a door would probably cause the floor to rupture and that this could well lead to the loss of the aircraft. Convair, the memo stated, could not avoid a degree of legal liability if this happened. Management concluded that Douglas must know about the problem and that as the design was a Douglas one then it would be better not to raise the issue. As a Convair employee put it, 'it is an interesting legal and moral dilemma'.

On the DC10, however, it was possible for the handle to be operated even if the locking pins were not in place as part of the mechanism was so long that it could be bent with very little force.

The problems became publically apparent early in the DC10's history when a rear cargo door detached from an American Airlines flight that had just departed Detroit and was over Windsor, Ontario. The flight had not reached altitude and was lightly loaded. There was depressurisation and the floor was damaged. Skilful piloting brought the aircraft down without the injuries being too serious.

Rather than this incident being followed by a formal investigation, a 'gentlemen's agreement' was reached between McDonnell Douglas (as the company had then become), the four US airlines flying the DC10 at the time and the Federal Aviation Authority (FAA) to institute remedial measures. No formal Airworthiness Directive which would have compelled action and would have been in the public domain was issued.

The decision was made by McDonnell Douglas to fit a support bracket to alleviate the bending in the mechanism, extend the length of the locking pins and to provide a visual indicator in the door that it had been shut correctly. The latter consisted of a small window with an indicator that could be viewed from outside

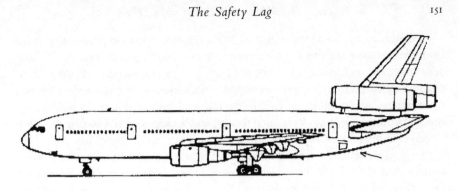

DC10 rear cargo door. (R. Cartwright)

by a baggage handler closing the door. Not a perfect solution but it should have been enough to ensure safety until a new design could be put in place.

To be failsafe the indicator should have been driven by the locking pin mechanism – if the locking pins moved correctly then the indicator would move into the safe position. For some reason McDonnell Douglas engineers ran the indicator off the handle mechanism; there was no direct link between the indicator and the locking pins. If the actuator stalled then moving the handle down would cause the pins to jam against the mechanism. If the support bracket failed part of the mechanism would bend and the handle could be pulled fully down. The pins would not be in place but the indicator would show safe. It was unlikely that the support bracket would fail but what if it was not present?

The aircraft already in service were retro-fitted with the new measures and new aircraft had them fitted automatically. There were, however, some aircraft at the factory that had not been sold as they were part of a cancelled order; one of them was hull No.29. Hull 29 was eventually sold to Turkish Airlines.

On 3 March 1974 the aircraft took off from Paris on the final leg of an Istanbul to London flight. It was full with 346 passengers and crew. Luggage had been loaded and the baggage handler, an Algerian, had checked the indicator in the little window.

At just under 12,000ft altitude the rear cargo door failed. The floor collapsed under the force of the air and the weight of the passengers. The plane crashed into the forest of Ermenonville just north of Paris – there were no survivors.

Crash investigators recovered the rear cargo door some distance away from the crash. Two things were evident immediately. Firstly the locking pins were wrongly adjusted and secondly the support bracket had never been fitted. It had not been removed; it had never been there in the first place. Records held by McDonnell Douglas clearly showed that the work had been completed and signed off. There has never been a satisfactory explanation for this.

Almost immediately McDonnell Douglas blamed the baggage handler whom they described as 'illiterate'. He spoke and read fluent French and Arabic but as he was less proficient in English the company described him as illiterate. McDonnell Douglas was soon forced to apologise.

Clearly McDonnell Douglas, Convair, the FAA and perhaps the airline were negligent. It was not until a court case for compensation by relatives of the dead that denials stopped. In order to prevent more and more of the failings of those involved coming to light out of court settlements were reached. However, there was an investigation by Paul Eddy and his colleagues at the *Sunday Times* newspaper (their findings have since been published as *Destination Disaster* – see bibliography) and the full facts published.

The similarities with *Titanic* and the investigations into that disaster are compelling. First blame somebody else – Captain Lord/the baggage handler, then try to ensure that officialdom is protected at all costs. Sixty-two years after *Titanic* whitewashes were still being attempted but in 1974 the media was more powerful than in 1912.

Just as White Star was able to bring the *Olympic* up to standard with extra lifeboats and so on immediately after the *Titanic* disaster, so too were McDonnell Douglas able to provide a properly functioning rear cargo door for the DC10 extremely quickly.

Andrea Doria

Radar was a development of the Second World War. On the night of 25 July 1956 the pride of the Italian Merchant Marine, the beautiful 29,100 GRT SS *Andrea Doria* of the Italian Line, with a capacity for 1,241 passengers and 500 crew, was approaching the coast off Nantucket bound for New York. It was foggy that night. Coming in the opposite direction out of New York was the smaller, 12,396 GRT, *Stockholm* of the Swedish American Line bound for Gothenburg. Both ships had radar sets. Through a series of errors and misreading of the radar plots they apparently manoeuvred into each other in what can be described as a 'radar assisted collision'. They could hear each other, they could see each other on their radars but they still collided. A last desperate manoeuvre by the *Andrea Doria* misfired and she presented her flank to the ice-strengthened bow of the *Stockholm*. The Swedish ship reversed out of the deep V-sided gash she had caused and the *Andrea Doria* began to fill with water and list to starboard. The list rendered her lifeboats on one side unable to be lowered.

Stockholm carried lifeboat spaces for 2,000 (more than needed for a full complement of passengers and crew). The passengers on *Titanic* had not been so lucky, but with half the lifeboats unable to be used the passengers on the *Andrea Doria* were in dire peril.

Stockholm was too badly damaged to render much assistance; she had had five crew killed but no passengers. Distress calls went out but unless help came soon then a major disaster was in the making. Forty-four years after *Titanic* had foundered, the cold waters of the North Atlantic off North America were the scene of another maritime drama.

Fortunately assistance did come. The ship that played the role of *Carpathia* was the elegant *Ile de France* of the French Line. Heading for Europe she was just out of the edge of the area within which she would be expected to respond. Her captain, Baron Raoul de Beaudéan, did not hesitate and turned the ship around and headed west to join the smaller ships that were beginning to arrive.

Forty-six people died on the *Andrea Doria* but 1,660 lived – it was almost a reversal of the *Titanic* disaster. The *Andrea Doria* capsized and sank the following morning.

The incident and its aftermath were heavily covered by the news media on both sides of the Atlantic. While the rescue efforts were both successful and commendable, the cause of the collision and the loss of *Andrea Doria* generated much interest in the media and many lawsuits. Largely because of an out-of-court settlement agreement between the two shipping companies during hearings immediately after the disaster, no determination of the cause was ever formally published. Although greater blame appeared initially to fall on the *Andrea Doria*, it is now believed that both ships may have misinterpreted their radar plots. Studies of the disaster suggest that a misreading of radar on the Swedish ship may have initiated the collision course, leading to some errors on both ships and resulting in disaster.

Andrea Doria was the last major transatlantic passenger vessel to sink before the jet airliner became the normal and accepted method of travel. The incident indicated the need for better training with radar. The technology was there but the safety lag was still apparent in terms of psychological responses – how well did the officers on the bridges of the two ships trust their radars? Was it a lack of familiarity with the new radar technology – a safety lag that was the true reason for the accident?

Andrea Doria lies at the bottom of the ocean but the *Stockholm* had a long career ahead of her after she was repaired. In 1960 she became the East German *Völkerfreundschft*, then in 1986 she was converted into a refugee accommodation ship in Oslo and renamed *Fridtjot Nansen*. In 1990 she was rebuilt as a cruise ship and has had a number of names, finally becoming the *Athena* for Classic International Cruises under whose flag she still sails. In her main foyer is a display detailing her encounter with the *Andrea Doria*.

Chapter 8

Conclusions

There were errors in the construction of *Titanic*, errors in the way she was operated and errors in the evacuation. However, a disaster can happen even if the majority of the parties are doing the right thing – they can just be in the wrong place at the wrong time.

BEA (British European Airways) flight 476 from London to Istanbul on 10 September 1976 had been instructed to fly at 33,000ft over what was then Yugoslavia but a catalogue of errors by air traffic control resulted in the aircraft colliding with another climbing aircraft. Both aircrews were doing precisely what they had been instructed to do. If the BEA pilot had been flying a little slower or a little faster or had he not been so precise in flying at exactly the proscribed altitude or if the other aircraft had climbed a little slower, and so on, then 176 lives would not have been lost. The blame (shades of *Titanic*) fell on a lowly air traffic controller when it was really the out-dated system that was at fault. The controller was given a two-year jail sentence but rightly released after international pressure. He was not solely to blame; it was also the system's fault. This was in the days of totalitarian Yugoslavia and the system must never be seen to be faulty. So it was in 1912.

If *Titanic* had actually collided with the *New York* at Southampton (see chapter 3) and the maiden voyage had been delayed and if *Olympic* had not needed repairs that resulted in a delay in the completion of *Titanic*, how would history have been changed?

What were the chances that an iceberg calved in the Arctic would have made its way down the Atlantic, carried by the Labrador Current, would meet the world's largest liner and that they would collide? They must be millions if not billions to one.

Titanic was not the only ship to sink on her maiden voyage. Perhaps the second most famous was the Swedish warship *Vasa* (sometimes referred to as the *Wasa*), the brand new pride of the Swedish Navy in the 1620s when Sweden was a major European power with its own empire. As the display in the wonderful *Vasa* Museum in Stockholm reads:

In 1628 the ship was ready. Sunday August 10 was the day of the *Vasa*'s maiden voyage. The beaches around Stockholm were filled with spectators, among them foreign diplomats. The maiden voyage was to be an act of propaganda for the ambitious Swedish king Gustavus Adolphus.

The *Vasa* set sail and fired a salute. But only after a few minutes of sailing the ship began to heel over. She righted herself slightly – and heeled over again. Water started to gush in through the open gunports. And, to everyone's horror and disbelief, the glorious and mighty warship suddenly sank! Of the 150 people on board, 30-50 died in the disaster. When *Vasa* had been salvaged in 1961, archaeologists found the remains of 25 skeletons.

The 16,990 GRT liner *Georges Philippar* was built in France and was launched on 6 November 1930, ready for delivery to her owners Compagnie des Messageries Maritimes in January 1932. She had been ordered as a replacement for the *Paul Lacat*, which had been destroyed by fire in December 1928. Prior to the commencement of her maiden voyage, the French police warned her owners that threats had been made to destroy the ship, by who is not clear but there was considerable political unrest in France at the time. Her outbound maiden voyage to Japan passed without incident. She was sailing home via Colombo with 347 crew and 518 passengers on board and a cargo including bullion.

On 16 May while *Georges Philippar* was 145 nautical miles off the Horn of Africa a fire broke out in one of the cabins. There was a delay in reporting the fire, which had spread by the time the captain made the decision to try and beach the ship at Aden, and increased speed, which only made the fire burn more fiercely. The order to abandon ship was given and a distress call made. Although rescue ships soon arrived, fifty-four people died in the fire. *Georges Philippar* sank in the Gulf of Aden. To this day it is not known whether the fire was an accident or started deliberately.

It could be argued that *Georges Philippar* had successfully completed her maiden voyage as she was on the return trip but come what may she had a very short and ultimately tragic life.

Another Harland & Wolff vessel that had a very short life was the SS *Magdalena* of Royal Mail Lines which sank in 1949 after hitting rocks off the coast of Brazil in April 1949. Like the *Georges Philippar* she was brand new, had completed her maiden voyage from London to Buenos Aires and was returning to London via Santos which she left on 24 April, initially bound for Rio de Janeiro. Although her course out of Santos had been carefully plotted she appeared to be consistently north of it.

The *Magdalena* sailed from Santos on the afternoon of 24 April 1949, taking her departure from a point south of the Isle of Moela at 4.28 p.m. and setting a course to pass some 2 miles south of Boi Point on the Isle of San Sebastian. The draught on sailing was 27ft 5in forward and 27ft 7in aft.

It quickly became apparent that the vessel was, in fact, making a more northerly course than was intended and at 6 p.m. and again at 7 p.m., on the orders of her master, course was altered slightly to starboard, and at 7.56 p.m. Boi Point was abeam at a distance of about 2 miles. The course was then altered to 62 degrees by gyro compass to pass about half-a-mile to the northward of Palmas Island Light. It was again found that the vessel was to the northward of her intended course and at 2.30 a.m. the senior second officer, who was the officer of the watch, reported to the master that the vessel was some 2 or 2½ miles to the northward of her course line.

On leaving Santos the master was on the bridge, and remained either on the bridge or in his room immediately below the bridge. Even when he retired to bed he left instructions to be called if there were any problems. He was informed of the ship's progress from time to time but was not made aware of any difficulties. The captain was due back on the bridge at 4.30 a.m. but as he was dressing the ship struck part of the Tijucas Rocks and became stranded.

After stranding, an attempt was made to lay out the starboard anchor but, owing to rising wind and sea, was abandoned, and the vessel remained ashore until about 11.34 p.m. On the rising tide in very rough sea, with a heavy swell, the vessel came afloat and blew clear of the rocks when both anchors were let go. About 6.50 a.m. on 26 April the anchors were hove up and, with tug assistance, an attempt was made to tow the vessel into port. The wind had risen, with considerable swell, and the *Magdalena* had made considerable water and was down by the head. Shortly after midday, whilst passing to the eastward of Cotuntuba Island, she struck the ground, bumped heavily and broke her back, becoming a total loss.

Some of the crew used their own lifeboats, one group ending up making an unscheduled visit to the famous Copacabana Beach which was where their lifeboat came ashore.

Unlike *Titanic* there was a full and vigorous inquiry that censored the captain, the first officer and to a lesser extent the second officer for failing to take appropriate action especially as it was known that the ship was off track.

One of the unluckiest ships was the *Principessa Iolanda* (sometimes called the *Principessa Jolanda*). She was a 9,200 GRT vessel designed for the Italy to South America service for NGI (Navigazione Generale Italiana). Her launching, in front of a crowd that included Italian nobility, was in September 1907. The ship appeared to be being launched to plan when something went wrong and she slowly rolled over and sank. The wreck was later scrapped on the spot, although the engines were salvaged and reutilised

Myth?

Ice is no longer a problem for shipping

In chapters 1 and 2 it was related how Guion Line's *Arizona* had hit an iceberg head on in 1879 and survived. It is interesting to consider what might have been the result if *Titanic* had not been turned. A head-on collision would have caused massive damage and would have crumpled her bow but she might have survived. One cannot criticise First Officer Murdoch for taking the action he did – it would be human nature to try to manoeuvre away from a collision.

Even today despite ice patrols, radar, satellite imagery and the like, ice is still a problem. Two fairly recent examples demonstrate this.

In June 1989 the Russian cruise liner (operating in Western markets to gain hard currency for what was then, but only just, the USSR) *Maxim Gorkiy* hit an ice floe (not an iceberg) while on a cruise near the Svalbard Archipelago, north of Norway and well into the Arctic Circle, and began to sink rapidly. All passengers and a third of the crew were instructed to abandon ship, while the Norwegian Coast Guard vessel *Senja* was dispatched to assist. By the time the *Senja* arrived on the scene some three hours later, the *Maxim Gorkiy* was already partially submerged. The passengers, who were mainly West Germans, were evacuated from the lifeboats and ice floes by helicopters and the *Senja*, eventually being flown back to Germany. Meanwhile the crew of the *Senja* had managed to stop the *Maxim Gorkiy's* sinking, by which time her bow had already sunk down to the level of the main deck. On 21 June the *Maxim Gorkiy* was towed to Spitsbergen where quick repairs were made to make her watertight enough to survive a return to Germany for repairs. She sailed back under her own power and after repairs was back on service on 17 August – a lucky escape.

The *Explorer* was a specially designed small cruise ship for Arctic and Antarctic service, originally commissioned and operated by the Swedish explorer Lars-Eric Lindblad. She was formerly named *Lindblad Explorer*. By 2004 she was being operated by a Canadian expedition holiday company.

The *Explorer* was the first cruise ship designed specifically to sail the icy waters of the Antarctic Ocean. On 23 November 2007 she struck an unidentified submerged object, reported to be ice, which caused a 10 x 4in gash in her hull. The *Explorer* was abandoned after taking on water and listing heavily. The normally stormy waters were, thankfully, relatively calm. Fortunately the Norwegian Coastal Voyage vessel the *Nord Norge* was also in the area – the Norwegian company has been using its spare vessels in the Antarctic during the Northern winter. There were no losses and the lifeboats performed their role well, but again a major potential tragedy was only averted by the fortuitous presence of another vessel in the area.

Much more tragic was the 1959 case of the *Hans Hedtoft* – a case which mirrors that of *Titanic* sixty-seven years earlier almost exactly. A small ship with a double bottom and seven watertight compartments, an armoured bow and stern, she was designed for Arctic conditions as she was intended for the year-round service between Denmark and Greenland. Like *Titanic*, *Hans Hedtoft* had a riveted hull, a feature which some criticised as being less resistant to ice pressure than a welded hull.

Hans Hedtoft sailed from Copenhagen on her maiden voyage on 7 January 1959. Her voyage to Greenland was made in record time. On 29 January, she began her return journey with forty crew, fifty-five passengers and a cargo of frozen fish on board. The next day *Hans Hedtoft* collided with an iceberg about 35 miles south of Cape Farewell, the southernmost point of Greenland. A distress call was put out that was answered by a number of vessels. Within an hour, another message was sent stating that the engine room was flooded. At 3.12 p.m. it was announced that the ship was sinking. A final message was sent at 5.41 p.m. stating the ship was slowly sinking and requesting immediate assistance. On 31 January, the US Coast Guard cutter USCGC *Campbell* reported that conditions were the worst seen and there was no sign of *Hans Hedtoft* or her passengers and crew. The search was called off on 7 February. The only piece of wreckage ever recovered was a lifebelt which washed ashore some months after the ship sank. Before her disastrous maiden voyage it had been claimed that the *Hans Hedtoft* was the safest ship afloat and 'unsinkable' – shades of *Titanic?*

Myth?

It remains the worst peacetime shipping disaster ever

Up to 1987 *Titanic* was the worst peacetime shipping disaster with 1,513 dead. Nearly as many or even more lives had been lost in other sinkings but these were during wartime, for example the *Lusitania*, torpedoed in 1915 with the loss of 1,198 lives; the *Lancastria* in 1940, 5,000-plus dead when capsized after being bombed whilst evacuating troops from France; the *Laconia* torpedoed whilst carrying troops and (ironically) Italian prisoners of war in 1942 – around 2,500 dead; and the *Wilhelm Gustloff* sunk in the Baltic by a Russian submarine whilst evacuating troops and refugees – over 5,200 dead.

However, in peacetime *Titanic's* terrible record was broken in 1987 when the ferry *Doña Paz*, a Philippine-registered passenger ferry travelling from Leyte Island to Manila, sank after colliding with a tanker on 20 December. With a death toll of, at most, 4,375 people, the collision resulted in the deadliest ferry disaster in history and is now considered as the worst ever peacetime maritime disaster.

In recent times large casualties have mainly resulted when passenger ferries have sunk, to give just three examples:

Herald of Free Enterprise	Zeebrugge	1987	193 dead
Estonia	Baltic	1984	852 dead
al-Salam Boccaccio '98	Red Sea	2006	1,400+ dead

There has been a major liner disaster since the *Andrea Doria* sank. On 31 August 1986 the *Admiral Nakimov*, built in 1925 as the German vessel *Berlin*, collided with a cargo vessel and sank in the Black Sea 8 miles from Novorossysk. Eight hundred and thirty-six people were rescued but 423 lives were lost.

It is paradoxical that the worst air disaster ever involved passengers who were flying across the Atlantic to join a cruise ship. Sixty-five years after the *Titanic* disaster the airliner had taken over from the ocean passenger liner completely. On Sunday 27 March 1977 a bomb, which caused no loss of life, damaged the passenger terminal at Las Palmas airport in the Canary Islands. As a result flights were diverted to Los Rodeos Airport on neighbouring Tenerife.

Amongst the flights diverted were a KLM Boeing 747 bound for Las Palmas on a charter holiday flight from Amsterdam and a Pan American 747 operating

a charter for Royal Cruise Lines. Most of the 364 passengers were of retirement age and had boarded at Los Angeles for the first stage of a charter flight
to Gran Canaria. They were due to join the line's *Golden Odyssey* for a twelve-
day Mediterranean cruise. Departing LAX late the previous afternoon they had
flown direct to John F. Kennedy Airport in New York. The aircraft was refuelled,
fourteen additional passengers boarded, and there was a change of crew.

When Los Palmas airport opened there was a need to deal with the congestion
at Tenerife. The KLM flight taxied to the end of the runway in somewhat misty
conditions. The plan was for the Pan Am flight to taxi part of the way along the
runway and then to turn off onto a taxi way. In the mist the turning was missed
and at the same time the KLM pilot believed he had take-off permission. His co-
pilot challenged this assumption but then did nothing more. The captain was one
of the most senior on the KLM roster and yet despite not having confirmed permission to take-off he commenced the run down the runway catching his co-pilot
offguard. The aircraft was almost airborne when the Pan Am aircraft was spotted.
Despite efforts to avoid a collision by both pilots there was a massive conflagration.
All 248 people on the KLM flight died and only sixty-one out of the 396 on the
Pan Am flight survived. The death toll was a massive 583. It was a clear case of pilot
error, although the errors were compounded by confusion about call signs. Once
again a human being had somehow over-ridden all of the safety systems. Getting
away as quickly as possible had caused risks to be taken. Just as with *Titanic* time
and again there would not have been another aircraft on the runway just as there
would not have been an iceberg in front of the ship. On both occasions fate and
circumstances conspired to make what was recklessness into a major disaster.

Challenger

The Space Shuttle *Challenger* disaster occurred on Tuesday 28 January 1986, when
the orbiter and its launch components broke apart 73 seconds into its flight, after
the main fuel tank exploded. All seven crew members died. *Challenger* disintegrated over the Atlantic Ocean, off the coast of central Florida.

Disintegration of the entire vehicle began after an O-ring seal in its right solid
rocket booster failed at lift-off, allowing pressurised hot gas from within the solid
rocket motor to reach the outside and impinge upon the external fuel tank causing an explosion.

The crew compartment and many other vehicle fragments were eventually
recovered from the ocean floor after a lengthy search and recovery operation.
Although the exact timing of the death of the crew is unknown, several crew
members are known to have survived the initial breakup of the spacecraft.
However, the shuttle had no escape system and the astronauts did not survive the
impact of the crew compartment with the ocean surface.

The disaster resulted in a thirty-two-month delay in the shuttle program and
the formation of the Rogers Commission, a special commission to investigate
the accident. The Rogers Commission found that NASA's organisational cul-

ture and decision-making processes had been a key contributing factor to the accident. NASA managers were well aware that the design of the boosters contained a potentially catastrophic flaw in the O-rings since 1977, but they failed to address it properly. They also disregarded warnings from engineers about the dangers of launching posed by the low temperatures of that morning and had failed to adequately report these technical concerns to their superiors. The Rogers Commission offered NASA nine recommendations that were to be implemented before shuttle flights resumed.

Just like the DC10 over Paris, people knew that there could be a catastrophe. The final section of this chapter considers whether Captain Smith, an experienced mariner, should have known and also should his officers have known that speeding in the vicinity of ice was dangerous. When we go on a bus, or on an aeroplane or on a ship, we make the assumption that the driver is rational and competent, but is that a fair assumption?

The shuttle *Columbia* was destroyed on 1 February 2003 while re-entering the atmosphere after a sixteen-day mission. The investigation determined that a hole was punctured in the leading edge on one of *Columbia*'s wings – which had formed when a piece of insulating foam from the external fuel tank had peeled off during the launch sixteen days earlier and struck the shuttle's wing. During the intense heat of re-entry, hot gases penetrated the interior of the wing, destroying the support structure and causing the rest of the shuttle to break apart. The break off of the foam had been observed during the launch but once the craft was in the air there was little that could be done. *Columbia* was a tragic accident whilst what happened to *Challenger* could and should have been prevented as there was clear evidence before the launch that there were unresolved issues.

Titanic – the legacy

On 3 August 1991, the *Oceanos*, a small Greek cruise ship, was off South Africa when she suffered an engine room explosion. The engine room flooded and the ship began to list dangerously. By good fortune she was just within the range of the South African's military helicopters and all the passengers and crew were rescued. The captain did not endear himself to anybody by being one of the first survivors into a helicopter. At least Captain Smith stayed with *Titanic*. As the disaster unfolded on board *Titanic* the officers, crew and – to their credit – many of the male passengers adhered to the principle of 'women and children first'. Sadly, this principle has not always been adhered to since, despite the example set on the *Titanic*. The real heroes of the *Oceanos* were the ship's entertainers who worked hard to assist the guests.

Titanic has become more than a ship – the word has entered the vocabulary. Management consultants are fond of describing the restructuring of companies in dire financial circumstances as 'rearranging the deck chairs on the *Titanic* after she hit the iceberg', i.e. worrying about small things whilst there is a major disaster happening around you. Comedians often refer to *Titanic* in their acts.

The authors were amazed to see, after the 1997 movie was released, cruise companies providing backdrops of the Grand Staircase of *Titanic* for passengers to have their photographs taken against. As a matter of interest the authors were informed by somebody connected with the making of the movie that the staircase used in it is in fact 1.5 times the size of the actual one – apparently the real staircase was not quite big enough for Hollywood.

It was after *Titanic* sank that new rules regarding the number of lifeboat places that ships had to be fitted with were amended to one place for every passenger and member of the crew. That it needed a major disaster and over 1,500 deaths to accomplish this beggars belief. The disaster brought about standardisation in the use of radio at sea and this alone has saved countless lives. The International Ice Patrol also stems from the *Titanic* disaster.

From 1912 onwards it was considered negligent for a captain to speed in dangerous conditions, especially fog and ice.

On 8 September 1923, seven destroyers of Destroyer Squadron ELEVEN (DesRon 11) went hard aground and were wrecked with the loss of twenty-three lives at Honda Point, California, due to navigational error. Completely exposed to wind and waves, and often obscured by fog, this is a dangerous and rocky shore.

Just over twelve hours earlier DesRon 11 had left San Francisco Bay and formed up for a morning of combat manoeuvres. In an important test of engineering efficiency, this was followed by a 20-knot run south, including a night passage through the Santa Barbara Channel. In late afternoon the fourteen destroyers fell into column formation, led by their flagship, USS *Delphy*.

Poor visibility ensured that the squadron commander and two other experienced navigators on board *Delphy* had to work using dead reckoning. Soundings could not be taken at 20 knots, but they checked their chartwork against bearings obtained from the radio direction finding (RDF) station at Point Arguello, a few miles south of Honda. At the time they expected to turn into the Channel, the Point Arguello station reported they were still to the northward. However, RDF was still new and not completely trusted, so this information was discounted and DesRon 11 was ordered to turn eastward, with each ship following *Delphy*.

However, the squadron was actually several miles north and further east than *Delphy*'s navigators believed. It was very dark and almost immediately the ships entered a dense fog bank. About five minutes after making her turn, *Delphy* slammed into the Honda shore and stuck fast. A few hundred yards astern, USS *S.P. Lee* saw the flagship's sudden stop and turned sharply to port, but quickly struck the hidden coast to the north of *Delphy*. Following her, USS *Young* had no time to turn before she ripped her hull open on submerged rocks and came to a stop just south of *Delphy* and rapidly turned over on her starboard side. The next two destroyers in line, USS *Woodbury* and *Nicholas*, turned right and left respectively, but also hit the rocks. Steaming behind them, USS *Farragut* backed away with relatively minor damage, USS *Fuller* ran aground near the USS *Woodbury*; USS *Percival* and *Somers* both narrowly evaded the catastrophe, but as USS *Chauncey* tried to rescue the men clinging to the capsized *Young* she herself went aground nearby. The last four destroyers, USS *Kennedy*, *Paul Hamilton*, *Stoddert* and *Thompson*, successfully turned clear of the coast and were unharmed.

It seems incredible that just eleven years after *Titanic*, experienced naval officers could make such an error as to lead to a mass grounding of so many vessels. Clearly there was too much reliance on new technology and less on old-fashioned seamanship.

These rules also failed to prevent the collision between the *Andrea Doria* and the *Stockholm* covered in the previous chapter. Approaching the fog bank off Nantucket the *Andrea Doria* had slowed down but it was only a token reduction; 21.8 knots from 23 knots. They had radar so why slow down too much and delay their arrival in New York? She also had much better watertight division than *Titanic* and this did keep her afloat for longer but she still sank.

The disaster had a profound impact on many lives. Families were torn asunder. The hopes of a fresh start in the New World destroyed for those hapless steerage passengers who saw in America an escape from poverty and persecution. The survivors had to live with the disaster for the rest of their lives. As this book went to print the authors met a lady who told them another piece of interesting family history akin to the 'mumps' story on page 63. The lady's grandfather had gone to sign on as a crew member on *Titanic*. He was newly married and had risen late that morning – too late to sign on, in fact: there were enough men before him in the signing-on line. By a dint of fate he never sailed on the ship and the family was saved the anguish of bereavement.

It took until the 1990s for the reputation of Captain Lord of the *Californian* to be partially restored and his struggle was one legacy of *Titanic* that should have been laid to rest many years earlier. Captain Smith's reputation, however, has not really suffered. His last words to the crew of 'look after yourself lads' bring a feeling of pride to British hearts. If he had crashed his ship he had at least the dignity of dying a hero's death! In fact it is probable that he did not 'go down with the ship'. He is reported to have been swimming towards a lifeboat (some say with a baby in his arms or even held by his teeth – the authors consider this to be rather unlikely) in an attempt to save himself. If he had survived it is likely that the press would have hounded him as they hounded Ismay.

The surviving officers had their careers blighted, in particular Lightoller. The Royal Navy considered him suitable for command but not White Star – he was, after all, the most senior surviving officer of the *Titanic*: not a good thing to put on your CV!

Captain Smith was the senior captain of White Star. He was the highest paid seaman in the world. In legal terms he was 'Master under God'. Bruce Ismay may have been his chairman but he did not have to impress him or indeed take instructions that could have endangered his ship. It is often forgotten that Smith, as captain of *Olympic*, had quite recently been in collision with HMS *Hawke* in the Solent. True *Olympic* had the pilot on board but the captain was still in command and responsible for the safety of his vessel, passengers, crew and cargo. It used to be that the only place where the captain handed over responsibility to the pilot was in the Panama Canal, but even that has changed.

The ultimate legacy? The authors photographed against a backdrop of the *Titanic* staircase whilst on board the *Black Watch*. (Authors' collection)

The master of a ship is a man or woman with legal and moral authority (in 2011 a female captain took command of the new *Queen Elizabeth* for Cunard but she is still the 'master'). It is not surprising that his officers did not question Smith's decisions. There have been many examples, particularly in the military, where foolish orders have had to be obeyed unquestioningly – discipline demands it and this causes problems when it comes to juniors exercising initiative. It is of paramount importance, therefore, that those in authority guard against arrogance and complacency and that they listen as well as direct – a good captain knows this and acts on it. He or she knows that they are not invulnerable. A captain in the years up to the great Depression of the 1920s and '30s was a man of statue. There is a photograph of the captain of the White Star liner *Majestic* in the 1920s conducting his Sunday inspection. Not only is he dressed in his best uniform which had his medals displayed, he is also wearing a sword and is trailed by his junior officers.

Fate was unkind to *Titanic*. A few minutes either way or a little better visibility or a bigger rudder and she would have sailed past the iceberg. She was the biggest ship in the world but would have soon lost that honour to one of the new German liners then building. She would never have been the fastest. She would have arrived in New York and been given a wonderful reception. She would have sailed on as did her sister *Olympic. Olympic* became known as the loved; *Britannic* because of her short career, the forgotten; but the legacy of *Titanic* is always to be the damned – a symbol of mankind's vulnerability. If she had not encountered the iceberg she would have probably sailed until the mid-1930s,

A voyage that never happened – an advertisement for the return voyage of *Titanic* from New York. (Authors' collection)

become obsolete and been broken up. She would have been just a footnote in the history of the North Atlantic.

One of the most poignant items in the authors' collection of *Titanic*-related items is a copy of a poster for her return voyage – a voyage she was never destined to make.

Nicolas Monsarrat entitled his classic novel about the Battle of the Atlantic in the Second World War, *The Cruel Sea*. The sea is not cruel; it is indifferent to mere humans. We may believe that we control nature but it is a legacy of *Titanic* that, as we consider her story, we realise just how little we do control on this planet and that for the people on *Titanic* that cold April night in 1912 it was, to quote the title of Walter Lord's book (and the movie made from it), truly:

A night to remember.

Timeline

Date	Time	Details
2 March 1871		White Star commences Atlantic operations with SS *Oceanic*
4 November 1879		SS *Arizona* strikes iceberg head on and survives
28 December 1879		Tay Bridge collapses
1907		*Mauretania* and *Lusitania* enter service for Cunard
31 March 1909		The keel of *Titanic* laid
29 July 1908		The design for the *Titanic* approved
20 October 1910		*Olympic* launched
31 May 1911	12 p.m.	The hull of *Titanic* successfully launched
January 1912		Sixteen wooden lifeboats fitted on board the *Titanic*
31 March 1912		The fitting out of *Titanic* completed
2 April 1912		*Titanic* sea trials scheduled then postponed
2 April 1912	6 p.m.	*Titanic* sea trials, then ship sails for Southampton
3 April 1912		*Titanic* arrives in Southampton
10 April 1912	9.30–11.30 a.m.	Passengers arrive in Southampton and begin boarding the ship
10 April 1912	12 p.m.	*Titanic* sets sail on her maiden voyage
10 April 1912	6.30 p.m.	*Titanic* reaches Cherbourg, France
11 April 1912	11.30 a.m.	*Titanic* reaches Queenstown, Ireland
12/13 April 1912		*Titanic* sails through calm waters
14 April 1912		Throughout the day seven iceberg warnings are received
14 April 1912	11.40 p.m.	Lookout Frederick Fleet spots an iceberg dead ahead. *Titanic* strikes the iceberg on the starboard (right) side of her bow
14 April 1912	11.50 p.m.	Water pours in and rises 14ft in the front part of the ship
15 April 1912	12 a.m.	The captain is told the ship can only stay afloat for a couple of hours. He gives the order to call for help over the radio
15 April 1912	12.05 a.m.	The orders are given to uncover the lifeboats and to get passengers and crew ready on deck. There is only room in the lifeboats for half of the estimated 2,227 on board

Date	Time	Details
15 April 1912	12.25 a.m.	The lifeboats begin being loaded with women and children first. The *Carpathia*, south-east of the *Titanic* by about 58 miles, picks up the distress call and begins sailing to rescue passengers
15 April 1912	12.45 a.m.	The first lifeboat is safely lowered away. Although it could carry sixty-five people, it leaves with only twenty-eight on board. The first distress rocket is fired
15 April 1912	2.05 a.m.	The last lifeboat leaves the ship. There are still over 1,500 people left on the ship. The tilt of *Titanic's* deck grows steeper and steeper
15 April 1912	2.17 a.m.	The last radio message is sent. The captain announces 'Every man for himself'
15 April 1912	2:20 a.m.	*Titanic's* broken-off stern settles back into the water, becoming more level for a few moments. Slowly it fills with water and tilts its end high into the air before sinking into the sea. People in the water slowly freeze to death
15 April 1912	3.30 a.m.	*Carpathia's* rockets were spotted by the survivors
15 April 1912	4.10 a.m.	The first lifeboat is picked up by the *Carpathia*
15 April 1912	8.50 a.m.	*Carpathia* leaves the area bound for New York. She had on board 705 survivors of the *Titanic* disaster
18 April 1912	9.00 p.m.	*Carpathia* arrives in New York
20 April 1912		*Titanic* scheduled to leave New York on return voyage
19–25 May 1912		US Inquiry into the disaster held
22 April–15 May 1912		Several ships sent to the disaster site to recover bodies. A total of 328 bodies are found floating in the area
2–3 July 1912		British Inquiry into the disaster held
31 March 1913		J.P. Morgan dies
26 February 1914		*Britannic* launched
29 May 1914		*Empress of Ireland* sinks after collision in the St Lawrence
7 May 1915		*Lusitania* torpedoed and sunk
1916		*Britannic* sunk in the Aegean
1 January 1927		White Star acquired by Kyslant (Lord Kyslant was chairman) group of companies (Royal Mail Group)
1928		*Oceanic* laid down but never completed; part of the steel worked into RMS *Queen Mary*
1932		Last White Star vessel, MV *Georgic* enters service
1934		White Star sold and merged with Cunard as Cunard White Star
August 1935		*Olympic* sold to breakers
17 October 1937		Bruce Ismay dies
30 January 1945		*Wilhelm Gustloff* torpedoed and sunk
8 December 1952		Charles Lightoller dies
26–26 July 1956		*Andrea Doria* collides with the *Stockholm* and sinks

Date	Time	Details
1958		The film *A Night to Remember* is released
24 January 1962		Captain Stanley Lord of *Californian* dies
3 March 1974		DC 10 disaster over Paris
1 September 1985		Robert Ballard discovers *Titanic* at the bottom of the North Atlantic
28 January 1986		*Challenger* Space Shuttle disaster
1989		A consortium, led by John Parker and Norwegian ship owner Fred Olsen and including management and employees, purchases Harland & Wolff
1990		Partial re-opening of *Titanic* Inquiry by UK Department of Transport
1992		UK Department of Transport report presented
1995		Robert Ballard surveys wreck of *Britannic*
1998		Cunard becomes part of Carnival
1979		SOS *Titanic* – television movie
3 August 1991		*Oceanus* sinks off South Africa
1997		James Cameron's *Titanic* movie released
1 February 2003		*Columbia* Space Shuttle disaster
2006		Tender *Nomadic* returns to Belfast
23 November 2007		MV *Explorer* strikes ice flow in the Antarctic and sinks
31 May 2009		Millvina Dean, the last *Titanic* survivor, dies
14–15 April 2012		100th anniversary of the *Titanic* disaster

Royal Mail Steamer *Titanic*

Laid down	21 March 1909
Launched	31 May 1911
Gross Registered Tonnage	46,329
Length	882ft
Beam	92ft
Draft	34ft
First class*	905
Second class*	564
Third class (steerage)*	1,134
Crew	944
Trials	2 April 1912
Maiden voyage	10 April 1912
Intended route	Southampton – Cherbourg – Queenstown (Cobh) – New York
Hit iceberg	14 April 1912
Sank	15 April 1912
Sisters	*Olympic* – entered service 14 June 1911
	Broken up 1937
	Britannic (*Gigantic*) – entered service as a hospital ship 8 December
1915	Mined and sank 21 November 1916

Bibliography

Titanic in books, plays, poems, films and art

There has probably been no single incident in history (perhaps Jack the Ripper runs it close) that has inspired so many factual and fictional books, movies, plays and even a musical than *Titanic*. The First and Second World Wars and the American Civil War may have more titles about them but they were events that lasted years. Using *Titanic* as a 'keyword' on Amazon produced an incredible 16,805 results for books and 205 results for DVDs. While many of them would be new editions etc., it is still a prodigious number. By comparison Jack the Ripper produced only 765 hits.

Even today *Titanic* continues to fascinate writers and producers with new offerings (including of course this one) coming out on a regular basis.

Books directly related to Titanic

Amongst the myriad of factual offerings about *Titanic* the authors consider that the following are well worth reading, being in their personal collection. This does not imply that there are not other deserving volumes, only that they have not had time to read them yet! Publishers are not exclusive; different editions may well have different publishers.

BALLARD Robert D., *The Discovery of the Titanic*, Hodder & Stoughton
—, *Exploring the Titanic*, Scholastic
—, *The Lost Ships of Robert Ballard*, Patrick Stephens
BALLARD Robert D. & SWEENEY, Michael S., *Return to Titanic*, National Geographic
BERGFELDER Tim and STREET Sarah, *The Titanic in Myth and Memory: Representations in Visual and Literary Culture*, I.B. Tauris
BEVERIDGE Bruce, HALL, Steve, KLISTORNER Daniel, ANDREWS Scott & BRAUNSCHWEIGER Art, *Titanic – The Ship Magnificent, Volumes I & II*, The History Press
—, *Titanic in Photographs*, The History Press
BRYCESON Dave (compiler), *The Titanic Disaster: As Reported in the British National Press April-July 1912*, W.W. Norton
BUTLER Daniel Allen, *The Other Side of the Night - The Carpathia, the Californian, and the Night the Titanic Was Lost*, Casemate Books
CAMERON Stephen, *Titanic – Belfast's Own*, Wolfhound
CARROLL Yvonne, *A Hymn For Eternity –The Story of Wallace Hartley, Titanic Bandmaster*, The History Press

CARTWRIGHT R., *The Pitkin Guide to Titanic*, Pitkin Publishing

CHIRNSIDE Mark, *The Olympic Class Ships – Olympic, Titanic, Britannic*, The History Press

COLLINS L.M., *The Sinking of the Titanic: The Mystery Solved*, Souvenir Press

COOPER Gary, *Titanic Captain: The Life of Edward John Smith*, The History Press

DAVIE Michael, *Titanic – The Full Story of a Tragedy*, Grafton

DOEDEN Matthew, *Sinking of the Titanic*, Raintree

EATON John P. & HAAS Charles A., *Titanic – Triumph and Tragedy*, Patrick Stephens

—, *Titanic – Destination Disaster*, Patrick Stephens

EVERETT Marshall, *Wreck & Sinking of the Titanic*, L.H. Walter (1912)

GARDINER Robin, *Titanic – The Ship That Never Sank*, Ian Allan

GARDINER Robin & VAN DER VAT Dan, *The Riddle of the Titanic*, Weidenfeldt & Nicolson

GARRISON Webb, *A Treasury of Titanic Tales*, Rutledge Hill Press

GIBSON Allen, *The Unsinkable Titanic*, The History Press

GRACIE Archibald, *Titanic: A Survivor's Story*, The History Press

GREEN Rod, *Building the Titanic*, Carlton Books

HALL, Steve & BEVERIDGE Bruce, *Titanic or Olympic: Which Ship Sank?*, The History Press

HEYER Paul, *Titanic Legacy – Disaster as Media Event & Myth*, Praeger

HOOPER McCARTY Jennifer & FOECKE Tim, *New Forensic Discoveries – What Really Sank the Titanic*, Citadel press

HUTCHINGS David, *The Titanic Story*, The History Press

JEFFERS Alan & GORDON Rob, *Titanic Halifax – a guide to sites*, Nimbus Publishing

MARCUS Geoffrey, *The Maiden Voyage*, George Allen & Unwin

MARSHALL Logan (ed.), *On board the Titanic – the complete story with eyewitness accounts*, Dover

—, *The Sinking of the Titanic*, The History Press

MAXTON-GRAHAM John, *Titanic Survivor – The Memoirs of Violet Jessop, Stewardess*, Sutton Publishing

MCCAULEY Dana, ARCHBOLD, Rick and LORD Walter, *Last Dinner on the Titanic: Menus and Recipes from the Legendary Liner*, Hyperion

McCLUSKY Tom, SHARPE Michael & MARRIOT Leo, *Titanic and her sisters Olympic and Britannic*, PRC Publishing

McMILLAN Beverley & LEHRER Stanley, *Titanic: Fortune and Fate: personal effects from those on the lost ship*, Simon & Schuster

MOLONY Senan, *Titanic: Victims and Villains*, The History Press

—, *Titanic and the Mystery Ship*, The History Press

MOWBRAY Jan, *The Sinking of the Titanic*, Dover Publications

MYLON Patrick, *The White Star Collection: A Shipping Line in Postcards*, The History Press

NILSSON Sally, *The Man Who Sank Titanic: The Troubled Life of Quartermaster Robert Hichens*, The History Press

RIFFENBURGH Beau, *The Titanic Experience*, The Five Mile Press

TARSHIS Lauren & DAWSON Scott (illustrator), *I Survived the Sinking of the Titanic, 1912*, Scholastic

TIBBALLS Geoff, *The Mammoth Book of How it Happened – Titanic*, Robinson

WILLIAMS Thomas B. & KAMPS R. (ed.), *Titanic and the Californian*, Tempus Publishing

WINOCOUR Jack (ed.), & BEESLEY Lawrence, GRACIE Archibald, BRIDE Harold & LIGHTOLLER Charles (survivors), *The Story of Titanic as told by its Survivors*, Dover

Useful websites

British Titanic Society
www.britishtitanicsociety.com

David Hoddinott – 'Date with Destiny' painting
www.davehoddinott.ca

Encyclopaedia Titanica
www.encyclopedia-titanica.org

Harland & Wolff
www.harland-wolff.com

Maritime Museum of the North Atlantic
museum.gov.ns.ca/mma/about/about.html

The Maritime Museum, Southampton
www.southampton.gov.uk/s-leisure/artsheritage/museums-galleries/maritimemuseum.aspx

Mark Chirnside's Reception Room: *Olympic, Titanic & Britannic*
www.markchirnside.co.uk

Merseyside Maritime Museum
www.liverpoolmuseums.org.uk/maritime

Steiff bears (*Titanic* mourning bear)
www.steiffteddybears.co.uk

Titanic's Dock and Pump House (Belfast)
www.titanicsdock@nisp.co.uk

Titanic Historical Society
www.titanichistoricalsociety.org

Titanic International Society
www.titanicinternationalsociety.org

Titanic Inquiry (electronic copies of the US and British Inquiries)
www.titanicinquiry.org

Titanic Reproductions Ltd
www.titanicreproductions.co.uk

Titanic – the Experience
www.titanictheexperience.com

Titanic – the Ship Magnificent
www.titanic-theshipmagnificent.com

Titanic Titanic
www.titanic-titanic.com

Ulster Folk & Transport Museum
www.nmni.com/uftm

White Star Momentos [sic] – gifts from the birthplace of the *Titanic* including 100th Anniversary memorabilia
www.whitestarmomentos.co.uk

Movies and stage plays

Whilst the 1997 *Titanic* movie is well known there have been other films and even a musical about the ship. A selection are listed below.

TITANIC THE MUSICAL

Opened on Broadway in 1997. It won five Tony Awards including the award for Best Musical.

A NIGHT TO REMEMBER (1956)

Television movie that formed the basis for the 1958 feature (see below).

A NIGHT TO REMEMBER (1958)

The best film about *Titanic* is the 1958 movie *A Night to Remember* starring Kenneth Moore as Charles Lightoller.

RAISE THE TITANIC

Based on a 1976 novel by Clive Cussler (see under fiction), that tells the fictional story of efforts to bring the remains of the ill-fated ocean liner to the surface. In 1980, the book was adapted for a film and one of the financiers is reported to have said that 'it would have been cheaper to lower the Atlantic'.

S.O.S. TITANIC

1979 television movie starring David Janssen and Cloris Leachman. Quite a good interpretation of the disaster.

ATLANTIC

The first full-length feature film about the disaster, *Atlantic* was an early 'talkie' from 1929. Interestingly, although the film is clearly about *Titanic* the name of the ship is never mentioned.

THE UNSINKABLE MOLLY BROWN

A 1964 film adaptation of the musical. Debbie Reynolds starred in the title role with Marilu Henner taking over for the television mini-series. Kathy Bates played the role in the 1997 *Titanic* movie.

TITANIC (1997)

Titanic is an American romantic and disaster movie starring Leonardo DiCaprio as Jack Dawson and Kate Winslet as Rose DeWitt Bukater, members of different social classes who fall in love aboard the ship during its ill-fated maiden voyage. Though the central roles and love story are fictitious, some characters are based on historical figures.

The film contains some notable inaccuracies. There is smoke coming out of the fourth funnel. Jack and Rose run through the engine areas in evening dress, areas that in reality would have been full of heat, smoke and coal dust. Passengers could not access the bow of *Titanic* and in 1912 no third-class passenger would have been allowed in first class even if invited.

The 1997 film is another version of *West Side Story* and *Porgy and Bess*, which in turn are derived from *Romeo and Juliet*, and the score contains some memorable music.

Myth?

Jack Dawson did exist

J. Dawson did exist – he was actually Joseph Dawson, a coal trimmer on *Titanic* and his grave is at Fairview Lawn Cemetery in Halifax. The name of the character was taken from the headstone.

TITANIC II

A direct to DVD production, the action takes place in April 2012, 100 years after the sinking of *Titanic*. A new luxury cruise liner, the *Titanic II*, has been christened, and is soon to embark on her maiden voyage, on the same route the *Titanic* took 100 years earlier (however *Titanic II* begins her voyage in the United States and is scheduled to finish in the United Kingdom).

During the voyage effects of global warning cause a large glacier in Greenland to collapse, creating a disastrous tsunami that sends an iceberg crashing into the *Titanic II*, crushing the entire starboard side of the ship and putting immense pressure on the liner's turbines. As people struggle against the rising waters, the turbines eventually explode, which creates an immense fire in the middle of the listing vessel.

Another tsunami then capsizes her drowning most of the people still on board.

NO GREATER LOVE

1996 television movie based on Danielle Steel's novel of the same name.

TITANIC (1943)

Perhaps one of the most unusual of the 'mainstream' films about *Titanic* (there have been spoofs and even pornographic films featuring the ship) was this version of the story produced by the Nazi Government in Germany with, naturally, a heroic, Aryan German first officer!

Titanic has also featured as part of the plot of the UK drama series *Upstairs, Downstairs* (see quote at the beginning of this book) and also at the very start of the 2010 series *Downton Abbey*.

Given the huge number of books about *Titanic* a complete list of fiction and poems requires a book of its own. Readers are directed to the excellent *Titanic in Print and on Screen* by D. Brian Anderson, published by McFarland & Company, where there are very useful lists and synopses.

Other references to support this book:

BONNER Kit & BONNER Carolyn, *Great Ship Disasters*, MBI Publishing

BRINDLE Steven, *Brunel – the man who built the world*, Weidenfeld & Nicolson (Orion)

BURGESS Douglas R., *Seize the Trident – The Race for Superliner Supremacy and How it Altered the Great War*, McGraw Hill

CHIRNSIDE Mark, *RMS Olympic – Titanic's Sister*, The History Press

CROAL James, *Fourteen Minutes – the sinking of the Empress of Ireland*, Sphere Books

De KERBRECH Richard, *Ships of the White Star Line*, Ian Allan

EMMONS Frederick, *The Atlantic Liners, 1927–70*, David & Charles

FOX Stephen, *The Ocean Railway*, Harper Collins

GARDINER Robin, *The History of the White Star Line*, Ian Allan

HOFFER William, *Saved – the Sinking of the Andrea Doria*, MacMillan

KLUDAS Arnold, *Record Breakers of the North Atlantic*, Chatham Publishing

McAULEY Robert, *The Liners*, Boxtree

McCLUSKY Tom, *No Place for a Boy – A Life at Harland & Wolff*, The History Press

MASSIE Robert K., *Castles of Steel*, Pimlico

MILLER William, *Picture History of the Cunard Line*, Dover Books

—, *The Fabulous Interiors of the Great Ocean Liners*, Dover Books

—, *Picture History of British Ocean Liners, 1900 to the Present*, Dover Books

STEEL Nigel & HART Peter, *Jutland 1916*, Cassell

Index

THE TITANIC COLLECTION

THE 100TH ANNIVERSARY OF THE SINKING OF TITANIC 15TH APRIL 2012

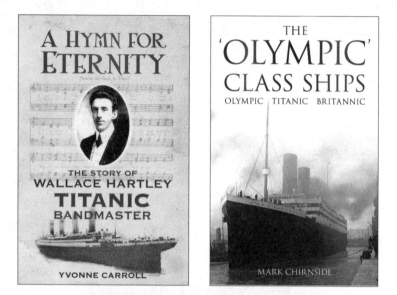

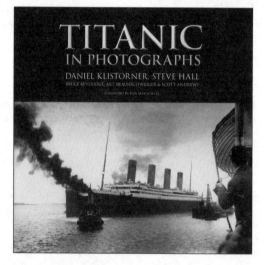

For the full Titanic experience visit The History Press website and follow the Titanic link. For stories and articles about Titanic, join us on Facebook.

www.thehistorypress.co.uk